CASSELL
Dictionary of
Cynical Quotations

Jonathon Green

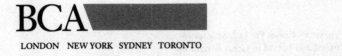

LONDON NEW YORK SYDNEY TORONTO

This edition published 1994
by BCA
by arrangement with Cassell Plc

CN 9094

Typeset by Colset Pte Ltd, Singapore
Printed and bound in Great Britain by
Mackays of Chatham PLC, Chatham, Kent

CONTENTS

ACTING

Actresses will happen in the best regulated families.
Addison Mizner and Oliver Herford, *The Entirely New Cynic's Calendar*, 1905

Musical comedy is the Irish stew of drama. Anything may be put into it, with the certainty that it will improve the general effect.
P.G. Wodehouse, *The Man with Two Left Feet*, 1917

When actors begin to think, it's time for a change. They are not fitted for it.
Stephen Leacock, *The Decline of Drama*, 1921

If you have a message [in the theatre] call for Western Union.
George S. Kaufman, quoted in *Wits End* by J.R. Gaines, 1977

Satire is what closes Saturday night.
George S. Kaufman

Theatre director: a person engaged by the management to conceal the fact that the players cannot act.
James Agate, *Ego*, 1935–48

A character actor is one who cannot act and therefore makes an elaborate study of the disguise and stage tricks by which acting can be grotesquely simulated.
George Bernard Shaw

Acting is like roller skating – once you know how to do it, it is neither stimulating nor exciting.
George Sanders

For an actor, success is simply delayed failure.
Graham Greene

The art of acting consists in keeping people from coughing.
Sir Ralph Richardson, in the *Observer*, 1947

They shot too many pictures and not enough actors.
Walter Winchell

Some of the greatest love affairs I've known have involved one actor, unassisted.

**Wilson Mizner, quoted in *The Incredible Mizners*
by A. Johnson, 1953**

You can pick out the actors by the glazed look that comes into their eyes when the conversation wanders away from themselves.

Michael Wilding

Musicals: a series of catastrophes ending with a floorshow.

Oscar Levant

Glamour in the theatre is usually twenty chorus girls in a line all doing the same thing. It is assumed that twenty women are more glamorous than one.

Peter Ustinov

Acting is the expression of a neurotic impulse.

Marlon Brando

An actor is not quite a human being – but then, who is?

George Sanders

An actor's a guy who, if you ain't talkin' about him, ain't listening.

Marlon Brando, quoted in the *Observer*, 1956

A good many inconveniences attend play-going in any large city, but the greatest of them is usually the play itself.

Kenneth Tynan, in the *New York Herald Tribune*, 1957

Show me a congenital eavesdropper with the instincts of a Peeping Tom and I will show you the makings of a dramatist.

Kenneth Tynan, *Pausing on the Stairs*, 1957

Acting is all about honesty. If you can fake that, you've got it made.

George Burns

Modesty is the artifice of actors, similar to passion in call-girls.

Jackie Gleason

The relationship between the make-up man and the film actor is that of accomplices in crime.

Marlene Dietrich

The best audience is intelligent, well-educated and a little drunk.
Alben W. Barkley

Galaxy: five or six actresses.
J.B. Morton ('Beachcomber'), in the *Daily Express*, passim

The man was a major comedian, which is to say that he had the compassion of an icicle, the effrontery of a carnival shill and the generosity of a pawnbroker.
S.J. Perelman

The question actors most often get asked is how can they bear saying the same things over and over again, night after night, but God knows what the answer to that is. Don't we all anyway; might as well get paid for it.
Elaine Dundy, *The Dud Avocado*, 1958

That's a lot to see buggers jump.
Nigel Bruce, commenting on the cost of ballet tickets

Generally speaking, the . . . theatre is the aspirin of the middle classes.
Wolcott Gibbs, *More in Sorrow*, 1958

Fans are people who let an actor know he's not alone in the way he feels about himself.
Anonymous

The whole motivation for any performer: 'Look at me, Ma!'
Lenny Bruce

Acting is largely a matter of farting about in disguises.
Peter O'Toole

A fan club is a group of people who tell an actor he is not alone in the way he feels about himself.
Jack Carson, quoted in *The Wit of the Theatre*, ed. R. May, 1969

One begins with two people on a stage, and one of them had better say something pretty damn quick.
Moss Hart, on writing plays, quoted in *Contemporary Dramatists*, 1977

The more you do for an actor the worse it hates you.

Percy Hammond, quoted in *Selected Letters of James Thurber*, ed. H. Thurber and E. Weeks, 1981

A starlet is any woman under thirty not actively employed in a brothel.

Anonymous, quoted in *Halliwell's Filmgoer's Companion*, 1985

Casting: deciding which of two faces the public is least tired of.

Anonymous, quoted in *Halliwell's Filmgoer's Companion*, 1985

There are two kind of directors in the theatre: those who think they are God and those who are certain of it.

Rhetta Hughes

See also HOLLYWOOD

ADULTS

When childhood dies, its corpses are called adults and they enter society, one of the politer names of hell. That is why we dread children, even if we love them. They show us the state of our decay.

Brian Aldiss, in the *Guardian*, 1971

See also CHILDREN, FAMILIES, PARENTS

ADVERTISING

Advertising is legalised lying.

H.G. Wells

Advertising may be described as the science of arresting the human intelligence long enough to get money from it.

Stephen Leacock, *Garden of Folly*, 1924

Advertising is the rattling of a stick inside a swill bucket.

George Orwell

Advertising is the whip which hustles humanity up the road to the Better Mousetrap. It is the vision which reproaches man for the paucity of his desires.

E.S. Turner, *The Shocking History of Advertising*, 1952

You can fool all the people all of the time if the advertising is right and the budget is big enough.

Joseph E. Levine

From any cross-section of ads, the general advertiser's attitude would seem to be: if you are a lousy, smelly, idle, underprivileged and over-sexed, status-seeking neurotic moron, give me your money.

Kenneth Bromfield, in *Advertisers' Weekly* magazine, 1962

If the package doesn't say 'New' these days, it had better say 'Seven Cents Off'.

Spencer Klaw, in *Fortune* magazine, 1963

It has been said that Public Relations is the art of winning friends and getting people under the influence.

Jeremy Tunstall, *The Advertising Man*, 1964

The essence of good advertising is not to inspire hope, but to create greed.

Charles Adams, *Common Sense in Advertising*, 1966

Advertising is the art of making whole lies out of half truths.

Edgar A. Shoaff, quoted in *Peter's Quotations* by L. Peter, 1977

When the client moans and sighs
Make his logo twice the size.
If he still should prove refractory,
Show a picture of his factory.
Only in the gravest cases
Should you show the clients' faces.

Anonymous advertising agency jingle, quoted in *Ogilvy on Advertising* by David Ogilvy, 1983

ADVICE

The expert: an ordinary man, away from home, giving advice.

Anonymous

Old men are fond of giving good advice to console themselves for their inability to set a bad example.

François, Duc de La Rochefoucauld, *Maxims*, 1665

Few listen without a desire of conviction to those who advise them to spare their money.

Samuel Johnson, *The Idler*, 1758–60

To appear more warlike, you should ride with your sword drawn; but take care you do not cut your horse's ear off.

Captain Francis Grose, *Advice to Officers of the British Army*, 1782

The advice that is wanted is commonly unwelcome, and that which is not wanted is evidently impertinent.

Samuel Johnson, in the letters to Hester Thrale, 1788

Advice is seldom welcome, and those who want it most always like it least.

Lord Chesterfield, *Letters to his Son*, 1774

Advice is that which we ask for when we want approbation.

Charles Caleb Colton, *Lacon*, 1820

Good advice is one of those injuries which a good man ought, if possible, to forgive, but at all events to forget at once.

'Horace' Smith, *Gaieties and Gravities*, 1826

When we ask advice, we are usually looking for an accomplice.

Marquis de La Grange, *Pensées*, 1872

It is always a silly thing to give advice, but to give good advice is absolutely fatal.

Oscar Wilde, *The Portrait of Mr W.H.*, 1889

I always pass on good advice. It is the only thing to do with it. It is never any good to oneself.

Oscar Wilde, *An Ideal Husband*, 1895

The best careers advice to give to the young is 'Find out what you like doing best and get someone to pay you for doing it'.

Katherine Whitehorn, in the *Observer*, 1975

See also OPINIONS

AFFAIRS

A painted face fills the husband with suspicion and the gallant with hope.
Anonymous Swedish proverb

Nobody knows how to manage a wife but a bachelor.
George Colman the Elder, *The Jealous Wife*, 1761

Love and a cottage, eh, Fanny! Ah, give me indifference and a coach and six!
George Colman the Elder, *The Clandestine Marriage*, 1766

The one charm of marriage is that it makes a life of deception absolutely necessary for both parties.
Oscar Wilde, *The Picture of Dorian Gray*, 1891

To our sweethearts and wives. May they never meet.
***Toasts for All Occasions*, 19th century**

Nothing looks so like innocence as indiscretion.
Oscar Wilde, *Lady Windermere's Fan*, 1892

There is nothing in the world like the devotion of a married woman. It's a thing no married man knows anything about.
Oscar Wilde, *Lady Windermere's Fan*, 1892

The happiness of a married man depends on the women he has not married.
Oscar Wilde, *A Woman of No Importance*, 1893

In married life, three is company and two is none.
Oscar Wilde, *The Importance of Being Earnest*, 1895

A husband should tell his wife everything that he is sure she will find out, and before anybody else does.
Lord Thomas Dewar

Fidelity, n. A virtue peculiar to those who are about to be betrayed.
Ambrose Bierce, *The Devil's Dictionary*, 1911

No modern woman with a grain of sense ever sends little notes to an unmarried man – not until she is married, anyway.

Arthur Binstead, *Pitcher's Proverbs*, **1909**

A bachelor has to have inspiration for making love to a woman, a married man needs only an excuse.

Helen Rowland

One man's folly is another man's wife.

Helen Rowland

Every man wants a woman to appeal to his better side, his nobler instincts and his higher nature – and another woman to help him forget them.

Helen Rowland, *A Guide to Men*, **1922**

The follies which a man regrets most in his life are those which he didn't commit when he had the opportunity.

Helen Rowland, *A Guide to Men*, **1922**

There can only be one end to marriage without love, and that is love without marriage.

John Churton Collins, in *The English Review*, **1914**

Husbands never become good. They merely become proficient.

H.L. Mencken, *Sententiae*, **1916**

Jealousy is the theory that some other fellow has just as little taste.

H.L. Mencken, *Sententiae*, **1916**

No matter how happily a woman may be married, it always pleases her to discover that there is a nice man who wishes she were not.

H.L. Mencken, *A Mencken Chrestomathy*, **1949**

He would, wouldn't he.

Mandy Rice-Davies, on being informed that Lord Astor had denied her allegations of 'impropriety' during the Profumo Affair, 1963

Never tell. Not if you love your wife . . . In fact, if your old lady walks in on you, deny it. Yeah. Just flat out and she'll believe it: 'I'm tellin' ya. This chick came downstairs with a sign around her neck "Lay On Top Of Me Or I'll Die". I didn't know what I was gonna do . . .'

Lenny Bruce, quoted in *The Essential Lenny Bruce*, **ed J. Cohen, 1967**

There is little wife-swapping in suburbia . . . It is unnecessary, the females being all so similar.

Richard Gordon

Like Mariana of the Moated Grange, who hated late afternoon most of all, the unfaithful wife dreads the coming of 5.30, when the danger zone of her husband returning home has been entered and she knows now it's too late for the lover to telephone.

Jilly Cooper, *The British in Love*, 1980

See also DIVORCE, HUSBANDS, LOVE, LOVERS, MARRIAGE, SEX, WIVES

AGE

All would live long, but none would be old.

Benjamin Franklin

Old men and comets have been reverenced for the same reason: their long beards and pretences to foretell events.

Jonathan Swift, *Thoughts on Various Subjects*, 1706

Tomorrow is an old deceiver, and his cheat never grows stale.

Samuel Johnson, *The Idler*, 1758–60

One of the pleasures of reading old letters is the knowledge that they need no answer.

George Gordon, Lord Byron, quoted in *The Oxford Book of Aphorisms*, ed. J. Gross, 1983

Grey hair is a sign of age, not of wisdom.

Anonymous

She may very well pass for forty-three
In the dusk, with a light behind her.

W.S. Gilbert, *Trial by Jury*, 1875

Many a man that couldn't direct you to the drugstore on the corner when he was thirty will get a respectful hearing when age has further impaired his mind.

Finley Peter Dunne, *Mr Dooley On Making A Will*, 1919

Age, n. That period of life in which we compound for the vices that we still cherish by reviling those that we have no longer the enterprise to commit.

Ambrose Bierce, *The Devil's Dictionary***, 1911**

No one thinks he looks as old as he is.

Edgar Watson Howe, *Country Town Sayings***, 1911**

She always believed in the old adage – leave them while you're looking good.

Anita Loos, *Gentlemen Prefer Blondes***, 1925**

The denunciation of the young is a necessary part of the hygiene of older people, and greatly assists the circulation of their blood.

Logan Pearsall Smith, *Afterthoughts***, 1931**

As I grow older and older
And totter towards the tomb
I find that I care less and less
Who goes to bed with whom.

Dorothy L. Sayers

There is only one cure for grey hair. It was invented by a Frenchman. It is called the guillotine.

P.G. Wodehouse, *The Old Reliable***, 1951**

If you live long enough, you'll see that every victory turns into a defeat.

Simone de Beauvoir, *All Men are Mortal***, 1955**

Maturity is behaviour determined by the plans other people have in mind.

David Mercer, *Let's Murder Vivaldi***, 1968**

Most men do not mature, they simply grow taller.

Leo Rosten, in the *Saturday Review***, 1970**

Remember that as a teenager you are in the last stage of your life when you will be happy to hear that the phone is for you.

Fran Lebowitz, *Social Studies***, 1981**

Anniversaries, those meaningless indicator boards in decimals which command us to exhume feeling.

Neal Ascherson, in the *Observer***, 1986**

See also DEATH

AMBITION

What seems to be generosity is often only disguised ambition – which despises small interests to gain great ones.

François, Duc de La Rochefoucauld, *Maxims*, 1665

There are hardly two Creatures of a more differing Species than the same Man, when he is pretending to a Place, and when he is in possession of it.

George Savile, Marquis of Halifax, *Political, Moral and Miscellaneous Thoughts and Reflexions*, c.1694

Ambition often puts Men upon doing the meanest offices, so climbing is performed in the same position with creeping.

Jonathan Swift, *Thoughts on Various Subjects*, 1706

Ambition is but avarice on stilts, and masked.

Walter Savage Landor

Ambition is the last refuge of the failure.

Oscar Wilde, *Phrases and Philosophies for the Use of the Young*, 1894

Ambition, n. An overmastering desire to be vilified by enemies while living and made ridiculous by friends when dead.

Ambrose Bierce, *The Devil's Dictionary*, 1911

The higher a monkey climbs, the more you can see of his behind.

General 'Vinegar Joe' Stilwell

See also APPLAUSE, EGOTISM, FAME, SUCCESS

APPLAUSE

I know mankind too well to think they are capable of receiving the truth, much less of applauding it.

Lady Mary Wortley Montagu, letter to the Countess of Bute, 1763–7

When the million applaud, you ask yourself what harm you have done; when they censure you, what good.

Charles Caleb Colton, *Lacon*, 1820

Applause, n. The echo of a platitude from the mouth of a fool.
  Ambrose Bierce, *The Devil's Dictionary*, 1911

When I hear a man applauded by the mob I always feel a pang of pity for him. All he has to do to be hissed is to live long enough.
  H.L. Mencken, *Minority Report*, 1956

Do not fear when your enemies criticise you. Beware when they applaud.
  Vo Dong Giang, in *Time* magazine, 1978

See also AMBITION, EGOTISM, FAME, SUCCESS

ARCHITECTURE

A doctor can bury his mistakes, but an architect can only advise his client to plant vines.
  Frank Lloyd Wright

In my experience, if you have to keep the lavatory door shut by extending your left leg, it's modern architecture.
  Nancy Banks-Smith, in the *Guardian*, 1969

Post-war architecture is the accountant's revenge on the pre-war businessman's dreams.
  Rem Koolhaas, *Delirious New York*, 1978

What has happened to architecture since the Second World War that the only passers-by who can contemplate it without pain are those equipped with a white stick and a dog?
  Bernard Levin, in *The Times*, 1983

Architecture is very much like the oldest profession: it has only one aim, and that is to please for a fee.
  Philip Johnson, 1984

Suburbia is where the developer bulldozes out the trees, then names the streets after them.
  Bill Vaughan

The relationship between architects and the media is based on trust and understanding. The architects don't trust the media and the media don't understand the architects.
  Building Design Magazine, 1986

You have to give this much to the Luftwaffe – when it knocked down our buildings it did not replace them with anything more offensive than rubble. We did that.

H.R.H. Charles, Prince of Wales, 1987

ARISTOCRACY

Nobility is nothing but ancient riches.

John Ray, *A Collection of English Proverbs*, 1670

Send your noble blood to market and see what it will bring.

Thomas Fuller, M.D., *Gnomologia*, 1732

The cure for admiring the House of Lords [is] to go and look at it.

Walter Bagehot, *The English Constitution*, 1867

We in the House of Lords are never in touch with public opinion. That makes us a civilised body.

Oscar Wilde, *A Woman of No Importance*, 1893

You should study the Peerage, Gerald . . . it is the best thing in fiction the English have ever done.

Oscar Wilde, *A Woman of No Importance*, 1893

Aristocracies, as a rule, all the world over, consist, and have always consisted, of barbaric conquerors or their descendants, who remain to the last, on the average of instances, at a lower grade of civilization and morals than the democracy they live among.

Grant Allen, quoted in *The Westminster Gazette*, 1894

Aristocracy is like the cheese: the older it is the higher it becomes.

David Lloyd George, speech, 1910

If there is any man today who believes that the object of the eternal struggle for existence will evolve a higher type, an aristocracy of class, nation or race, that man has failed to read the history of mankind. In other words, he is a hopeless optimist.

Norman Lindsay, *Creative Effort*, 1924

Democracy means government by the uneducated, while aristocracy means government by the badly educated.

G.K. Chesterton, in the *New York Times*, 1931

The House of Lords has a value – it is good evidence of life after death.
Lord Soper

See also CLASS, GENTLEMEN

ART

The emperor loves art in the same way a butcher loves a fat ox.
Napoleon Bonaparte

Painting, n. The art of protecting flat surfaces from the weather and exposing them to the critic.
Ambrose Bierce, *The Devil's Dictionary*, 1911

It's easy to understand modern art: if it hangs on the wall it's a painting, if you can walk around it it's a sculpture.
Anonymous

If more than ten per cent of the public likes a painting, it should be burned.
George Bernard Shaw

Buy old masters. They fetch a better price than old mistresses.
Lord Beaverbrook

Sculptures are mud-pies which endure.
Cyril Connolly

Johnny, keep it out of focus. I want to win the foreign picture award.
Billy Wilder, to his cameraman John Seitz, during the shooting of *Sunset Boulevard*, 1949

Modern art is what happens when painters stop looking at girls and persuade themselves that they have had a better idea.
John Ciardi

Modern art is when you buy a picture to cover a hole in the wall and then decide that the hole looks much better.
Anonymous

If it sells, it's art.
Frank Lloyd, in *The Legacy of Mark Rothko* by Lee Seldes, 1978

Art for art's sake is a philosophy of the well-fed.

Cao Yu, in the *Observer*, 1980

The market is always converting works of art into passive fictions of eternity and immutability, of transcendent value for which no price may necessarily be too high. When the word 'priceless' crops up, the haggling has only just begun . . . A fair price is the highest one a collector can be induced to pay.

Robert Hughes, in the *New York Review of Books*, 1984

See also ARTISTS

ARTISTS

Good painters imitate art, bad ones spew it up.

Miguel de Cervantes

He who anticipates his century is generally persecuted when living and is always pilfered when dead.

Benjamin Disraeli

The artistic temperament is a disease that afflicts amateurs.

G.K. Chesterton, *Heretics*, 1905

When we speak of the artistic temperament, we are usually referring to the sum of qualities which hinder the artist in producing.

Arthur Schnitzler

Most of those who call themselves artists are in reality picture dealers, only they make the pictures themselves.

Samuel Butler, *Notebooks*, 1912

Artists hate the enlightened amateur, unless he buys.

Ernest Dimnett, *What We Live By*, 1932

The moment you cheat for the sake of beauty, you know you are an artist.

Max Jacob, *Art Poétique*, 1922

I had a private income – the young artist's best friend.

P.G. Wodehouse, *Quick Service*, 1940

A primitive artist is an amateur whose work sells.
Grandma Moses

I always suspect an artist who is successful before he is dead.
John Murray Fitzgibbon

Remember I'm an artist. And you know what that means in a court of law: the next worst thing to an actress.
Joyce Cary, *The Horse's Mouth*, 1944

Artists can colour the sky red because they know it's blue. The rest of us, who aren't artists, must colour things the way they really are, or people might think we're stupid.
Jules Feiffer

Everyone wants an artist on the wall or on the shelf, but nobody wants him in the house.
James Baldwin

No poet or novelist wishes he was the only one who ever lived, but most of them wish they were the only one alive, and quite a number fondly believe their wish has been granted.
W.H. Auden, *The Dyer's Hand*, 1963

Immature artists imitate, mature artists steal.
Lionel Trilling, in *Esquire* magazine, 1962

Generation to generation . . . nothing changes in Bohemia.
Nik Cohn, *Awopbopaloobopalopbamboom*, 1969

He will lie even when it is inconvenient: the sign of a true artist.
Gore Vidal, *Two Sisters*, 1970

The key to building a superstar is to keep their mouth shut. To reveal an artist to the people can be to destroy him. It isn't to anyone's advantage to see the truth.
Bob Ezrin

Creators are the sacrificial objects of a bored society.
David Williamson, *A Handful of Friends*, 1976

It is very good advice to believe only what an artist does, rather than what he says about his work.
David Hockney, *David Hockney*, 1976

Photography is the 'art form' of the untalented.

Gore Vidal, in the New Statesman magazine, 1978

Creativity is dead. The name of the game . . . is positioning.

Al Ries and Jack Trout, Positioning, 1981

Aesthetic value is often the by-product of the artist striving to do something else.

Evelyn Waugh, The Letters of Evelyn Waugh, ed. Mark Amory, 1980

The fashionable drawing rooms of London have always been happy to welcome outsiders – if only on their own, albeit undemanding terms. That is to say, artists, so long as they are not too talented, men of humble birth, so long as they have since amassed several million pounds, and socialists so long as they are Tories.

Christopher Booker, in Now magazine, 1981

The artist is a member of the leisured classes who cannot pay for his leisure.

Cyril Connolly, Journal 1928-1937, ed. D. Pryce-Jones, 1983

The word 'masterpiece' . . . used to mean a work that proved an artist's graduation into full professional skill, but now means an object whose aura and accumulated myth strike people blind temporarily and render their judgement timid.

Robert Hughes, quoted in the New York Review of Books, 1984

See also ART

AUTHORS

The praise of ancient authors proceeds not from the reverence of the dead, but from the competition and mutual envy of the living.

Thomas Hobbes, Leviathan, 1651

Of all artificial relations formed between mankind, the most capricious and variable is that between author and reader.

Earl of Shaftesbury, Characteristics of Men, Manners, Opinions, Times, 1711-13

An author is a fool who, not content with having bored those who have lived with him, insists on boring future generations.

Charles de Secondat, Baron de Montesquieu, *Persian Letters*, 1721

Novels are receipts to make a whore.

Matthew Green, *The Spleen*, 1737

The reciprocal civility of authors is one of the most risible scenes in the farce of life.

Samuel Johnson, *Works* vol. vi, 1787

The promises of authors are like the vows of lovers.

Samuel Johnson, *Works* vol. vii, 1787

I consider an author's literary reputation to be alive only while his name will ensure a good price for his copy from the booksellers.

Oliver Goldsmith, quoted in *The Life of Samuel Johnson* by J. Boswell, 1791

Take away from Genesis the belief that Moses was the author, on which only the strange belief that it is the word of God has stood, and there remains nothing of Genesis but an anonymous book of stories, fables, and traditonary or invented absurdities, or of downright lies.

Thomas Paine, *The Age of Reason*, 1793

Some books seem to have been written not to teach us anything, but to let us know that the author has known something.

Johann Wolfgang von Goethe, *Poetry and Truth*, 1811–31

If an author writes better than his contemporaries, they will term him a plagiarist; if as well, a pretender, but if worse, he may stand some chance of commendation as a genius of some promise, from whom much may be expected by a due attention to their good counsel and advice.

Charles Caleb Colton, *Lacon*, 1820

The hater of property and of government takes care to have his warranty deed recorded, and the book written against fame and learning has the author's name on the title page.

Ralph Waldo Emerson, *Journals*, 1909–14

I never saw an author in my life . . . that did not purr as audibly as a full-grown cat on having his fur stroked the right way by a skilful hand.

Oliver Wendell Holmes, *The Autocrat of the Breakfast-Table*, **1857–8**

One should not be too severe on English novelists. They are the only relaxation of the intellectually unemployed.

Oscar Wilde

There is no amount of praise which a man and an author cannot bear with equanimity. Some authors can even stand flattery.

Maurice Baring, *Dead Letters*, **1910**

It is a mean thief, or a successful author that plunders the dead.

Austin O'Malley

An author, like any other so-called artist, is a man in whom the normal vanity of all men is so vastly exaggerated that he finds it a sheer impossibility to hold it in. His over-powering impulse is to gyrate before his fellow men, flapping his wings and emitting defiant yells. This being forbidden by the police of all civilized nations, he takes it out by putting his yells on paper. Such is the thing called self-expression.

H.L. Mencken, *Prejudices*, **1919–27**

Every author really wants to have letters printed in the papers. Unable to make the grade, he drops down a rung on the ladder and writes novels.

P.G. Wodehouse, *Louder and Funnier*, **1932**

It is part of prudence to thank an author for his book before reading it, so as to avoid the necessity of lying about it afterwards.

George Santayana

Authors are easy to get on with – if you're fond of children.

Michael Joseph, in the *Observer*, **1949**

What an author likes to write most is his signature on the back of a cheque.

Brendan Francis

An author's first duty is to let down his country.

Brendan Behan, in the *Guardian*, **1960**

It is usually a mistake to confuse the author's point of view with the form he has discovered for it. When the second is admirable, we give him the Nobel Prize for the first.

Nigel Dennis, quoted in the *New York Review of Books*, 1971

There can be no society of authors.

Geoffrey Grigson, *The Private Art*, 1982

See also BEST-SELLERS, BOOKS, WRITING

BEAUTY

A beautiful woman should break her mirror early.

Baltasar Gracian, *The Art of Worldly Wisdom*, 1647

All heiresses are beautiful.

John Dryden, *King Arthur*, 1691

No woman can be a beauty without a fortune.

George Farquhar, *The Beaux Stratagem*, 1707

The blush is beautiful, but sometimes it is inconvenient.

Carlo Goldoni

If Jack's in love, he's no judge of Jill's beauty.

Benjamin Franklin, *Poor Richard's Almanack*, 1733-58

Women have, in general, but one object, which is their beauty; upon which, scarce any flattery is too gross for them to swallow. Nature has hardly formed a woman ugly enough to be insensible to flattery upon her person.

Lord Chesterfield, *Letters to his Son*, 1774

Women's beauty like men's wit, is generally fatal to the owners.

Lord Chesterfield, *Letters to his Son*, 1774

Rank is a great beautifier.

Edward George Bulwer-Lytton, Baron Lytton, *The Lady of Lyons*, 1838

When God provides a beautiful woman, the devil at once retorts with a fool to keep her.

Jules-Amédée Barbey d'Aurevilly

It is better to be beautiful than to be good, but . . . it is better to be good than to be ugly.

Oscar Wilde, *The Picture of Dorian Gray*, 1891

He has nothing. He looks everything. What more can one desire?

Oscar Wilde, *The Importance of Being Earnest*, 1895

I always say beauty is only sin deep.

Saki (H.H. Munro), *Reginald's Choir Treat*, 1904

Somehow a bachelor never quite gets over the idea that he is a thing of beauty and a boy for ever.

Helen Rowland, *A Guide to Men*, 1922

Beauty, n. The power by which a woman charms a lover and terrifies a husband.

Ambrose Bierce, *The Devil's Dictionary*, 1911

Man admire devotion in their wives – and beauty in other women.

Mae West

If a man hears much that a woman says, then she is not beautiful.

Henry Haskins, *Meditations in Wall Street*, 1940

Beauty is still supposed to arouse desire. This is not the case. Beauty has nothing to do with the physical jerks underneath the coverlet. Ugliness is one of the most reliable stimulants.

Henry de Montherlant, *The Goddess Cypris*, 1944

The average girl would rather have beauty than brains because she knows the average man can see much better than he can think.

Anonymous, quoted in *Ladies Home Journal*, 1947

If beauty isn't genius it usually signals at least a high level of animal cunning.

Peter York, in *London Collection* magazine, 1978

All God's children are not beautiful. Most of God's children are, in fact, barely presentable.

Fran Lebowitz, *Metropolitan Life*, 1978

Most beautiful but dumb girls think they are smart and get away with it, because other people, on the whole, aren't much smarter.

Louise Brooks, quoted in *Show People* by Kenneth Tynan, 1980

Distance is the soul of beauty.

Simone Weil, quoted in the *New York Review of Books*, 1981

BELIEF

Everyone prefers belief to the exercise of judgement.

Lucius Annaeus Seneca

When men are in doubt, they always believe what is most agreeable.

Flavius Arrianus, *The Anabasis of Alexander the Great*, c.AD150

Nothing is so firmly believed as that which we least know.

Michel de Montaigne, *Essays*, 1595

It is gross ignorance that produces the dogmatic spirit. The man who knows next to nothing is always eager to teach what he has just learned.

Jean de La Bruyère, *The Characters*, 1688

We are inclined to believe those whom we do not know because they have never deceived us.

Samuel Johnson, *The Idler*, 1758–60

Our prejudices are our mistresses; reason is at best our wife, very often heard indeed, but seldom minded.

Lord Chesterfield, *Letters to his Son*, 1774

Prejudice is never easy unless it can pass itself off for reason.

William Hazlitt, *Sketches and Essays*, 1839

For those who do not think, it is best to rearrange their prejudices once in a while.

Luther Burbank

The whole history of civilization is strewn with creeds and institutions which were invaluable at first, and deadly afterward.

Walter Bagehot, *Physics and Politics*, 1872

Fanaticism consists in redoubling your effort when you have forgotten your aim.

George Santayana, *The Life of Reason*, 1905–6

Bigot, n. One who is obstinately and zealously attached to an opinion that you do not entertain.
Ambrose Bierce, *The Devil's Dictionary*, 1911

Doctrinaires are the vultures of principle. They feed upon principle after it is dead.
David Lloyd George

You can't learn too soon that the most useful thing about a principle is that it can always be sacrificed to expediency.
W. Somerset Maugham, *The Circle*, 1921

Every man thinks his own beliefs are the culmination of two and a half thousand years of Western philosophy.
Alfred North Whitehead, quoted in the *Independent*, 1993

Just as every conviction begins as a whim, so does every emancipator serve his apprenticeship as a crank. A fanatic is a great leader who is just entering the room.
Heywood Broun, 1928

The fact that an opinion has been widely held is no evidence whatsoever that it is not utterly absurd. Indeed, in view of the silliness of the majority of mankind, a widespread belief is more likely to be foolish than sensible.
Bertrand Russell, *Marriage and Morals*, 1929

That which has been believed by everyone, always and everywhere, has every chance of being false.
Paul Valéry, *Tel quel*, 1943

Only one more indispensable massacre of Capitalists or Communists or Fascists or Christians or Heretics and there we are – there we are in the Golden Future.
Aldous Huxley, *Time Must Have a Stop*, 1945

It is characteristic of all movements and crusades that the psychopathic elements rise to the top.
Robert Linder, *Must You Conform*, 1956

Human beings are perhaps never more frightening than when they are convinced beyond doubt that they are right,
Laurens van der Post, *The Lost World of the Kalahari*, 1958

When the need is strong there are those who will believe anything.
Arnold Lobel, *Fables*, 1980

The more ridiculous a belief system, the higher the probability of its success.
Wayne R. Bartz, quoted in *Human Behaviour* magazine, 1975

Not every problem someone has with his girlfriend is necessarily due to the capitalist mode of production.
Herbert Marcuse, in *The Listener* magazine, 1978

An absurdity is anything advanced by our opponents, contrary to our own practice, or above our comprehension.
**'Horace' Smith, quoted in *Definitive Quotations*,
ed. J. Ferguson, 1981**

See also FAITH, IDEALS, IDEAS, MORALS, RELIGION, TRUE BELIEVERS, TRUTH

BEST-SELLERS

The best-seller is the golden touch of mediocre talent.
Cyril Connolly, *Journal 1928–1937*, ed. D. Pryce-Jones, 1983

Religion, aristocracy, sex and mystery: 'Christ,' said the Duchess, 'I'm pregnant. Whodunnit?'
W. Somerset Maugham, proposed recipe for a good story

If we should ever inaugurate a hall of fame, it would be reserved exclusively and hopefully for authors who, having written four best-sellers, still refrained from starting out on a lecture tour.
E.B. White

The principle of procrastinated rape is said to be the ruling one in all the great best-sellers.
V.S. Pritchett, *The Living Novel*, 1946

The best-seller . . . gives an idea of what is read on the periphery of literacy, the reading matter of those who have graduated from the literature of the lavatory wall to the printed word.
Arthur Calder-Marshall, in the *Author* magazine, 1951

A best-seller was a book which somehow sold well simply because it was selling well.

Daniel J. Boorstin, *The Image,* **1962**

See also AUTHORS, BOOKS, WRITING

BIOGRAPHY

Every great man nowadays has his disciples, and it is always Judas who writes the biography.

Oscar Wilde, *The Critic as Artist,* **1891**

Biography, like big-game hunting, is one of the unrecognised forms of sport, and it is as unfair as only sport can be.

Philip Guedalla, *Supers and Supermen,* **1920**

Autobiography is an unrivalled vehicle for telling the truth about other people.

Philip Guedalla, *Supers and Supermen,* **1920**

I enjoy reading biographies because I want to know about the people who messed up the world.

Marie Dressler, *Passing Show,* **1934**

To write one's memoirs is to speak ill of everyone but oneself.

Henri-Philippe Pétain, 1946

When you put down the good things you ought to have done, and leave out the bad ones you did do – that's Memoirs.

Will Rogers, *The Autobiography of Will Rogers,* **1949**

Just how difficult it is to write biography can be reckoned by anybody who sits down and considers just how many people know the real truth about his or her love affairs.

Rebecca West, in *Vogue* **magazine, 1952**

Look out for yourself – or they'll pee on your grave.

Louis B. Mayer

Autobiography: a book of gossip about other people.

J.B. Morton ('Beachcomber')

The purpose of Presidential office is not power, or leadership of the Western world, but reminiscence, best-selling reminiscence.
Roger Jellinek, in *New York Times Book Review*, 1969

Autobiography: probably the most respectable form of lying.
New York Times, 1982

Biography: voyeurism embellished with footnotes.
Robert Skidelsky, 1987

BOOKS

Satire is a sort of glass, wherein beholders do generally discover everybody's face but their own.
Jonathan Swift, *The Battle of the Books*, 1697

Weak men are the worse for the good sense they read in books because it furnisheth them only with more matter to mistake.
George Savile, Marquis of Halifax, *Political, Moral and Miscellaneous Thoughts and Reflexions*, c.1694

Books . . . only teach people to talk about what they do not understand.
Jean-Jacques Rousseau, *Émile*, 1762

The majority of books of our time give one the impression of having been manufactured in a day out of the books read the day before.
Nicolas de Chamfort, *Maximes et pensées*, 1805

The success of many books is due to the affinity between the mediocrity of the author's ideas and those of the public.
Nicolas de Chamfort, *Maximes et pensées*, 1805

There can hardly be a stranger commodity in the world than books. Printed by people who don't understand them; sold by people who don't understand them; bound, criticised and read by people who don't understand them, and now even written by people who don't understand them.
Georg Christoph Lichtenberg, *Aphorisms*, 1764–99

When a new book is published, read an old one.
Samuel Rogers

Many books require no thought from those that read them, and for a very simple reason – they made no such demand upon those who wrote them.
  Charles Caleb Colton, *Lacon*, 1820

Books are made not like children but like pyramids . . . and they're just as useless! and they stay in the desert! . . . Jackals piss at their foot and the bourgeois climb up them.
  Gustave Flaubert, letter, 1857

Books for general reading always smell badly; the odour of common people hangs about them.
  Friedrich Wilhelm Nietzsche, *Beyond Good and Evil*, 1886

The good end happily, the bad unhappily. That is what fiction means.
  Oscar Wilde, *The Importance of Being Earnest*, 1895

A classic is something that everyone wants to have read and nobody wants to read.
  Mark Twain, *The Disappearance of Literature*, 1900

Publishers . . . like Methodists . . . love to keep the Sabbath and anything else they can lay their hands on.
  Anna Ross, 1910

Novel, n. A species of composition bearing the same relation to literature that the panorama bears to art.
  Ambrose Bierce, *The Devil's Dictionary*, 1911

The greatest masterpiece in literature is only a dictionary out of order.
  Jean Cocteau, *Le Potomak*, 1919

Publisher: the patron saint of the mediocre.
  Elbert Hubbard, *The Roycroft Dictionary*, 1923

The chief knowledge that a man gets from reading books is the knowledge that very few of them are worth reading.
  H.L. Mencken

There are two motives for reading a book: one, that you enjoy it, the other that you can boast about it.
  Bertrand Russell, *The Conquest of Happiness*, 1930

Literature: proclaiming in front of everyone what one is careful to conceal from one's immediate circle.

Jean Rostand, *Journal d'un caractère,* **1931**

Books – what they make a movie out of for television.

Leonard L. Levinson

The best part of the fiction in many novels is the notice that the characters are purely imaginary.

Franklin P. Adams (F.P.A.)

As repressed sadists are said to become policemen or butchers so those with an irrational fear of life become publishers.

Cyril Connolly, *Enemies of Promise,* **1938**

Literature is the orchestration of platitudes.

Thornton Wilder, in *Time* **magazine, 1953**

The possession of a book becomes a substitute for reading it.

Anthony Burgess, in *New York Times Book Review,* **1966**

Having been unpopular in high school is not just cause for book publication.

Fran Lebowitz

The ratio of literacy to illiteracy is constant, but nowadays the illiterates can read.

Alberto Moravia, quoted in the *Observer,* **1979**

An optimist is one who believes everything he reads on the jacket of a new book.

Milwaukee Journal

Great literature is like moral leadership: everyone deplores the lack of it, but there is a tendency to prefer it from the safely dead.

Shirley Hazzard, 1982

If pregnancy were a book they would cut the last two chapters.

Nora Ephron, *Heartburn,* **1983**

Fiction is licensed lie-telling

William Amos, *The Originals,* **1985**

See also AUTHORS, BEST-SELLERS, WRITING

BORES

We often forgive those who bore us, but we cannot forgive those whom we bore.

François, Duc de La Rochefoucauld, *Maxims*, 1665

Every hero becomes a bore at last.

Ralph Waldo Emerson, *Representative Men*, 1850

All men are bores, except when we want them.

Oliver Wendell Holmes

Bore, n. A person who talks when you wish him to listen.

Ambrose Bierce, *The Devil's Dictionary*, 1911

Virtuous people often revenge themselves for the constraints to which they submit by the boredom which they inspire.

Gustave Le Bon, *Aphorismes du temps présent*, 1913

Make [the reader] laugh and he will think you a trivial fellow, but bore him in the right way and your reputation is assured.

W. Somerset Maugham, *The Gentleman in the Parlour*, 1930

Perhaps the world's second worst crime is boredom. The first is being a bore.

Cecil Beaton

A gossip is one who talks to you about others, a bore is one who talks to you about himself; and a brilliant conversationalist is one who talks to you about yourself.

Lisa Kirk, quoted in *New York Journal American*, 1954

Dear World, I am leaving you because I am bored. I am leaving you with your worries. Good luck.

George Sanders, his suicide note, 1972

In heaven they will bore you, in hell you will bore them.

Katherine Whitehorn

A bore is a fellow talking who can change the subject back to his topic of conversation faster than you can change it back to yours.

Laurence J. Peter, *Peter's Quotations*, 1977

See also EGOTISM, TALK

BOYS

A bachelor never quite gets over the idea that he is a thing of beauty and a boy for ever.

Helen Rowland

Boys will be boys, and so will a lot of middle-aged men.

Kin Hubbard

I never see any difference in boys. I only know two sorts of boys. Mealy boys and beef-faced boys.

Charles Dickens, *Oliver Twist*, **1838**

Teenage boys, goaded by their surging hormones, run in packs like the primal horde. They have only a brief season of exhilarating liberty between control by their mothers and control by their wives.

Camille Paglia, *Sex, Art and American Culture*, **1992**

See also CHILDREN

BRAVERY

Courage is the fear of being thought a coward.

'Horace' Smith

People are only heroes when they can't do anything else.

Paul Claudel

Show me a hero, and I will write you a tragedy.

F. Scott Fitzgerald, *The Crack-Up*, **1936**

There is no such thing as bravery – only degrees of fear.

John Wainwright, quoted in *The Times*, **1980**

BUREAUCRACY

Bureaucracy . . . the giant power wielded by pygmies.

Honoré de Balzac, *Les Employés*, **1838**

A memorandum is written not to inform the reader but to protect the writer.

Dean Acheson

The perfect bureaucrat everywhere is the man who manages to make no decisions and escape all responsibility.

Brooks Atkinson, *Once Around the Sun*, **1951**

The speed of exit of a civil servant is directly proportional to the quality of his service.

Ralph Nader

A basic rule of bureaucracies: the longer the title, the lower the rank.

Hugh Rawson, *A Dictionary of Euphemisms*, **1983**

See also COMMITTEES

BUSINESS

Corruption is simply business without scruples.

Anonymous

A market is a place set apart for men to deceive and get the better of one another.

Anacharsis, quoted in *Lives and Opinions of Eminent Philosophers* **by Diogenes Laertius, c.225**

There is no kind of idleness by which we are so easily seduced as that which dignifies itself by the appearance of business.

Samuel Johnson, *The Idler*, **1758–60**

Here's the rule for bargains: 'Do other men, for they would do you'. That's the true business precept.

Charles Dickens, *Martin Chuzzlewit*, **1843–4**

It is well known what a middle man is: he is a man who bamboozles one party and plunders the other.

Benjamin Disraeli, speech, 1845

Everyone lives by selling something.

Robert Louis Stevenson

A financier is a pawnbroker with imagination.

Arthur Pinero, 1893

Look, we trade every day out there with hustlers, deal-makers, shysters, con-men. That's the way businesses get started. That's the way this country was built.
   Hubert Allen

Financial sense is knowing that certain men will promise to do certain things and fail.
   Edgar Watson Howe, *Sinner Sermons*, 1926

When two men in a business always agree, one of them is unnecessary.
   William Wrigley Jr

Don't take a nickel, just hand them your business card.
   Richard M. Daley, advising on the safe enjoyment of graft

The trouble with the profit system has always been that it was highly unprofitable to most people.
   E.B. White, *One Man's Meat*, 1944

There is a good deal of solemn cant about the common interests of capital and labour. As matters stand, their only common interest is that of cutting each other's throat.
   Brooks Atkinson, *Once Around the Sun*, 1951

There is little that can be said about most economic goods. A tooth-brush does little but clean teeth. Aspirin does little but dull pain. Alcohol is important mostly for making people more or less drunk . . . There being so little to be said, much is to be invented.
   John Kenneth Galbraith, *Economics, Peace and Laughter*, 1971

Crime is a logical extension of the sort of behaviour that is often considered perfectly respectable in legitimate business.
   Robert Rice, *The Business of Crime*, 1956

An actuary is someone who moved out of accountancy because he couldn't stand the excitement.
   Anonymous

A hustler is a man who will talk you into giving him a free ride and make it seem as if he is doing you a great favour.
   Bill Veeck, 1965

Commercialism is doing well that which should not be done at all.
Gore Vidal

The only promotion rules I can think of are that a sense of shame is
to be avoided at all costs and there is never any reason for a hustler to
be less cunning than more virtuous men. Oh yes . . . whenever you
think you've got something really great, add ten per cent more.
Bill Veeck, 1965

The value of anything is not what you get paid for it, nor what it cost
to produce, but what you can get for it at an auction.
William Lyon Phelps, quoted in the *National Observer*, 1969

In a hierarchy every employee tends to rise to his level of incompetence . . . in time every post tends to be occupied by an employee who
is incompetent to carry out its duties . . . Work is accomplished by
those employees who have not yet reached their level of incompetence.
Laurence J. Peter, *The Peter Principle*, 1969

An office party is not, as is sometimes supposed, the Managing Director's chance to kiss the tea-girl. It is the tea-girl's chance to kiss the
Managing Director (however bizarre an ambition this may seem to
anyone who has seen the Managing Director face on).
Katherine Whitehorn

As long as people will accept crap, it will be financially profitable to
dispense it.
Dick Cavett, in *Playboy* magazine, 1971

The first myth of management is that it exists. The second myth of
management is that success equals skill.
Robert Heller, *The Great Executive Dream*, 1972

Nothing is illegal if one hundred businessmen decide to do it.
Andrew Young, 1976

An accountant is a man hired to explain that you didn't make the
money you did.
Anonymous

If you hype something and it succeeds, you're a genius – it wasn't a
hype. If you hype it and it fails, then it was just a hype.
Neil Bogart

It comes down to that . . . business tactic: the guy that yells loudest is right.

Irving Azoff, quoted in *Rolling Stone* magazine, 1976

The business world worships mediocrity. Officially we revere free enterprise, initiative and individuality. Unofficially we fear it.

George Lois, *The Art of Advertising*, 1977

The arms business is founded on human folly. That is why its depths will never be plumbed and why it will go on forever. All weapons are defensive and all spare parts are non-lethal. The plainest print cannot be read through a solid gold sovereign, or a ruble or a golden eagle.

Sam Cummings, 1978

The salary of the chief executive of the large corporation is not a market award for achievement. It is frequently in the nature of a warm personal gesture by the individual to himself.

John Kenneth Galbraith, *Annals of an Abiding Liberal*, 1980

Management: an activity or art where those who have not yet succeeded and those who have proved unsuccessful are led by those who have not yet failed.

Paulsson Frenckner, speech, 1984

Contract: an agreement that is binding on the weaker party.

Frederick Sawyer

Supermarkets . . . symbols of man's inhumanity to women.

Philip Adams, in *The Dictionary of Australian Quotations*, 1984

See also MONEY, THE RICH

CENSORSHIP

To forbid us anything is to make us have a mind for it.

Michel de Montaigne, *Essays*, 1595

Wherever they burn books, they will also, in the end, burn people.

Heinrich Heine, *Almansor*, 1823

A satire which the censor is able to understand deserves to be banned.

Karl Kraus

Assassination is the extreme form of censorship.

George Bernard Shaw, *The Rejected Statement*, 1916

I wouldn't tell the people anything until the war is over, and then I'd tell them who won.

Anonymous American military censor, on the ideal use of the media in war, 1943

Obscenity is what happens to shock some elderly and ignorant magistrate.

Bertrand Russell, in *Look* magazine, 1954

When there is official censorship it is a sign that speech is serious. When there is none, it is pretty certain that the official spokesmen have all the loudspeakers.

Paul Goodman, *Growing Up Absurd*, 1960

The First Amendment forbids any law 'abridging the freedom of speech'. It doesn't say, 'except for commercials on children's television' or 'unless somebody says "cunt" in a rap song or "chick" on a college campus'.

P.J. O'Rourke, *Parliament of Whores*, 1991

Obscenity is whatever gives a judge an erection.

Anonymous American lawyer

See also TALK, WRITING

CHARITY

An open hand makes a blind eye.

Francis Quarles, *Enchyridion*, 1641

All are apt to shrink from those that lean upon them.

George Savile, Marquis of Halifax, *Political, Moral and Miscellaneous Thoughts and Reflexions*, c.1694

He that feeds upon charity has a cold dinner and no supper.

Thomas Fuller, M.D., *Gnomologia*, 1732

Everyone in this world has as much as they can do in caring for themselves, and few have leisure really to think of their neighbour's

distresses, however they may delight their tongues with talking of them.
Samuel Johnson

The most genuine and efficacious charity is that which greases the paws of the priests; such charity covers a multitude of sins.
Voltaire, *Philosophical Dictionary*, 1764

Charity, like nature, abhors a vaccuum. Next to putting it into the bank, men like to squander their superfluous wealth on those to whom it is sure of doing the least possible good.
William Hazlitt, *Butts of Different Sorts*, 1829

We do not quite forgive a giver. The hand that feeds us is in some danger of being bitten.
Ralph Waldo Emerson, *Journals*, 1909–14

Take egotism out, and you would castrate the benefactors.
Ralph Waldo Emerson, *Journals* 1909–14

The worst of charity is, that the lives you are asked to preserve are not worth preserving.
Ralph Waldo Emerson

One can always be kind to people about whom one cares nothing.
Oscar Wilde, *The Picture of Dorian Gray*, 1891

Altruism: the art of doing unselfish things for selfish reasons.
Anonymous

Charity is the sterilised milk of human kindness.
Oliver Herford

People who mean well – always a poisonous class.
E.V. Lucas

Philanthropy seems to me to have become simply the refuge of people who want to annoy their fellow creatures.
Oscar Wilde, *An Ideal Husband*, 1895

Man is the only animal which esteems itself rich in proportion to the number and voracity of its parasites.
George Bernard Shaw, *Man and Superman*, 1903

Self-sacrifice enables us to sacrifice other people without blushing.
George Bernard Shaw, *Man and Superman*, 1903

The Princess had always defended a friend's complexion if it was really bad. With her . . . charity began at homeliness and did not generally progress much further.
Saki (H.H. Munro), *Reginald in Russia*, 1910

Dependent, adj. Reliant upon another's generosity for the support which you are not in a position to exact from his fears.
Ambrose Bierce, *The Devil's Dictionary*, 1911

When a benefactor has no other confidant than the beneficiary, his secret, as a rule, is only too safe.
Alexandre Vinet, quoted in *A Cynic's Breviary* by J.R. Solly, 1925

You can only help one of your luckless brothers
By trampling down a dozen others.
Bertolt Brecht, *The Good Person of Szechuan*, 1943

We'd all like a reputation for generosity, and we'd all like to buy it cheap.
Mignon McLaughlin, *The Neurotic's Notebook*, 1963

There is only one word for aid that is genuinely without strings and that word is blackmail.
Colm Brogan

Without the skeleton at the feast, it is questionable whether the feast tastes good.
George Buchanan

Compassion is a luxury of the affluent.
Tony Randall, quoted in *Playboy* magazine, 1974

See also LIBERALS, MONEY, RELIGION

CHILDREN

The reason why parents love the younger children best is because they now have so little hope that the elder will do well.
Japanese proverb

You are to have as strict a Guard upon yourself among your Children as if you were among your Enemies.

George Savile, Marquis of Halifax, *Political, Moral and Miscellaneous Thoughts and Reflexions*, c.1694

As fathers commonly go, it is seldom a misfortune to be fatherless; and considering the general run of sons, as seldom a misfortune to be childless.

Lord Chesterfield, *Letters to his Son*, 1774

Bachelors' wives and old maids' children are always perfect.

Nicolas de Chamfort, *Maximes et pensées*, 1805

When I consider how little of a rarity children are . . . I cannot for the life of me tell what cause for pride there can possibly be in having them.

Charles Lamb, *Essays of Elia*, 1823

Children are never too tender to be whipped: like tough beefsteaks, the more you beat them the more tender they become.

Edgar Allen Poe, in *Graham's Magazine*, 1850

If you desire to drain to the dregs the fullest cup of scorn and hatred that a human fellow creature can pour out for you, let a young mother hear you call her baby 'it'.

Jerome K. Jerome, *Idle Thoughts of an Idle Fellow*, 1886

Children begin by loving their parents. After a time they judge them . . . rarely, if ever, do they forgive them.

Oscar Wilde, *A Woman of No Importance*, 1893

It must have been some unmarried fool that said 'A child can ask questions that a wise man cannot answer'; because, in any decent house, a brat that starts asking questions is promptly packed off to bed.

Arthur Binstead, *Pitcher's Proverbs*, 1909

The parent who could see his boy as he really is would shake his head and say, 'Willie is no good. I'll sell him.'

Stephen Leacock, *Literary Lapses*, 1910

Childhood, n. The period of human life intermediate between the idiocy of infancy and the folly of youth – two removes from the sin of manhood and three from the remorse of age.

Ambrose Bierce, *The Devil's Dictionary*, 1911

The best way to keep children at home is to make the home atmosphere pleasant – and to let the air out of the tyres.
   Dorothy Parker

Nature makes boys and girls lovely to look upon so they can be tolerated until they acquire some sense.
   William Lyon Phelps

Beat your son every day; you may not know why, but he will.
   Anonymous

The effects of infantile instruction, like those of syphilis, are never completely cured.
   Robert Briffault, *Sin and Sex*, 1931

Anyone who hates children and dogs can't be all bad.
   W.C. Fields

Destroy him as you will, the bourgeois always bounces up. Execute him, expropriate him, starve him out *en masse*, and he reappears in your children.
   Cyril Connolly, 1937

There is no more sombre enemy of good art than the pram in the hall.
   Cyril Connolly, *Enemies of Promise*, 1938

Adolescence: a stage between infancy and adultery.
   Anonymous, quoted in *H.L. Mencken's Dictionary of Quotations*, 1942

The state of innocence contains the germs of all future sin.
   Alexandre Arnoux

What is an adult? A child blown up by age.
   Simone de Beauvoir, *The Woman Destroyed*, 1969

I love children. Especially when they cry – for then someone takes them away.
   Nancy Mitford

Children have never been very good at listening to their elders, but they have never failed to imitate them.
   James Baldwin, in *Esquire* magazine, 1960

The easiest way for your children to learn about money is for you not to have any.

Katherine Whitehorn, *How To Survive Children*, 1975

It is no wonder people are so horrible when they start life as children.

Kingsley Amis, *One Fat Englishman*, 1963

Children are cruel, ruthless, cunning and almost incredibly self-centred. Far from cementing a marriage, children more frequently disrupt it. Child-rearing is on the whole an expensive and unrewarding bore, in which more has to be invested, both materially and spiritually, than ever comes out in dividends.

Nigel Balchin, quoted in the *Sunday Express*, 1965

Society highly values its normal men. It educates children to lose themselves and to become absurd, and thus be normal. Normal men have killed perhaps 100,000,000 of their fellow normal men in the last fifty years.

R.D. Laing, *The Politics of Experience*, 1967

I know what 'custody' [of the children] means. 'Get even'. That's all custody means. Get even with your old lady.

Lenny Bruce, quoted in *The Essential Lenny Bruce*, ed. J. Cohen, 1967

Children's talent to endure stems from their ignorance of alternatives.

Maya Angelou, *I Know Why the Caged Bird Sings*, 1969

The Jewish man with parents alive is a fifteen-year-old boy and will remain a fifteen-year-old boy until they die.

Philip Roth, *Portnoy's Complaint*, 1967

Cleaning your house while your kids are still growing
Is like shovelling the walk before it stops snowing.

Phyllis Diller

Boys will be boys. And even that wouldn't matter if we could prevent girls from being girls.

Anthony Hope (Sir Anthony Hope Hawkins), *The Dolly Dialogues*, 1894

See also ADULTS, BOYS, FAMILIES, GIRLS, PARENTS

CHRISTIANS

Men of simple understanding, little inquisitive and little instructed, make good Christians.
   Michel de Montaigne, *Essays*, 1595

Christ: a parish demagogue.
   Percy Bysshe Shelley

What is more harmful than any vice? Practical sympathy for the botched and weak – Christianity.
   Friedrich Wilhelm Nietzsche, *The Antichrist*, 1888

Christianity has done love a great service by making it a sin.
   Anatole France, *The Garden of Epicurus*, 1894

People may say what they like about the decay of Christianity; the religious system that produced green Chartreuse can never really die.
   Saki (H.H. Munro), *Reginald on Christmas Presents*, 1904

Popular Christianity has for its emblem a gibbet, for its chief sensation a sanguinary execution after torture, for its central mystery an insane vengeance brought off by a trumpery expiation.
   George Bernard Shaw, *Major Barbara*, 1907

Christian, n. One who believes that the New Testament is a divinely inspired book admirably suited to the spiritual need of his neighbour.
   Ambrose Bierce, *The Devil's Dictionary*, 1911

Heaven: the Coney Island of the Christian imagination.
   Elbert Hubbard, *The Notebook*, 1927

Christ died for our sins. Dare we make his martyrdom meaningless by not committing them?
   Jules Feiffer, quoted in *Peter's Quotations*, ed. L. Peter, 1977

See also BELIEF, THE CLERGY, FAITH, GOD, HYPOCRISY, MORALS, RELIGION

CIVILISATION

Our civilisation is founded on the shambles, and every individual existence goes out in a lonely spasm of helpless agony.
William James, *Varieties of Religious Experience*, 1902

Civilisation is the lamb's skin in which barbarism masquerades.
Thomas B. Aldrich, *Ponkapog Papers*, 1903

There is a vast difference between the savage and civilised man, but it is never apparent to their wives until after breakfast.
Helen Rowland, *A Guide to Men*, 1922

The major advances in civilisation are processes that all but wreck the societies in which they occur.
Alfred North Whitehead

Civilisation is nothing else but the attempt to reduce force to being the last resort.
José Ortega y Gasset, *The Revolt of the Masses*, 1930

It is so stupid of modern civilisation to have given up believing in the devil when he is the only explanation of it.
Ronald Knox, *Let Dons Delight*, 1939

The civilised are those who get more out of life than the uncivilised, and for this the uncivilised have not forgiven them.
Cyril Connolly (Palinurus), *The Unquiet Grave*, 1944

The civilisation of one epoch becomes the manure of the next.
Cyril Connolly (Palinurus), *The Unquiet Grave*, 1944

You can't say civilisation don't advance . . . for in every war they kill you a new way.
Will Rogers, *The Autobiography of Will Rogers*, 1949

We are born princes and the civilising process makes us frogs.
Eric Berne, *The Games People Play*, 1964

All that is left for the civilised man is to laugh at the absurdity of the human condition.
Auberon Waugh, in *Esquire* magazine, 1968

We are all born charming, fresh and spontaneous and must be civilised before we are fit to participate in society.

Judith Martin, *Miss Manners' Guide to Excruciatingly Correct Behaviour*, 1983

See also HUMANITY, LIFE

CLASS

The difference between what is commonly called ordinary company and good company is only hearing the same things said in a little room or in a large salon, at small tables or at great tables, before two candles or twenty sconces.

Alexander Pope

Barbarians, Philistines, Populace . . . the three great classes into which our society is divided.

Matthew Arnold, *Culture and Anarchy*, 1869

The danger is not that a particular class is unfit to govern. Every class is unfit to govern.

Sir J.E.E. Dalberg, first Baron Acton, letter to Mary Gladstone, 1881

It is only by not paying one's bills that one can hope to live in the memory of the commercial classes.

Oscar Wilde, *Phrases and Philosophies for the Use of the Young*, 1894

Never speak disrespectfully of society – only people who can't get into it do that.

Oscar Wilde, *The Importance of Being Earnest*, 1895

I think she must have been very strictly brought up, she's so desperately anxious to do the wrong thing correctly.

Saki (H.H.Munro), *Reginald on Worries*, 1904

I don't think you want too much sincerity in society. It would be like an iron girder in a house of cards.

W. Somerset Maugham, *The Circle*, 1921

Society is like the air: neccessary to breathe, but insufficient to live on.

George Santayana

Broadly speaking, human beings may be divided into three classes: those who are billed to death, those who are worried to death and those who are bored to death.
Sir Winston Churchill

A broad definition of crime in England is that it is any lower-class activity that is displeasing to the upper class.
David Frost and Antony Jay

The genius of our ruling class is that it has kept a majority of the people from ever questioning the inequity of a system where most people drudge along paying heavy taxes for which they get nothing in return.
Gore Vidal

Class: when they're running you out of town, to look like you're leading the parade.
Bill Battie, in *Sports Illustrated* magazine, 1976

The working classes have a reputation for potency and being good in bed – a myth probably started by middle-class novelists and by graphologists who claim that anyone with loopy writing must be highly sexed.
Jilly Cooper, *Class*, 1979

See also ARISTOCRACY, GENTLEMEN, THE MASSES

THE CLERGY

A priest is a man who is called Father by everyone except his own children, who are obliged to call him Uncle.
Anonymous Italian saying

The Clergy would have us believe them against our own reason, as the woman would have had her husband against his own eyes, when he took her with another man, which she yet stoutly denied: 'What, will you believe your own eyes before your own sweet wife?'
John Selden, *Table Talk*, 1689

A clergyman is one who feels himself called upon to live without working at the expense of the rascals who work to live.
Voltaire

To the philosophical eye the vices of the clergy are far less dangerous than their virtues.

Edward Gibbon, *Decline and Fall of the Roman Empire*, 1776–88

Priests and conjurors are of the same trade.

Thomas Paine, *The Age of Reason*, 1793

And priests dare babble of a God of peace,
Even whilst their hands are red with guiltless blood,
Murdering the while, uprooting every germ
Of truth, exterminating, spoiling all,
Making the earth a slaughter-house!

Percy Bysshe Shelley, *Queen Mab*, 1813

In every country and in every age the priest has been hostile to liberty. He is always in alliance with the despot, abetting his abuses in return for protection of his own.

Thomas Jefferson, letter, 1814

Mothers, wives and maids,
These be the tools with which priests manage men.

Robert Browning, *The Ring and the Book*, 1868–9

How large a share of vanity must spur the piety of the missionary. There is something melodramatic in landing on some Fiji island, in baptising, debauching and ultimately murdering the unsuspecting savage; then in taking his land in the name of the Most High.

Richard Birnie, *Essays*, 1879

In all ages hypocrites, called priests, have put crowns on the heads of thieves, called kings.

Robert G. Ingersoll, 1884

'Sins' are indispensable to every society organized on an ecclesiastical basis; they are the only reliable weapons of power; the priest lives upon sins; it is necessary to him that there be 'sinning'.

Friedrich Wilhelm Nietzsche, *The Antichrist*, 1888

Priests . . . these turkey-cocks of God.

Friedrich Wilhelm Nietzsche, *The Antichrist*, 1888

Clergyman, n. A man who undertakes the management of our spiritual affairs as a method of bettering his temporal ones.

Ambrose Bierce, *The Devil's Dictionary*, 1911

Parsons always seem to be specially horrified about things like sun-bathing and naked bodies. They don't mind poverty and misery and cruelty to animals nearly as much.

Susan Ertz

Of learned men, the clergy show the lowest development of profes-sional ethics. Any pastor is free to cadge customers from the divines of rival sects, and to denounce the divines themselves as theological quacks.

H.L. Mencken, *Minority Report*, 1956

See also BELIEF, FAITH, GOD, HYPOCRISY, MORALS, RELIGION

COMMITTEES

A committee should consist of three men, two of whom are absent.

Sir Herbert Beerbohm Tree

A committee is a group that keeps the minutes and loses hours.

Milton Berle, 1954

A conference is a gathering of important people who singly can do nothing but together can decide that nothing can be done.

Fred Allen

What is a committee? A group of the unwilling, picked from the unfit, to do the unnecessary.

Richard Harkness, quoted in the *New York Herald Tribune*, 1960

Meetings are indispensable when you don't want to do anything.

John Kenneth Galbraith, *Ambassador's Journal*, 1969

A committee is a cul-de-sac down which ideas are lured and then quietly strangled.

Sir Barnett Cocks, in *New Scientist* magazine, 1973

See also BUREAUCRACY

COMPUTERS

If you put tomfoolery into a computer, nothing comes out but tom-foolery. But this tomfoolery, having passed through a very expensive machine, is somehow ennobled and no-one dares criticise it.

Pierre Gallois

Machines from the Maxim gun to the computer are for the most part means by which a minority can keep free men in subjection.

Kenneth Clark, *Civilisation*, **1969**

To err is human, but to really foul things up requires a computer.

Farmers' Almanac, 1978

CONFORMITY

                      . . . and obedience,
Bane of all genius, virtue, freedom, truth,
Makes slaves of men, and, of the human frame,
A mechanised automaton.

Percy Bysshe Shelley, *Queen Mab*, **1813**

Conformity, humility, acceptance – with these coins we are to pay our fares to paradise.

Robert Lindner, *Must You Conform?*, **1956**

See also CONSERVATIVES, CONSISTENCY

CONSCIENCE

Conscience is, in most men, an anticipation of the opinions of others.

Sir Henry Taylor, *The Statesman*, **1836**

Conscience and cowardice are really the same things. Conscience is the trade-name of the firm.

Oscar Wilde, *The Picture of Dorian Gray*, **1891**

So long as there are earnest believers in the world, they will always wish to punish opinions, even if their judgement tells them that it is unwise and their conscience that it is wrong.

Walter Bagehot, *Literary Studies*, **1879–95**

The conscience is a watch that everyone sets by the time of his own country.

Aurelien Scholl, quoted in *Reflections on the Art of Life*
by J.R. Solly, 1902

A guilty conscience is the mother of invention.

Carolyn Wells

Pangs of conscience are the sadistic stirrings of Christianity.
Karl Kraus, *Half Truths and One and a Half Truths*, 1986

Conscience is a cur that does not stop us from passing but that we cannot prevent from barking.
**Nicolas de Chamfort, quoted in *A Cynic's Breviary*
by J.R. Solly, 1925**

Most people sell their souls, and live with a good conscience on the proceeds.
Logan Pearsall Smith, *Afterthoughts*, 1933

If you really want to do something new, the good won't help you with it. Let me have men about me that are arrant knaves. The wicked, who have something on their conscience, are obliging, quick to hear threats, because they know how it's done, and for booty. You can offer them things because they will take them. Because they have no hesitations. You can hang them if they get out of step. Let me have men about me that are utter villains – provided that I have the power, the absolute power, over life and death.
Hermann Göring

One lives with so many bad deeds on one's conscience and some good intentions in one's heart.
Pierre Reverdy, *Le livre de mon bord*, 1948

Living with a conscience is like driving a car with the brakes on.
Budd Schulberg, *What Makes Sammy Run?*, 1941

Conscience is what your mother told you before you were six years old.
Dr Brock Chisholm, quoted in *Ladies Home Journal*, 1949

Conscience is the inner voice that warns us that someone might be looking.
H.L. Mencken, *A Mecken Chrestomathy*, 1949

The Anglo-Saxon conscience does not prevent the Anglo-Saxon from sinning, it merely prevents him from enjoying his sin.
Salvador de Madariaga

A conscience which has been bought once will be bought twice.
Norbert Wiener, *The Human Use of Human Beings*, 1954

See also HONESTY, HYPOCRISY

CONSERVATIVES

Tory: a cant term, derived, I suppose, from an Irish word, signifying savage.

Samuel Johnson, *A Dictionary of the English Language*, 1755

There are only two great currents in the history of mankind: the baseness which makes conservatives and the envy which makes revolutionaries.

Edmond and Jules de Goncourt, *Diary*, 12, July 1867

Conservatism . . . is mainly due to want of imagination . . . Conservatism, in the lump, is a euphemism for selfishness . . . Stupid people can only see their own side of a question; they cannot even imagine any other side possible. So, as a rule stupid people are Conservative.

Grant Allen, quoted in *The Westminster Gazette*, 1894

Radicalism, n. The conservatism of tomorrow injected into the affairs of today.

Ambrose Bierce, *The Devil's Dictionary*, 1911

Conservative, n. A statesman who is enamoured of existing evils, as distinguished from the Liberal who wishes to replace them with others.

Ambrose Bierce, *The Devil's Dictionary*, 1911

A conservative is a man who is too cowardly to fight and too fat to run.

Elbert Hubbard, *The Notebook*, 1927

The radical invents the views. When he has worn them out, the conservative adopts them.

Mark Twain, *Notebook*, 1935

How can wealth persuade poverty to use its political freedom to keep wealth in power? Here lies the whole art of Conservative politics in the 20th century.

Aneurin Bevan, *In Place of Fear*, 1952

There is nothing more disgusting in British political life than a Conservative who thinks he has public opinion behind him.

Auberon Waugh, in the *Spectator* magazine, 1986

See also CONFORMITY, CONSISTENCY, GOVERNMENT, PARTIES, POLITICIANS, POLITICS

CONSISTENCY

There is nothing in this world constant but inconstancy.

Jonathan Swift, *A Critical Essay upon the Faculties of Mind,*
1707

No perverseness equals that which is supported by system, no errors
are as difficult to root out as those which the understanding has pledged
its credit to uphold.

William Wordsworth, *Poems,* **1815**

Consistency is the hobgoblin of little minds, adored by little statesmen
and philosophers and divines.

Ralph Waldo Emerson, *Essays,* **1841**

Consistency requires you to be as ignorant today as you were a year
ago.

Bernard Berenson, *Notebook,* **1892**

One is often kept in the right road by a rut.

Gustave Droz, quoted in *Reflections on the Art of Life*
by J.R. Solly, 1902

See also CONFORMITY, CONSERVATIVES

COWARDICE

Most of the time the word *realism* is a polite translation of the word
cowardice.

Jean Dutourd, *Taxis of the Marne,* **1957**

CRIME

All criminals turn preachers under the gallows.

Italian proverb

Successful and fortunate crime is called virtue.

Lucius Annaeus Seneca, *Hercules Furens,* **c.AD50**

Society . . . prepares crimes; criminals are only the instruments necessary for executing them.

L.A.J. Quételet

The state calls its own violence law, but that of the individual crime.

Max Stirner, *The Ego and His Own*, 1845

Thieves respect property; they merely wish the property to become their property that they may more perfectly respect it.

G.K. Chesterton, *The Man Who Was Thursday*, 1908

Organised crime is just the dirty side of the sharp dollar.

Raymond Chandler, *The Long Goodbye*, 1953

My fellow-prisoners seemed to me in no way morally inferior to the rest of the population though they were on the whole slightly below the usual level of intelligence, as was shown by their having been caught.

Bertrand Russell, *Autobiography*, 1967

What's the difference between a guy in the bighouse and the average guy you pass in the street? The guy in the bighouse is a Loser who tried.

Charles Bukowski, *Notes of a Dirty Old Man*, 1969

See also LAW

CRITICS & CRITICISM

Critics are the stupid who discuss the wise.

Anonymous

Critics are like brushers of nobleman's clothes.

Sir Henry Wotton

They who write ill and they who durst not write,
Turn critics out of mere revenge and spite.

John Dryden, *The Conquest of Granada*, 1670

Though by whim, envy or resentment led,
They damn those authors whom they never read.

Charles Churchill, *The Candidate*, 1764

The great contention of criticism is to to find the faults of the moderns and the beauties of the ancients. While an author is yet living we estimate his powers by his worst performance, and when he is dead we rate them by his best.

Samuel Johnson, *The Plays of Shakespeare*, 1765

I never read a book before reviewing it – it prejudices a man so.

Sydney Smith, quoted in *The Smith of Smiths* by Hesketh Pearson, 1934

As a bankrupt thief turns thief-taker, so an unsuccessful author turns critic.

Percy Bysshe Shelley, *Adonais*, 1821

Taking to pieces is the trade of those who cannot construct.

Ralph Waldo Emerson

Nature fits all her children with something to do,
He who would write and can't write, would surely review,
Can set up a small booth as a critic, and sell us his
Petty conceit and his pettier jealousies.

James Lowell, *A Fable for Critics*, 1848

You know who critics are? – the men who have failed in literature and art.

Benjamin Disraeli, *Lothair*, 1870

A man is a critic when he cannot be an artist, just as a man becomes a stool pigeon when he cannot be a soldier.

Gustave Flaubert

It is only an auctioneer who can equally and impartially admire all schools of art.

Oscar Wilde, *The Critic as Artist*, 1891

Caviler, n. A critic of our own work.

Ambrose Bierce, *The Devil's Dictionary*, 1911

Reviewing has one advantage over suicide: in suicide you take it out on yourself; in reviewing you take it out on other people.

George Bernard Shaw

Criticism is prejudice made plausible.
H.L. Mencken

Reviewers . . . seemed to fall into two classes: those who had little to say, and those that had nothing.
Max Beerbohm, *Seven Men*, 1919

Critics . . . are of two sorts: those who merely relieve themselves against the flower of beauty, and those, less continent, who afterwards scratch it up.
William Empson, *Seven Types of Ambiguity*, 1930

A critic is a gong at a railroad crossing clanging loudly and vainly as the train goes by.
Christopher Morley

Time is the only critic without ambition.
John Steinbeck

A critic is a legless man who teaches running.
Channing Pollock

A critic is a man who writes about things he doesn't like.
Anonymous, quoted in *H.L. Mencken's Dictionary of Quotations*, 1942

Any fool can criticise – and many of them do.
Cyril Garbett

A musicologist is a man who can read music but can't hear it.
Sir Thomas Beecham, quoted in *Beecham Remembered* by H. Proctor-Gregg, 1976

A critic is a man created to praise greater men than himself, but he is never able to find them.
Richard Le Gallienne

My native habitat is the theatre, I toil not, neither do I spin. I am a critic and a commentator. I am essential to the theatre – as ants to a picnic, as the boll weevil to a cotton field.
Joseph Mankiewicz, screenplay for *All About Eve*, 1950

A drama critic is a man who leaves no turn unstoned.
George Bernard Shaw, quoted in the *New York Times*, 1950

Be fairly ruthless, I think, with opponents of 'modern' painting. If you are lucky enough to find a man who still says 'I don't know about pictures but I know what I like' point out to him that because he does not know about pictures he does not know what he likes and repeat this in a thundering voice . . . If your man says of some picture 'Yes, but what does it mean?' ask him, and keep on asking him, what his carpet means, or the circular patterns on his rubber overshoes. Make him lift up his foot to look at them.

Stephen Potter, *One-Upmanship*, **1952**

What critics call 'dirty' in our films they call 'lusty' in foreign films.

Billy Wilder

Critics are like eunuchs in a harem: they know how it's done, they've seen it done every day, but they're unable to do it themselves.

Brendan Behan

Reviewmanship . . . 'how to be one up on the author without actually tampering with the text'. In other words how, as a critic, to show that it is really yourself who should have written the book, if you had had the time, and since you hadn't are glad that someone else has, although obviously it might have been done better.

Stephen Potter, *Supermanship*, **1958**

The avocation of assessing the failures of better men can be turned into a comfortable livelihood, providing you back it up with a Ph.D.

Nelson Algren, *Writers at Work* **1st series, 1958**

Critics are eunuchs at a gang-bang.

George Burns

A critic is a bundle of biases held loosely together by a sense of taste.

Whitney Balliett, *Dinosaurs in the Morning*, **1962**

Asking a working writer what he feels about critics is like asking a lamp-post what it feels about dogs.

John Osborne

A critic is a man who knows the way but can't drive the car.

Kenneth Tynan, in the *New York Times*, **1966**

Friendly attacks should begin with faint praise, but be careful not to use adjectives or phrases of which the publisher can make use in advertisements.

John Betjeman

It is wrong to read the books one reviews – it creates a prejudice.
George Croly

A good review from the critics is just another stay of execution.
Dustin Hoffman, quoted in *Playboy* magazine, 1975

A drama critic is a person who surprises a playwright by informing him what he meant.
Wilson Mizner, quoted in *The People's Almanac*, 1976

Criticism of the arts . . . taken by and large, ends in a display of suburban omniscience which sees no further than into the next-door garden.
Sir Thomas Beecham, quoted in *Beecham Stories* by Harold Atkins and Archie Newman, 1978

I read a good deal of criticism, but only as a vice: not so good as reading science fiction, rather better than reading mystery stories.
Gore Vidal

Pop music is the kind played so fast that you can't work out which classical composer it was pinched from.
Anonymous

See also ACTING, WRITING

CULTURE

Mass culture: a contradiction in terms.
Anonymous

Culture is an instrument wielded by professors to manufacture professors, who when their turn comes, will manufacture professors.
Simone Weil, *The Need for Roots*, 1952

Great cultural changes begin in affectation and end in routine.
Jacques Barzun, *The House of Intellect*, 1959

It is only the middle-class people who, quite mistakenly, imagine that a lively pursuit of the latest in reading or painting will advance their status in the world.
Mary McCarthy, *On the Contrary*, 1962

The old complaint that mass culture is designed for eleven-year-olds is of course a shameful canard. The key age has traditionally been more like fourteen.

Robert Christgau, in *Esquire* magazine, 1969

It strikes me as gruesome and comical that in our culture we have an expectation that a man can always solve his problems. This is so untrue that it makes me want to cry – or laugh.

Kurt Vonnegut Jr, in *Playboy* magazine, 1973

Culture . . . television programmes so boring that they cannot be classified as entertainment.

Quentin Crisp, *How To Become a Virgin*, 1981

Mass culture is a machine for showing desire. Here is what must interest you, it says, as if it guessed that men are incapable of finding out what to desire by themselves.

Roland Barthes, quoted in the *New York Review of Books*, 1982

CYNICISM

Cynic, n. A blackguard whose faulty vision sees things as they are, not as they ought to be.

Ambrose Bierce, *The Devil's Dictionary*, 1911

A cynic is not merely one who reads bitter lessons from the past, he is one who is prematurely disappointed in the future.

Sydney J. Harris, *On the Contrary*, 1962

Cynicism: an extension of ennui maintaining that not only are you bored, you are in a state of disbelief as well. And you cannot be convinced otherwise . . . more than a pose; it's also a handy time saver. By deflating your companion's enthusiasm, you can cut conversations in half.

Lisa Bernbach, *The Official Preppy Handbook*, 1981

See also TRUTH

DEATH

Death is life's answer to the question 'Why?'

Graffito

I desire to go hell, not heaven. In hell I shall enjoy the company of popes, kings and princes, but in heaven are only beggars, monks, hermits and apostles.

Niccolò Machiavelli, on his deathbed, 1527

Six feet of earth make all men equal.

James Howell, *Proverbs*, 1659

O Death, all-eloquent! you only prove
What dust we dote on, when 'tis man we love.

Alexander Pope, *Eloisa to Abelard*, 1717

The first breath is the beginning of death.

Thomas Fuller, M.D., *Gnomologia*, 1732

I know of nobody that has a mind to die this year.

Thomas Fuller, M.D., *Gnomologia*, 1732

In this world, nothing can be said to be certain but death and taxes.

Benjamin Franklin, letter, 1789

I have no relish for the country: it is a kind of grave.

Sydney Smith, letter, 1838

The play is the tragedy 'Man'
And its hero the conqueror, Worm.

Edgar Allen Poe, *The Raven and Other Poems*, 1845

To beings constituted as we are the monotony of singing psalms would be as great an affliction as the pains of hell, and might even be pleasantly interrupted by them.

Benjamin Jowett, from his introduction to Plato's *Phaedo*, 1871

It is not true that the dying man is generally more honest than the living. On the contrary, by the solemn attitude of the by-standers and the flowing or repressed streams of tears, everyone present is now inveigled into a comedy of vanity, now conscious, now unconscious.

Friedrich Wilhelm Nietzsche, *Human, All Too Human*, 1878

Nowhere probably is there more true feeling, and nowhere worse taste, than in a churchyard.

Benjamin Jowett, *Letters*, 1899

Razors pain you;
Rivers are damp;
Acids stain you;
And drugs cause cramp.
Guns aren't lawful;
Nooses give;
Gas smells awful;
You might as well live.

Dorothy Parker, *Résumé*, 1926

De mortuis nil nisi bunkum.

Harold Laski

A single death is a tragedy, a million deaths is a statistic.

Joseph Stalin

The living are the dead on holiday.

Maurice Maeterlinck

All our knowledge merely helps us to die a more painful death than the animals that know nothing.

Maurice Maeterlinck

I have no need of your God-damned sympathy. I only wish to be entertained by some of your grosser reminiscences.

Alexander Woollcott, to a visitor during his last illness, 1943

Millions long for immortality who do not know what to do with themselves on a rainy Sunday afternoon.

Susan Ertz, *Anger in the Sky*, 1943

One wants to stay alive, of course, but one only stays alive by virtue of the fear of death.

George Orwell, *Shooting an Elephant*, 1950

Many a man has decided to stay alive not because of the will to live, but because of the determination not to give assorted surviving bastards the satisfaction of his death.

Brendan Francis

Dying is a very dull, dreary affair. My advice to you is to have nothing whatever to do with it.

W. Somerset Maugham, attributed as his last words, 1965

Don't look forward to the day when you stop suffering. Because when it comes you'll know that you're dead.

Tennessee Williams, in the *Observer*, 1958

Many men on the point of an edifying death would be furious if they were suddenly restored to health.

Cesare Pavese, quoted in *The Faber Book of Aphorisms*,
ed. W.H. Auden and L. Kronenberger, 1964

For the unhappy man death is the commutation of a sentence of life imprisonment.

Alexander Chase, *Perspectives*, 1966

The destruction of this planet would have no significance on a cosmic scale. To an observer in the Andromeda nebula, the sign of our extinction would be no more than a match flaring for a second in the heavens.

Stanley Kubrick

Death is nature's way of telling you to slow down.

Severn Darden

Every suicide is a solution to a problem.

Jean Baechler, *Suicides*, 1980

We all end up as packaged goods.

Westbrook Pegler, quoted in the *New York Review of Books*,
1981

The past is the only dead thing that smells sweet.

Cyril Connolly, *Journal 1928–1937*, ed. D. Pryce-Jones, 1983

See also AGE

DECENCY

The only way for a woman to provide for herself decently is for her to be good to some man that can afford to be good to her.

George Bernard Shaw, *Mrs Warren's Profession*, 1898

Decency is indecency's conspiracy of silence.

George Bernard Shaw, *Maxims for Revolutionists*, 1903

All decent people live beyond their incomes nowadays, and those who aren't respectable live beyond other people's. A few gifted individuals manage to do both.

Saki (H.H. Munro), *The Match-maker,* **1911**

When you have told anyone you have left them a legacy the only decent thing to do is to die at once.

Samuel Butler, *Notebooks,* **1912**

Decency . . . must be an even more exhausting state to maintain than its opposite. Those who succeed seem to need a stupefying amount of sleep.

Quentin Crisp, *The Naked Civil Servant,* **1968**

See also HONESTY

DEMOCRACY

A democracy is a government in the hands of men of low birth, no property and vulgar employments.

Aristotle, *Politics,* **c.322BC**

Democracy is an aristocracy of blackguards.

George Gordon, Lord Byron

Democracy gives every man the right to be his own oppressor.

James Russell Lowell

Democracy becomes a government of bullies, tempered by editors.

Ralph Waldo Emerson, *Journals,* **1909–14**

Universal suffrage is the government of a house by its nursery.

Otto von Bismarck

High hopes were once formed of democracy, but democracy means simply the bludgeoning of the people, by the people, for the people.

Oscar Wilde, *The Soul of Man under Socialism,* **1891**

Parliaments are the great lie of our time.

Konstantin Pobedonostsev, 1896

Democracy substitutes election by the incompetent many for appointment by the corrupt few.

George Bernard Shaw, *Man and Superman*, 1903

Democracy is the name we give to the people each time we need them.

Robert, Marquis de Flers and Arman de Cavaillet, *L'habit vert*, 1912

Democracy is the art of running the circus from the monkey cage.

H.L. Mencken, *Sententiae*, 1916

Democracy is a form of religion. It is the worship of jackals by jackasses.

H.L. Mencken, *Sententiae*, 1916

That a peasant may become king does not render the kingdom democratic.

Woodrow Wilson, 1917

A democracy is a state which recognises the subjection of the minority to the majority, that is, an organisation for the systematic use of violence by one class against another, by one part of the population against another.

V.I. Lenin, *The State and Revolution*, 1917

Democracy is the theory that the common people know what they want, and deserve to get it good and hard.

H.L. Mencken, *A Book of Burlesques*, 1920

The most popular man under a democracy is not the most democratic man, but the most despotic man. The common folk delight in the exactions of such a man. They like him to boss them. Their natural gait is the goosestep.

H.L. Mencken

Democracy is a device which ensures that we shall be governed no better than we deserve.

George Bernard Shaw

Democracy is grounded upon so childish a complex of fallacies that they must be protected by a rigid system of taboos, else even halfwits would argue it to pieces. Its first concern must thus be to penalise the free play of ideas.

H.L. Mencken, *In Defence of Women*, 1923

An honest politician will not be tolerated by a democracy unless he is very stupid . . . because only a very stupid man can honestly share the prejudices of more than half the nation.

Bertrand Russell, Presidential Address to LSE students, 1923

Democracy . . . a form of government by popular ignorance.

Kin Hubbard, 1923

A man may have strong humanitarian and democratic principles, but if he happens to have been brought up as a bath-taking, shirt-changing lover of fresh air, he will have to overcome certain physical repugnances before he can bring himself to put these principles into practice.

Aldous Huxley, *Jesting Pilate*, 1926

The democratic disease which expresses its tyranny by reducing everything to the level of the herd.

Henry Miller, *The Wisdom of the Heart*, 1941

In Switzerland they had brotherly love, five hundred years of democracy and peace and what did they produce? The cuckoo clock!

Orson Welles and Graham Greene, screenplay for *The Third Man*, 1949

Democracy: in which you say what you like and do what you're told.

Gerald Barry

Our great democracies still tend to think that a stupid man is more likely to become honest than a clever man and our politicians take advantage of this by pretending to be even more stupid than nature made them.

Bertrand Russell, *New Hopes for a Changing World*, 1951

The blind lead the blind. It's the democratic way.

Henry Miller, *The Air-conditioned Nightmare*, 1945

Under democracy, one party always devotes its chief energies to trying to prove that the other party is unfit to rule – and both commonly succeed, and are right.

H.L. Mencken, *Minority Report*, 1956

Democracy: a festival of mediocrity.

E.M. Cioran

Democracy is the art of saying 'Nice doggie' until you can find a rock.
  Wynn Catlin

Those who set out nobly to be their brother's keeper sometimes end up by becoming his jailer. Every emancipation has in it the seeds of a new slavery, and every truth easily becomes a lie.
  I.F. Stone, 1969

The House of Commons: the longest running farce in the West End.
  Cyril Smith, 1973

Democracy consists of choosing your dictators, after they've told you what it is you think you want to hear.
  Alan Coren, in the *Daily Mail*, 1975

Democracy is a process by which the people are free to choose the man who will get the blame.
  Laurence J. Peter, *Peter's Quotations*, 1977

Democracy is an abuse of statistics.
  Jorge Luis Borges, quoted in *Prisoner Without a Name, Cell Without a Number* by Jacobo Timerman, 1981

Democracy is supposed to give you the feeling of choice, like Painkiller X and Painkiller Y. But they're both just aspirin.
  Gore Vidal, quoted in the *Observer*, 1982

Democrats are the party of government activism, the party that says government can make you richer, smarter, taller and get the chickweed out of your lawn. Republicans are the party that says government doesn't work, and then they get elected and prove it.
  P.J. O'Rourke, *Parliament of Whores*, 1991

Now majority rule is a precious, sacred thing worth dying for. But – like other precious, sacred things . . . it's not only worth dying for; it can make you wish you were dead. Imagine if all life were determined by majority rule. Every meal would be a pizza.
  P.J. O'Rourke, *Parliament of Whores*, 1991

See also ARISTOCRACY, EQUALITY, GOVERNMENT, LEADERS, POLITICS, POWER, VOTING

DIPLOMACY

An ambassador is an honest man sent abroad to lie for the good of his country.

Sir Henry Wotton, written in the autograph album of Christopher Fleckamore, 1604

I have discovered the art of deceiving diplomats: I speak the truth and they never believe me.

Camillo di Cavour

How is the world ruled and how do wars start? Diplomats tell lies to journalists, and they believe what they read.

Karl Kraus, *Aphorisms and More Aphorisms*, 1909

Diplomats: babies in silk hats playing with dynamite.

Alexander Woollcott

He seemed such a nice old gentleman I thought I would give him my autograph as a souvenir.

Adolf Hitler, on signing the Munich Pact; 'he' is Neville Chamberlain, 1938

Sincere diplomacy is no more possible than dry water or wooden iron.

Joseph Stalin

Power politics is the diplomatic name for the law of the jungle.

Ely Culbertson, *Must We Fight Russia?*, 1946

An appeaser is one who feeds a crocodile – hoping that it will eat him last.

Sir Winston Churchill, 1954

All diplomacy is a continuation of war by other means.

Chou En-lai, 1954

British education is probably the best in the world, if you can survive it. If you can't there is nothing left for you but the diplomatic corps.

Peter Ustinov

A diplomat is a person who can tell you to go to hell in such a way that you actually look forward to the trip.

Caskie Stinnett, *Out of the Red*, 1960

One function of diplomacy is to dress realism in morality.
Will and Ariel Durant

Treaties are like roses and young girls – they last while they last.
Charles de Gaulle, 1963

Diplomacy is letting someone else have your way.
Lester Pearson, 1965

A real diplomat is one who can cut his neighbour's throat without having his neighbour notice it.
Trygve Lie

Personal diplomacy has caused a lot of mischief and harm . . . It leads to a very great fallacy, the almost pathetic belief of some Foreign Ministers, that if they had lunch with someone and called him by his Christian name, they have changed the fundamental facts of relationships between nations.
Sir Paul Hasluck, 1982

Diplomacy is about surviving until the next century. Politics is about surviving until Friday afternoon.
Antony Jay and Jonathan Lynn, *Yes, Prime Minister,* **1986**

Foreign aid is taxing poor people in rich countries for the benefit of rich people in poor countries.
Bernard Rosenberg

See also PATRIOTISM

DIVORCE

Divorce is probably of nearly the same date as marriage. I believe, however, that marriage is some weeks the more ancient.
Voltaire, *Philosophical Dictionary,* **1764**

Alimony: the fine for speeding in the joy-ride of matrimony.
Oliver Herford and John Clay, *Cupid's Cyclopedia,* **1910**

Wedding: a necessary formality before securing a divorce.
Oliver Herford and John Clay, *Cupid's Cyclopedia,* **1910**

Love, the quest, marriage, the conquest; divorce, the inquest.
   Helen Rowland

Alimony – the ransom that the happy pay to the devil.
   H.L. Mencken, *A Book of Burlesques*, 1920

Judges, as a class, display, in the matter of arranging alimony, that reckless generosity which is found only in men who are giving away someone else's cash.
   P.G. Wodehouse, *Louder and Funnier*, 1932

Alimony is like buying oats for a dead horse.
   Arthur Baer

They say that in America marriage counts as reasonable grounds for divorce.
   William Douglas-Home, *The Manor of Northstead*, 1954

You don't know a woman until you've met her in court.
   Norman Mailer

The *vie de bohème* is a way of life that has two formidable enemies – time and marriage. Even hooligans marry, though they know that marriage is but for a little while. It is alimony that is for ever.
   Quentin Crisp, *The Naked Civil Servant*, 1968

There are four stages to a marriage. First there's the affair, then there's the marriage, then children and finally the fourth stage, without which you cannot know a woman, the divorce.
   Norman Mailer, in *Nova* magazine, 1969

Insanity is considered a ground for divorce, though by the very same token it is the shortest detour to marriage.
   Wilson Mizner, quoted in *The People's Almanac*, 1976

Alimony is the curse of the writing classes.
   Norman Mailer, 1980

See also AFFAIRS, HUSBANDS, LOVE, LOVERS, MARRIAGE, WIVES

DRINK

The wages of Gin is Debt.

Addison Mizner and Oliver Herford, *The Entirely New Cynic's Calendar*, 1905

Alcohol is a very necessary article . . . It enables Parliament to do things at eleven at night that no sane person would do at eleven in the morning.

George Bernard Shaw, *Major Barbara*, 1907

Abstainer, n. A weak person who yields to the temptation of denying himself a pleasure.

Ambrose Bierce, *The Devil's Dictionary*, 1911

Drinking makes such fools of people, and people are such fools to begin with, that it's compounding a felony.

Robert Benchley

Drink and dance and laugh and lie,
Love, the reeling midnight through
For tomorrow we shall die!
(But, alas, we never do.)

Dorothy Parker, *The Flaw in Paganism*, 1931

An alcoholic is someone you don't like who drinks as much as you do.

Dylan Thomas, quoted in *Life of Dylan Thomas* by Constantine Fitzgibbon, 1965

Work is the curse of the drinking classes.

Mike Romanoff

Ladies and Gentlemen, I give you a toast. It is: Absinthe makes the tart grow fonder!

Hugh Drummond, quoted in *The Vintage Years* by Seymour Hicks, 1943

Alcohol is like love: the first kiss is magic, the second is intimate, the third is routine. After that you just take the girl's clothes off.

Raymond Chandler, *The Long Goodbye*, 1953

Fishing, with me, has always been an excuse to drink in the daytime.

**Jimmy Cannon, quoted in *No Cheering in the Pressbox*
by J. Holtzman, 1973**

Drunks are rarely amusing unless they know some good songs and lose
a lot at poker.

Karl Roosevelt, in the *New York Times*, 1975

Most . . . drugs are self-limiting. If you drink you act like hell. But
if you keep drinking you pass out. Then your battered wife sets fire
to your bed and Farrah Fawcett stars in the TV movie about your brief,
sorry life.

P.J. O'Rourke, *Parliament of Whores*, 1991

DULLNESS

Anger makes dull men witty – but it keeps them poor.

Francis Bacon

What age was not dull? When were not the majority wicked? or what
progress was ever made by society? Society is always flat and foolish.

Ralph Waldo Emerson, 1850

Dullness is the coming of age of seriousness.

**Oscar Wilde, *Phrases and Philosophies for the Use of the
Young*, 1894**

Dullness is the first requisite of a good husband.

W. Somerset Maugham, *Lady Frederick*, 1907

It is the dull man who is always sure and the sure man who is always
dull.

H.L. Mencken, *Prejudices* 2nd series, 1922

The trouble with telling a good story is that it invariably reminds the
other fellow of a dull one.

Sid Caesar

The first requirement of a statesman is that he be dull. This is not
always easy to achieve.

Dean Acheson, 1970

DUTY

Whenever one person is found adequate to the discharge of a duty by close application thereto, it is worse executed by two persons and scarcely done at all if three or more are employed therein.

George Washington

The absurd duty, so often inculcated, of obeying a parent only on account of his being a parent, shackles the mind, and prepares it for a slavish submission to any power but reason.

Mary Wollstonecraft, *A Vindication of the Rights of Woman*, 1792

Duty is what one expects from others.

Oscar Wilde, *A Woman of No Importance*, 1893

When a stupid man is doing something he is ashamed of, he always declares that it is his duty.

George Bernard Shaw, *Caesar and Cleopatra*, 1901

Most affections are habits or duties we lack the courage to end.

Henry de Montherlant, *Queen After Death*, 1942

EDUCATION

Classical education in the English public schools consists of casting sham pearls in front of real swine.

Anonymous

The Vanity of teaching often tempteth a Man to forget he is a Blockhead.

George Savile, Marquis of Halifax, *Political, Moral and Miscellaneous Thoughts and Reflexions*, c.1694

Education is what remains when we have forgotten all that we have been taught.

George Savile, Marquis of Halifax, *Political, Moral and Miscellaneous Thoughts and Reflexions*, c.1694

An English university is a sanctuary in which exploded systems and obsolete prejudices find shelter and protection after they have been hunted out of every corner of the world.

Adam Smith, *The Wealth of Nations*, 1776

Anyone who has passed through the regular gradations of a classical education, and is not made a fool by it, may consider himelf as having had a very narrow escape.

William Hazlitt, *The Ignorance of the Learned*, 1821

A scholar is a man with this inconvenience, that, when you ask him his opinion of any matter, he must go home and look up his manuscripts to know.

Ralph Waldo Emerson

In large states public education will always be mediocre, for the same reason that in large kitchens the cooking is usually bad.

Friedrich Wilhelm Nietzsche, *Human, All Too Human*, 1878

The universities are a sort of lunatic asylum for keeping young men out of mischief.

Bishop Mandell Creighton

Education is fatal to anyone with a spark of artistic feeling. Education should be confined to clerks, and even them it drives to drink.

George Moore, *Confessions of a Young Man*, 1888

A college is a place where pebbles are polished and diamonds dimmed.

Robert G. Ingersoll

What is the task of higher education? To make man into a machine. What are the means employed? He is taught how to suffer being bored.

Friedrich Wilhelm Nietzsche, *The Twilight of the Idols*, 1889

Education is an admirable thing, but it is well to remember from time to time that nothing that is worth knowing can be taught.

Oscar Wilde, *The Critic as Artist*, 1891

Education is what you must acquire without any interference from your schooling.

Mark Twain

It is only the learned who care to learn, the ignorant who prefer to teach.

Edouard Le Berquier

In an examination those who do not wish to know ask questions of those who cannot tell.

Sir Walter Raleigh

A musical education is necessary for musical judgement. What most people relish is hardly music; it is rather a drowsy reverie relieved by nervous thrills.

George Santayana, *The Life of Reason*, 1905–6

It doesn't make much difference what you study so long as you hate it.

Finley Peter Dunne, *Mr Dooley Remembers*, 1910

You can't expect a boy to be vicious until he's been to a good school.

Saki (H.H.Munro), *The Baker's Dozen*, 1910

Education is a state-controlled manufactory of echoes.

Norman Douglas

University: . . . a place where rich men send their sons who have no aptitude for business.

Kin Hubbard, 1923

Education is the inculcation of the incomprehensible into the indifferent by the incompetent.

John Maynard Keynes

I have been in the scholastic profession long enough to know that nobody enters it unless he has some very good reason that he is anxious to conceal.

Evelyn Waugh, *Decline and Fall*, 1928

The difference between intelligence and education is this: intelligence will make you a good living.

Charles F. Kettering

Teaching is the last refuge of feeble minds with a classical education.

Aldous Huxley

A professor is a man whose job is to tell students how to solve the problems of life which he himself has tried to avoid by becoming a professor.

Anonymous

The first star a child gets in school for the mere performance of a needful task is its first lesson in graft.

Philip Wylie, *Generation of Vipers*, 1942

The average Ph.D. thesis is nothing but the transference of bones from one graveyard to another.

J. Frank Dobie, *A Texan in England*, 1945

I am inclined to think that one's education has been in vain if one fails to learn that most schoolmasters are idiots.

Hesketh Pearson

Education is what survives when what has been learnt has been forgotten.

B.F. Skinner, quoted in the *New Scientist* magazine, 1964

Education, the great mumbo-jumbo and fraud of the age, purports to equip us to live and is prescribed as a universal remedy for everything from juvenile delinquency to premature senility. For the most part it only serves to enlarge stupidity, inflate conceit, enchance credulity and put those subjected to it at the mercy of brain-washers with printing, presses, radio and TV at their disposal.

Malcolm Muggeridge, in the *Observer*, 1966

An education enables you to earn more than an educator.

Anonymous, quoted in *Resistance to Knowledge* by Hans Gaffron, 1970

That's the trouble with these people who went to state schools. They don't know how to confuse the public.

Alexander Buzo, *Martello Towers*, 1976

Education is a method whereby one acquires a higher grade of prejudices.

Laurence J. Peter, *Peter's Quotations*, 1977

Fourteen years in the professor dodge has taught me that one can argue ingeniously on behalf of any theory, applied to any piece of literature. This is rarely harmful, because normally no-one reads such essays.

Robert B. Parker, quoted in *Murder Ink*, ed. D. Wynn, 1977

Education is a progressive discovery of our own ignorance.

Will Durant, quoted in the *National Enquirer*, 1980

Do know the difference between education and experience? Education is when you read the fine print; experience is what you get when you don't.

Pete Seeger, quoted in *Loose Talk*, ed. L. Botts, 1980

Educational television should be absolutely forbidden. It can only lead to unreasonable disappointment when your child discovers that the letters of the alphabet do not leap up out of books and dance around with royal-blue chickens.
Fran Lebowitz, *Social Studies*, 1981

Of all human activities, education is the one most likely to give rise to cant, pomposity and fraudulent expertise.
John Rae, in the *Observer*, 1983

Education is what most people receive, many pass on and few have.
Karl Kraus, *Half Truths and One and a Half Truths*, 1986

EGOTISM

A cock has great influence on his own dunghill.
Publilius Syrus, *Moral Sayings*, c.50BC

What makes other people's vanity intolerable is that it wounds our own.
François, Duc de La Rochefoucauld, *Maxims*, 1665

The reason why so few people are agreeable in conversation is that each is thinking more about what he intends to say than about what others are saying, and we never listen when we are eager to speak.
François, Duc de La Rochefoucauld, *Maxims*, 1665

We would rather speak of ourselves than not talk at all.
François, Duc de La Rochefoucauld, *Maxims*, 1665

It is as easy to deceive oneself without perceiving it as it is difficult to deceive others without their perceiving it.
François, Duc de La Rochefoucauld, *Maxims*, 1665

If the commending others did not recommend ourselves, there would be few panegyrics.
George Savile, Marquis of Halifax, *Political Moral and Miscellaneous Thoughts and Reflexions*, c.1694

The greatest magnifying glasses in the world are a man's own eyes when they look upon his own person.
Alexander Pope, letter, 1705

I must complain the cards are ill-shuffled, until I have a good hand.
Jonathan Swift

There are many things we despise in order that we may not have to despise ourselves.
Luc de Clapiers, Marquis Vauvenargues, *Reflections and Maxims*, 1746

No cause more frequently produces bashfulness than too high an opinion of our own importance.
Samuel Johnson, *The Rambler*, 1749–52

Pride is a vice which pride itself inclines every man to find in others and to overlook in himself.
Samuel Johnson, *Works* vol. vi, 1787

He who is in love with himself has at least this advantage – he won't encounter many rivals.
Georg Christoph Lichtenberg, *Aphorisms*, 1764–99

There is nothing more likely to betray a man into absurdity than condecension when he seems to suppose his understanding too powerful for his company.
Samuel Johnson, *The Life of Samuel Johnson* by J. Boswell, 1791

We grow tired of everything but turning others into ridicule and congratulating ourselves on their defects.
William Hazlitt, *The Plain Speaker*, 1826

We are not satisfied to be right, unless we can prove others to be quite wrong.
William Hazlitt, *Conversations*, 1830

We go on fancying that each man is thinking of us, but he is not; he is like us: he is thinking of himself.
Charles Reade

Apology is only egotism wrong side out.
Oliver Wendell Holmes

We do what we must, and call it by the best names.
Ralph Waldo Emerson

It is in the ability to deceive oneself that one shows the greatest talent.
Anatole France

'I have done that', says my memory. 'I cannot have done that', says my pride, and remains silent. At last – memory yields.
Friedrich Wilhelm Nietzsche, *Beyond Good and Evil*, 1886

He who despises himself nevertheless esteems himself as a self-despiser.
Friedrich Wilhelm Nietzsche

The only thing that consoles man for the stupid things he does is the praise he always gives himself for doing them.
Oscar Wilde

Modesty: the gentle art of enhancing your charm by pretending not to be aware of it.
Oliver Herford

The least pain in our little finger gives us more concern and uneasiness than the destruction of millions of our fellow-beings.
William Hazlitt, *Collected Works*, 1904

Caution is the confidential agent of selfishness.
Woodrow Wilson, speech, 1909

Admiration, n. Our polite recognition of another's resemblance to ourselves.
Ambrose Bierce, *The Devil's Dictionary*, 1911

Egotist, n. A person of low taste, more interested in himself than in me.
Ambrose Bierce, *The Devil's Dictionary*, 1911

If one hides one's talent under a bushel, one must be careful to point out the exact bushel under which it is hidden.
Saki (H.H. Munro), *The Unbearable Bassington*, 1912

The craving to be understood may in the end be the merest egoism.
F.H. Bradley, *Essay on Truth and Reality*, 1914

Self-respect – the secure feeling that no-one, as yet, is suspicious.
H.L. Mencken, *Sententiae*, 1916

Vanity is other people's pride.

Sacha Guitry

We don't ask others to be faultless, we only ask that their faults should not incommode our own.

Gyp, quoted in *A Cynic's Breviary* by J.R. Solly, 1925

One is vain by nature, modest by necessity.

Pierre Reverdy, *En vrac*, 1956

Most people have a furious itch to talk about themselves and are restrained only by the disinclination of others to listen. Reserve is an artificial quality that is developed in most of us as the result of inumerable rebuffs.

W. Somerset Maugham, *The Summing Up*, 1938

Sentimentality – that's what we call the sentiment we don't share.

Graham Greene

The most difficult secret for a man to keep is his own opinion of himself.

Marcel Pagnol, 1954

Egotism is the anaesthetic that dulls the pain of stupidity.

Frank Leary, in *Look* magazine, 1955

Men are not against you; they are merely for themselves.

Gene Fowler, *Skyline*, 1961

Innocence ends when one is stripped of the delusion that one likes oneself.

Joan Didion, *On Self Respect*, 1961

Every stink that fights the ventilator thinks it is Don Quixote.

Stanislaw J. Lec, *Unkempt Thoughts*, 1962

If you do not raise your eyes, you will think that you are the highest point.

Antonio Porchia, *Voces*, 1968

Confidence is simply that quiet, assured feeling you have before you fall flat on your face.

Dr L. Binder, quoted in *Quote and Unquote*, 1970

The only time to believe any kind of rating is when it shows you at the top.

Bob Hope, quoted in *Playboy* magazine, 1973

Words of delight, praise and enthusiasm are like visiting-cards. The bigger the card, the less important the man; the bigger the word, the less important the emotion.

Francis King, in *The Listener* magazine, 1978

What matters isn't just that I should win, it's that you should lose.

Anonymous

See also BORES

ELECTIONS

People never lie so much as after a hunt, during a war or before an election.

Otto von Bismarck

Bad officials are elected by good citizens who do not vote.

George Jean Nathan

In general, we elect men of the type that subscribes to only one principle – to get re-elected.

Terry M. Townshend, speech 1940

Whatever politicians, activists and manipulators propose, it is the phlegmatic, indifferent, ingrained electorate which disposes.

Don Aitkin, quoted, 1969

Lansdale seized on the idea of using Nixon to build support for the [Vietnamese] elections . . . really honest elections, this time. 'Oh, sure, honest, yes, that's right,' Nixon said, 'so long as you win!' With that he winked, drove his elbow into Lansdale's arm and slapped his own knee.

Richard M. Nixon, quoted in *Sideshow* by William Shawcross, 1979

See also AMBITION, APPLAUSE, FAME, SUCCESS

ENEMIES

The pleasantest laughter is at the expense of our enemies.
Sophocles, *Ajax*, c.450BC

Our years, our debts, and our enemies are always more numerous than we imagine.
Charles Nodier

One should forgive one's enemies, but not before they are hanged.
Heinrich Heine

Contempt, n. The feeling of a prudent man for an enemy who is too formidable safely to be opposed.
Ambrose Bierce, *The Devil's Dictionary*, 1911

What is important is food, money and opportunities for scoring off one's enemies. Give a man these three things and you won't hear much squawking out of him.
Brian O'Nolan, *The Best of Myles*, 1968

An enemy is someone you haven't seen for a while.
Bob Ellis, 1977

See also HATRED

ENGLAND

The people of England are never so happy as when you tell them they are ruined.
Arthur Murray, *The Upholsterer*, 1758

The English people fancy they are free; it is only during the election of Members of Parliament that they are so. As soon as these are elected the people are slaves . . . In the brief moments of their liberation the abuse made of it fully deserves that it should be lost.
Jean-Jacques Rousseau, *The Social Contract*, 1761

It is only necessary to raise a bugbear before the English imagination in order to govern it at will. Whatever they hate or fear, they implicitly believe in, merely from the scope it gives to these passions.
William Hazlitt, *The Life of Napoleon Buonaparte*, 1828–30

Silence can be defined as a conversation with an Englishman.

Heinrich Heine

We know of no spectacle so ridiculous as the British public in one of its periodical fits of morality.

Thomas Babington Macaulay, Baron Macaulay, in the Edinburgh Review, 1831

One has often wondered whether upon the whole earth there is anything so unintelligent, so unapt to perceive how the world is really going as an ordinary young Englishman of our upper class.

Matthew Arnold, Culture and Anarchy, 1869

In our English popular religion the common conception of a future state of bliss is that of . . . a kind of perfected middle-class home, with labour ended, the table spread, goodness all around, the lost ones restored, hymnody incessant.

Matthew Arnold, Literature and Dogma, 1873

The Englishman has all the qualities of a poker, except its occasional warmth.

Daniel O'Connell

In England it is enough for a man to try and produce any serious, beautiful work to lose all his rights as a citizen.

Oscar Wilde, lecture, 1882

To disagree with three-fourths of the British public on all points is one of the first elements of sanity, one of the deepest consolations in all moments of spiritual doubt.

Oscar Wilde, lecture, 1882

Freedom of discussion is in England little else than the right to write or say anything which a jury of twelve shopkeepers think it expedient should be said or written.

A.V. Dicey, Introduction to the Study of the Law of the Constitution, 1885

Thinking is the most unhealthy thing in the world, and people die of it just as they die of any other disease. Fortunately, in England at any rate, thought is not catching.

Oscar Wilde, The Decay of Lying, 1891

An Englishman does everything on principle: he fights you on patriotic principles; he robs you on business principles; he enslaves you on imperial principles.

George Bernard Shaw, *The Man of Destiny,* **1898**

Englishmen never will be slaves; they are free to do whatever the government and public opinion allow them.

George Bernard Shaw, *Man and Superman,* **1903**

'English fair play' is a fine expression. It justifies the bashing of the puny draper's assistant by the big hairy blacksmith, and this to the perfect satisfaction of both parties, if they are worthy the name of Englishman.

Joseph Furphy, *Such Is Life,* **1903**

In England we have come to rely upon a comfortable time-lag or a century intervening between the perception that something ought to be done and a serious attempt to do it.

H.G. Wells, *The Work, Wealth and Happiness of Mankind,* **1934**

The English instinctively admire any man who has no talent and is modest about it.

James Agate, *Ego,* **1935–48**

It pays in England to be a revolutionary and a bible-smacker most of one's life, and then come round.

Lord Alfred Douglas, 1938

Continental people have a sex life; the English have hot-water bottles.

George Mikes, *How To Be an Alien,* **1946**

In Germany democracy died by the headsman's axe. In Britain it can be by pernicious anaemia.

Aneurin Bevan

The attitude of the English towards English history reminds one a good deal of the attitude of a Hollywood director towards love.

Margaret Halsey, *With Malice Toward Some,* **1938**

The English never smash in a face. They merely refrain from asking it to dinner.

Margaret Halsey, *With Malice Toward Some,* **1938**

A ready means of being cherished by the English is to adopt the simple expedient of living a long time.

Malcolm Muggeridge, in *Esquire* magazine, 1961

Fay: The British police force used to be run by men of integrity. Truscott: That is a mistake which has been rectified.

Joe Orton, *Loot*, 1966

The English think that incompetence is the same thing as sincerity.

Quentin Crisp, in the *New York Times*, 1977

About one thing the Englishman has a particularly strict code. If a bird says 'Cluk bik bik bik bik' and 'caw' you may kill it, eat it or ask Fortnums to pickle it in Napoleon brandy with wild strawberries. If it says 'tweet' it is a dear and precious friend and you'd better lay off it if you want to remain a member of Boodles.

Clement Freud, *Freud on Food*, 1978

The depressing thing about an Englishman's traditional love of animals is the dishonesty thereof . . . Get a barbed hook into the upper lip of a salmon, drag him endlessly around the water until he loses his strength, pull him to the bank, hit him on the head with a stone, and you may well become fisherman of the year. Shoot the salmon and you'll never be asked again.

Clement Freud, *Freud on Food*, 1978

I know why the sun never sets on the British Empire – God wouldn't trust an Englishman in the dark.

Duncan Spaeth, quoted in *The Book of Insults* by N. McPhee, 1978

English Law: where there are two alternatives: one intelligent, one stupid; one attractive, one vulgar; one noble, one ape-like; one serious and sincere, one undignified and false; one far-sighted, one short; EVERYBODY will INVARIABLY choose the latter.

Cyril Connolly, *Journal 1928–1937*, ed. D. Pryce-Jones, 1983

The two sides of industry have traditionally always regarded each other in Britain with the greatest possible loathing, mistrust and contempt. They are both absolutely right.

Auberon Waugh, in *Private Eye* magazine, 1983

England: the only country in the world where the food is more dangerous than the sex.

Jackie Mason, 1990

ENVY

The praise we give newcomers into the world arises from the envy we bear to those who are established.

François, Duc de La Rochefoucauld, *Maxims,* **1665**

Few envy the consideration enjoyed by the oldest inhabitant.

Ralph Waldo Emerson

Envy is the most stupid of vices, for there is no single advantage to be gained from it.

Honoré de Balzac, quoted in *Reflections on the Art of Life* **by J.R. Solly, 1902**

Envy is the sincerest form of flattery.

John Churton Collins, in *The English Review,* **1914**

EQUALITY

When security and equality are in conflict, it will not do to hesitate a moment – equality must yield.

Jeremy Bentham, *Introduction to Principles of Morals and Legislation,* **1789**

The defect of equality is that we desire it only with our superiors.

Henri Becque, *Querelles littéraires,* **1890**

All animals are created equal, but some animals are more equal than others.

George Orwell, *Animal Farm,* **1945**

We clamour for equality chiefly in matters in which we ourselves cannot hope to gain excellence.

Eric Hoffer, *The Passionate State of Mind,* **1954**

The social process requires the standardisation of man and this standardisation is called equality.

Erich Fromm, *The Art of Loving,* **1956**

There is no snobbishness like that of professional equalitarians.

Malcolm Muggeridge, *Chronicles of Wasted Time* **vol.i, 1978**

See also DEMOCRACY

EXCUSE

Any excuse will serve a tyrant.
Aesop, *Fables*, 550BC

Whores and priests will never want excuse.
Daniel Defoe, *The True-born Englishman*, 1701

Destiny, n. A tyrant's authority for crime and a fool's excuse for failure.
Ambrose Bierce, *The Devil's Dictionary*, 1911

Tyrants are always assassinated too late. That is their great excuse.
E.M. Cioran

Usually, terrible things that are done with the excuse that progress requires them are not really progress at all, but just terrible things.
Russell Baker, *The Sayings of Poor Russell*, 1972

Two wrongs don't make a right, but they make a good excuse.
Thomas Szasz, *The Second Sin*, 1974

EXPERIENCE

Experience is the name everyone gives to their mistakes.
Oscar Wilde, *Lady Windermere's Fan*, 1892

Experience: an expensive tutor.
Oliver Herford and John Clay, *Cupid's Cyclopedia*, 1910

The only thing experience teaches us is that experience teaches us nothing.
André Maurois

Experience enables you to recognise a mistake when you make it again.
Franklin P. Jones

You cannot create experience, you must undergo it.
Albert Camus, *Notebooks*, 1962

Yesterday's avant-garde experience is today's chic and tomorrow's cliché.
Richard Hofstadter, *Anti-Intellectualism in American Life*, 1963

Experience – a comb life gives you after you lose your hair.
   Judith Stern

See also LIFE, TIME

EXPERTS

A professional is a person who tells you what you know already, but in a way you cannot understand.
   Anonymous

No man can be a pure specialist without being in the strict sense an idiot.
   George Bernard Shaw, *Maxims for Revolutionists*, 1903

An expert is a man who has made all the mistakes which can be made, in a very narrow field.
   Niels Bohr

The mere eminence of a specialist makes him the more dangerous.
   Alexis Carrel, *L'Homme cet inconnu*, 1935

An expert is a mechanic away from home.
   Charles E. Wilson

Sooner or later an expert will say, 'But I'm talking too much' – always a prelude to talking some more.
   Stephen Potter, *Some Notes on Lifemanship*, 1950

An expert is a man who has stopped thinking. Why should he think? He is an expert.
   Frank Lloyd Wright, quoted in the *Daily Express*, 1959

The function of the expert is not to be more right than other people, but to be wrong for more sophisticated reasons.
   Dr David Butler, in the *Observer*, 1969

To spot the expert, pick the one who predicts the job will take the longest and cost the most.
   **Warren's Rule, quoted in *Murphy's Law Book Two*
   by A. Bloch, 1980**

Specialists are people who always repeat the same mistakes.

Walter Gropius, quoted in *Contemporary Architects*, 1980

FAILURE

Every failure teaches a man something; to wit, that he will probably fail again the next time.

H.L. Mencken, *Sententiae*, 1916

Calamity, n. A more than commonly plain and unmistakable reminder that the affairs of this life are not of our own ordering. Calamities are of two types: misfortune to ourselves, and good fortune to others.

Ambrose Bierce, *The Devil's Dictionary*, 1911

FAITH

Faith is a necessary fraud at best.

Charles Churchill, *Gotham*, 1764

The beast faith lives on its own dung.

A.C. Swinburne, *Dirae*, 1875

A casual stroll through a lunatic asylum shows that faith does not prove anything.

Friedrich Wilhelm Nietzsche

A miracle is an event described by those to whom it was told by people who did not see it.

Elbert Hubbard, *The Philistine*, 1909

Delusion, n. The father of a most respectable family, comprising Enthusiasm, Affection, Self-Denial, Faith, Hope, Charity and many other goodly sons and daughters.

Ambrose Bierce, *The Devil's Dictionary*, 1911

Faith, n. Belief without evidence in what is told by one who speaks without knowledge, of things without parallel.

Ambrose Bierce, *The Devil's Dictionary*, 1911

Faith is an illogical belief in the occurrence of the improbable.

H.L. Mencken

Orthodoxy is a corpse that doesn't know it's dead.
Elbert Hubbard, *Epigrams*, 1923

A creed is an ossified metaphor.
Elbert Hubbard, *The Notebook*, 1927

I respect faith, but doubt is what gives you an education.
Wilson Mizner, quoted in *H.L. Mencken's Dictionary of Quotations*, 1942

Man is a credulous animal and must believe something. In the absence of good grounds for belief, he will be satisfied with bad ones.
Bertrand Russell, *Unpopular Essays*, 1950

There is no nonsense so arrant that it cannot be made the creed of the vast majority by adequate governmental action.
Bertrand Russell, *Unpopular Essays*, 1950

There lies at the back of every creed something terrible and hard for which the worshipper may one day be required to suffer.
E.M. Forster, *Two Cheers for Democracy*, 1951

I confused things with their names: that is belief.
Jean-Paul Sartre, *The Words*, 1964

Faith is much better than belief. Belief is when someone else does the thinking.
Buckminster Fuller, in *Playboy* magazine, 1972

In the name of religion, one tortures, persecutes, builds pyres. In the guise of ideologies, one massacres, tortures and kills. In the name of justice one punishes . . . in the name of love of one's country or of one's race one hates other countries, despises them, massacres them. In the name of equality and brotherhood there is suppression and torture. There is nothing in common between the means and the end, the means go far beyond the end . . . ideologies and religions . . . are the alibis of the means.
Eugène Ionesco, in *Esquire* magazine, 1974

Faith is that quality which enables us to believe what we know to be untrue.
Anonymous, quoted in *Definitive Quotations*, ed. J. Ferguson, 1981

See also BELIEF, CHRISTIANS, IDEALS, IDEAS, MORALS, RELIGION, TRUE BELIEVERS, TRUTH

FAME

The renown of great men should always be measured by the means which they have used to acquire it.
François, Duc de La Rochefoucauld, *Maxims*, 1665

Fame is but the breath of the people, and that is often unwholesome.
Thomas Fuller, M.D., *Gnomologia*, 1732

Fame is the advantage of being known by people of whom you yourself know nothing, and for whom you care as little.
Stanislaus Leszcynski, *Oeuvres du philosophe bien-faisant*, 1763

Many men and women enjoy popular esteem, not because they are known, but because they are unknown.
Nicolas de Chamfort

A good part of the fame of most celebrated men is due to the short-sightedness of their admirers.
Georg Christoph Lichtenberg, *Aphorisms*, 1764–99

He who comes up to his own idea of greatness must always have had a very low standard of it in his mind.
William Hazlitt

Fame is an undertaker that pays but little attention to the living, but bedizens the dead, furnishes out their funerals and follows them to the grave.
Charles Caleb Colton, *Lacon*, 1820

If a man was great while living, he becomes tenfold greater when dead.
Thomas Carlyle, *On Heroes, Hero-Worship and the Heroic in History*, 1840

Fame is proof that the people are gullible.
Ralph Waldo Emerson

Most celebrated men live in a condition of prostitution.
Charles-Augustin Sainte-Beuve, *Notebooks*, 1876

Martyrdom is the only way in which a man can become famous without ability.

George Bernard Shaw, *The Devil's Disciple*, **1901**

If you would be accounted great by your contemporaries, be not too much greater than they.

Ambrose Bierce, *Collected Works*, **1909–12**

Acquaintance, n. A person whom we know well enough to borrow from but not well enough to lend to. A degree of friendship called slight when the object is poor or obscure, and intimate when he is rich or famous.

Ambrose Bierce, *The Devil's Dictionary*, **1911**

A celebrity is one who is known to many persons he is glad he doesn't know.

H.L. Mencken, *Sententiae*, **1916**

What is glory? It is to have a lot of nonsense talked about you.

Gustave Flaubert, quoted in *A Cynic's Breviary* **by J.R. Solly, 1925**

Fame is the aggregate of all the misunderstanding that collects around a new name.

Rainer Maria Rilke

Fame is the beauty-parlour of the dead.

Benjamin DeCasseres, *Fantasia Impromptu*, **1933**

No one can make us hate ourselves like an admirer.

Cyril Connolly, *Enemies of Promise*, **1938**

A sign of a celebrity is that his name is often worth more than his services.

Daniel J. Boorstin, *The Image*, **1961**

A celebrity is a person who works hard all his life to become well-known, then wears dark glasses to avoid being recognised.

Fred Allen

Every society honours its live conformists and its dead troublemakers.

Mignon McLaughlin, *The Neurotic's Notebook*, **1963**

See also: AMBITION, APPLAUSE, EGOTISM, SUCCESS

FAMILIES

A family is but too often a commonwealth of malignants.
Jonathan Swift, *Thoughts on Various Subjects*, 1706

He that has no fools, knaves nor beggars in his family was begot by a flash of lightning.
Thomas Fuller, M.D., *Gnomologia*, 1732

The Family! Home of all social evils, a charitable institution for indolent women, a prison workshop for the slaving breadwinner and a hell for children.
August Strindberg, *The Son of a Servant*, 1886

Sacred family! . . . The supposed home of all the virtues, where innocent children are tortured into their first falsehoods, where wills are broken by parental tyranny, and self-respect smothered by crowded, jostling egos.
August Strindberg, *The Son of a Servant*, 1886

Relations are simply a tedious pack of people who haven't got the remotest knowledge of how to live, nor the smallest instinct about when to die.
Oscar Wilde, *The Picture of Dorian Gray*, 1891

Fathers should neither be seen nor heard. That is the only proper basis for family life.
Oscar Wilde, *An Ideal Husband*, 1895

Home is the girl's prison and the woman's workhouse.
George Bernard Shaw, *Maxims for Revolutionists*, 1903

Home life is no more natural to us than a cage is natural to a cockatoo.
George Bernard Shaw, *Getting Married*, 1908

'Home Sweet Home' must surely have been written by a bachelor.
Samuel Butler, *Notebooks*, 1912

Near relations are those that have a brilliant career. The others are only distant ones.
Charles Nairey, quoted in *A Cynic's Breviary* by J.R. Solly, 1925

Whenever a guy starts boasting to me about his family tree, I seem to smell a strong sniff of sap rising.

Mae West

The family is a court of justice which never shuts down for night or day.

Malcolm de Chazal, *Sens plastique*, 1949

Home is the place where, when you have to go there, they have to take you in.

Robert Frost

A 'good' family is one that used to be better.

Cleveland Amory, *Who Killed Society*, 1960

Far from being the basis of good society, the family, with its narrow privacy and tawdry secrets, is the source of all our discontents.

Edmund Leach, Reith lecture, 1967

Mother is the dead heart of the family, spending father's earnings on consumer goods to enhance the environment in which he eats, sleeps and watches the television.

Germaine Greer, *The Female Eunuch*, 1970

See also ADULTS, CHILDREN, PARENTS

FASHION

Fashion condems us to many follies; the greatest is to make oneself its slave.

Napoleon Bonaparte

Change in fashion is the tax which the industry of the poor levies on the vanity of the rich.

Nicolas de Chamfort, *Maximes et pensées*, 1805

Fashion is what one wears oneself. What is unfashionable is what other people wear.

Oscar Wilde, *An Ideal Husband*, 1895

Fashion is a form of ugliness so intolerable that we have to alter it every six months,

Oscar Wilde

Fashions, after all, are only induced epidemics.

George Bernard Shaw, *The Doctor's Dilemma*, 1906

Where's the man could ease a heart
Like a satin gown?

Dorothy Parker, *The Satin Dress*, 1927

Fashion: a barricade behind which men hide their nothingness.

Kin Hubbard, 1923

Fashion exists for women with no taste, etiquette for people with no breeding.

Marie, Queen of Romania

To call a fashion wearable is the kiss of death. No new fashion worth its salt is ever wearable.

Eugenia Sheppard, quoted in the *New York Herald Tribune*, 1960

FOOD

A man seldom thinks with more earnestness of anything than he does of his dinner.

Samuel Johnson, attrib. in *Anecdotes of the late Samuel Johnson* by Hester Thrale, 1786

There is no love sincerer than the love of food.

George Bernard Shaw, *Man and Superman*, 1903

A gourmet is just a glutton with brains.

Philip Haberman Jr, in *Vogue* magazine, 1961

FOOLS

Is there anything so assured, resolved, disdainful, contemplative, solemn and serious as an ass?

Michel de Montaigne, *Essays*, 1595

He who pleads his own cause has a fool for a client.

Anonymous proverb

If you wish to avoid seeing a fool you must first break your mirror.

François Rabelais

Promises are the pitfalls of fools.
   Baltasar Gracian, *The Art of Worldly Wisdom***, 1647**

There are more Fools than Knaves in the world, else the Knaves would not have enough to live on.
   Samuel Butler, *Prose Observations 1660–1680***, ed. Hugh de Quehen, 1980**

Men would not live long in society were they not the dupes of one another.
   François, Duc de La Rochefoucauld, *Maxims***, 1665**

Zeal is fit only for wise men, but is found mostly in fools.
   Thomas Fuller, M.D., *Gnomologia***, 1732**

Most fools think they are only ignorant.
   Benjamin Franklin, *Poor Richard's Almanack***, 1733–58**

A generous man is merely a fool in the eyes of a thief.
   Henry Fielding, *The History of Tom Jones***, 1749**

That the vulgar express their thoughts clearly is far from true; and what perspicuity can be found among them proceeds not from the easiness of their language, but the shallowness of their thoughts.
   Samuel Johnson, *The Idler***, 1758–60**

The number of wise men will always be small. It is true that it has increased; but that is nothing compared with the fools, and unfortunately it is said that God is always on the side of the big battalions.
   Voltaire, letter, 1770

He that teaches himself has a fool for a master.
   Benjamin Franklin

Ever since Adam fools have been in the majority.
   Casimir Delavigne

The greater the fool the better the dancer.
   Theodore Hook, *Sayings and Doings***, 1824–8**

There is nothing too monstrous for human credibility.
   Thomas Love Peacock, *Gryll Grange***, 1860–1**

I prefer rogues to imbeciles, because they sometimes take a rest.
   Alexander Dumas fils

You can generally make people ridiculous by taking them at their word.
   Jerome K. Jerome, *Three Men on the Bummel*, 1900

Whenever a man feels like publicly making a fool of himself, he can always find someone to egg him on by giving him a cheer.
   Arthur Binstead, *Pitcher's Proverbs*, 1909

Before a man speaks it is always safe to assume that he is a fool. After he speaks, it is seldom necessary to assume it.
   H.L. Mencken, *Sententiae*, 1916

What good are brains to a man? They only unsettle him.
   P.G. Wodehouse, *The Adventures of Sally*, 1920

As a rule men are foolish, ungrateful, jealous, covetous of others' goods, abusing their superiority when they are strong and rascals when they are weak.
   Voltaire, quoted in *A Cynic's Breviary* by J.R. Solly, 1925

The average man's opinions are much less foolish than they would be if he thought for himself.
   Bertrand Russell

Many a man is praised for his reserve and so-called shyness when he is simply too proud to risk making a fool of himself.
   J.B. Priestley, *All About Ourselves*, 1956

It's innocence when it charms us, ignorance when it doesn't.
   Mignon McLaughlin, *The Neurotic's Notebook*, 1963

A fellow who's always declaring that he's no fool usually has his suspicions.
   Wilson Mizner, quoted in *The People's Almanac*, 1976

Never argue with a fool – people might not know the difference.
   First Law of Debate, quoted in *Murphy's Law* by A. Bloch, 1979

Build a system that even a fool can use, and only a fool will want to use it.
   Shaw's System, quoted in *Murphy's Law* by A. Bloch, 1979

Earnestness is just stupidity sent to college.
   P.J. O'Rourke, *Holidays in Hell*, 1988

FREEDOM

When the People contend for their Liberty they seldom get anything
for their Victory but new Masters.
   **George Savile, Marquis of Halifax, *Political, Moral and
   Miscellaneous Thoughts and Reflexions*, c.1694**

Corruption . . . the most infallible symptom of constitutional liberty.
   **Edward Gibbon, *The Decline and Fall of the Roman Empire*,
   1776–88**

If any ask me what a free government is, I answer that for any practical
purposes, it is what the people think so.
   Edmund Burke, letter to the sheriffs of Bristol, 1777

It has been observed, that they who most loudly clamour for liberty
do not most liberally grant it.
   Samuel Johnson, *Works*, 1787

The great half-truth, liberty.
   William Blake, *The Marriage of Heaven and Hell*, 1790

Despotism sits nowhere so secure as under the effigy and ensigns of
Freedom.
   Walter Savage Landor

Freedom is the recognition of necessity.
   Friedrich Engels

The most essential mental quality for a free people, whose liberty
is to be progressive, permanent and on a large scale, is much stupidity.
   Walter Bagehot

Give a Frenchman twenty-five lashes, and if you only make a fine
speech to him about the freedom and dignity of man he will persuade
himself that he is not lashed at all.
   Otto von Bismarck, 1875

In our country we have three unspeakably precious things: freedom of
speech, freedom of conscience and the prudence never to practise either.
   Mark Twain, *Pudd'nhead Wilson's New Calendar*, 1894

Liberal institutions straightway cease from being liberal the moment they are soundly established: once this is attained, no more grievous and more thorough enemies of freedom exist than liberal institutions.
Friedrich Wilhelm Nietzsche, 1888

Liberty means responsibility, that is why most men dread it.
George Bernard Shaw, *Man and Superman*, 1903

Liberty, n. One of imagination's most precious possessions.
Ambrose Bierce, *The Devil's Dictionary*, 1911

It is true that liberty is precious: so precious that it must be rationed.
V.I. Lenin, *The State and Revolution*, 1917

Free speech is about as good a cause as the world has ever known. But it . . . gets shoved aside in favour of things which seem at a given moment more vital . . . everybody favours free speech in the slack moments when no axes are being ground.
Heywood Broun, 1926

It is often safer to be in chains than to be free.
Franz Kafka, *The Castle*, 1926

Liberty don't work as good in practice as it does in speech.
Will Rogers, 1927

Advocates of capitalism are very apt to appeal to the sacred principles of liberty, which are embodied in one maxim: The fortunate must not be restrained in the exercise of tyranny over the unfortunate.
Bertrand Russell, *Sceptical Essays*, 1928

Liberty is so much latitude as the powerful choose to accord to the weak.
Judge Learned Hand, 1930

Freedom – a drunken whore
Sprawling in a power maddened soldier's arms.
Marina Tsvetayeva

Freedom is the right to tell people what they do not want to hear.
George Orwell, *The Road to Wigan Pier*, 1937

Man is condemned to be free.

Jean-Paul Sartre, *Existentialism and Humanism,* **1947**

When people are free to do as they please, they usually imitate each other.

Eric Hoffer, *The Passionate State of Mind,* **1955**

If people have to choose between freedom and sandwiches, they will take sandwiches.

Lord Boyd-Orr, 1955

Most people want security in this world, not liberty.

H.L. Mencken, *Minority Report,* **1956**

What good is freedom if you've not got the money for it? It's all very fine to go on about Nora's escape at the end of *A Doll's House,* but just how was she planning to eat that night?

Lillian Hellman

If society fits you comfortably enough, you call it freedom.

Robert Frost, in *Esquire* **magazine, 1965**

The brotherhood of man is evoked by particular men according to their circumstances. But it seldom extends to all men. In the name of our freedom and our brotherhood we are prepared to blow up the other half of the world and to be blown up in our turn.

R.D. Laing, *The Politics of Experience,* **1967**

There's no such thing as a free lunch.

Milton Friedman

Freedom's just another word for nothing else to lose.

Kris Kristofferson, *Me and Bobby McGee,* **1969**

The more a regime claims to be the embodiment of liberty the more tyrannical it is likely to be.

Ian Gilmour, *Inside Right,* **1977**

Man persuades himself he is emancipated every time he decorates a new servitude with the name of liberty.

Achille Tournier, quoted in *The Oxford Book of Aphorisms,* **ed. J. Gross, 1983**

See also DEMOCRACY, REVOLUTION

FRIENDS

No-one ever really minds seeing a friend fall off a roof.

Confucius

In the misfortune of our friends we find something that is not displeasing to us.

François, Duc de La Rochefoucauld, *Maxims*, 1665

It is to receive a rare favour from a friend if, after he has achieved a high position in the world, he remembers you as an acquaintance.

Jean de La Bruyère, *The Characters*, 1688

I am no married man, and thou canst not lie with my wife. I am very poor, and thou canst not borrow money from me. Then what use am I as a friend?

William Congreve, *The Double Dealer*, 1694

I advise thee to visit Relations and friends, but I advise thee not to live too near them.

Thomas Fuller, M.D., *Introductio ad Sapientiam, or, The Art of Right Thinking*, 1731

Distrust all those who love you extremely upon a very slight acquaintance and without any visible reason.

Lord Chesterfield, *Letters to his Son*, 1774

Friendship is a disinterested commerce between equals; love, an abject intercourse between tyrants and slaves.

Oliver Goldsmith, *The Good-Natured Man*, 1768

Distance either of time or place is sufficient to reconcile weak minds to wonderful relations.

Samuel Johnson, *Works* vol. v, 1787

Friendship among women is only a suspension of hostilities.

Antoine Rivaroli, Comte de Rivarol

Never speak ill of yourself, your friends will always say enough on that subject.

Charles-Maurice de Talleyrand, quoted in *A Cynic's Breviary* by J.R. Solly, 1925

Most of our misfortunes are more supportable than the comments of our friends upon them.

Charles Caleb Colton, *Lacon*, **1820**

It is always safe to learn, even from our enemies – seldom safe to venture to instruct, even our friends.

Charles Caleb Colton, *Lacon*, **1820**

Never join with your friend when he abuses his horse or his wife, unless the one is about to be sold, the other to be buried.

Charles Caleb Colton, *Lacon*, **1820**

If you want enemies, excel others; if you want friends, let others excel you.

Charles Caleb Colton, *Lacon*, **1820**

Discussing the characters and foibles of common friends is a great sweetener and cement of friendship.

William Hazlitt, *Table Talk*, **1821–2**

Give me the avowed, the erect, amd manly foe,
Firm I can meet – perhaps may turn his blow!
But of all plagues, good Heaven, thy wrath can send,
Save me, oh, save me from the candid friend.

George Canning, *New Morality*, **1823**

I like a friend better for having faults that one can talk about.

William Hazlitt, *The Plain Speaker*, **1826**

Friendships last when each friend thinks he has a slight superiority over the other.

Honoré de Balzac

It is difficult to say who do you the worst mischief, enemies with the worst intentions or friends with the best.

Edward George Bulwer-Lytton, Baron Lytton

What is commonly called friendship is only a little more honour among rogues.

Henry David Thoreau

What men call social virtues, good fellowship, is commonly but the virtue of pigs in a litter, which lie close together to keep each other warm.

Henry David Thoreau, *Journal*, **1851**

Nobody ever forgets where he buried the hatchet.
Kin Hubbard, *Abe Martin's Broadcast*, 1926

The best way to keep your friends is not to give them away.
**Wilson Mizner, quoted in *The Incredible Mizners*
by A. Johnson, 1953**

God gives us our relatives; thank God, we can choose our friends.
**Addison Mizner and Oliver Herford, *The Cynic's Calendar*,
1901**

People say you mustn't love your friend's wife, but how are you to love
your enemy's wife?
George Moore

Distress, n. A disease incurred by exposure to the prosperity of a
friend.
Ambrose Bierce, *The Devil's Dictionary*, 1911

Friendless, adj. Having no favours to bestow. Destitute of fortune.
Addicted to utterance of truth and common sense.
Ambrose Bierce, *The Devil's Dictionary*, 1911

Beggar, n. One who has relied on the assistance of his friends.
Ambrose Bierce, *The Devil's Dictionary*, 1911

Acquaintance, n. A person whom we know well enough to borrow
from but not well enough to lend to. A degree of friendship called
slight when its object is poor or obscure, and intimate when he is rich
or famous.
Ambrose Bierce, *The Devil's Dictionary*, 1911

In prosperity our friends know us; in adversity we know our friends.
John Churton Collins, in *The English Review*, 1914

Friendship is a common belief in the same fallacies, mountebanks and
hobgoblins.
H.L. Mencken, *Sententiae*, 1916

When a man laughs at his troubles he loses a great many friends. They
never forgive the loss of their prerogative.
H.L. Mencken, *Sententiae*, 1916

The full potentialities of human fury cannot be reached until a friend
of both parties tactfully interferes.
  G.K. Chesterton

To find a friend one must close one eye; to keep him – two.
  Norman Douglas, *An Almanac*, 1941

Friendship will not stand the strain of very much good advice for very
long.
  Robert Lynd

A girl's best friend is her mutter.
  Dorothy Parker, quoted in *Wits End*, ed. R.E. Drennan, 1968

One of the most mawkish of human delusions is the notion that friendship should be lifelong. The fact is that a man of resilient mind outwears his friendships as certainly as he outwears his love affairs and his
politics.
  H.L. Mencken, *Prejudices*, 1919–27

The most disagreeable thing that your worst enemy says to your face
does not approach what your best friends say behind your back.
  **Alfred de Musset, quoted in *A Cynic's Breviary* by J.R. Solly,
  1925**

Lord, defend me from my friends; I can account for my enemies.
  **Charles d'Héricault, quoted in *A Cynic's Breviary*
  by J.R. Solly, 1925**

It's amazing how nice people are to you when they know you're going
away.
  Michael Arlen

I always choose my friends for their good looks and my enemies for their
good intellects. Man cannot be too careful in his choice of enemies.
  Albert Lewin, screenplay for *The Picture of Dorian Gray*, 1945

It's what the guests say as they swing out of the drive that counts.
  Anonymous, quoted in the *New York Times*, 1947

No one is completely unhappy at the failure of his best friend.
  Groucho Marx

When you are down and out something always turns up – and it is usually the noses of your friends.

Orson Welles, in the *New York Times*, 1962

A stranger loses half his charm the day he is no longer a stranger.

Genevieve Antoine-Dariaux, *The Men in Your Life*, 1968

A Code of Honour: never approach a friend's girlfriend or wife with mischief as your goal. There are too many women in the world to justify that sort of dishonourable behaviour. Unless she's really attractive.

Bruce J. Friedman, *Sex and the Lonely Guy*, 1977

Rough diamonds are a girl's best friend.

Jilly Cooper, *Class*, 1979

GENIUS

When a true genius appears in the world you may know him by this sign: that all the dunces are in confederacy against him.

Jonathan Swift, *Thoughts on Various Subjects*, 1706

I have always thought geniuses much inferior to the plain sense of a cookmaid, who can make a good pudding and keep the kitchen in order.

Lady Mary Wortley Montagu, letter to the Countess of Pomfret, 1739

Sometimes men come by the name of genius in the same way that certain insects come by the name of centipede: not because they have a hundred feet, but because most people can't count above fourteen.

Georg Christoph Lichtenberg, *Reflections*, 1799

Genius, in one respect, is like gold; numbers of persons are constantly writing about both, who have neither.

Charles Caleb Colton, *Lacon*, 1820

Genius is the talent of a man who is dead.

Edmond de Goncourt

The dull pray, the geniuses are light mockers.

Ralph Waldo Emerson

Unless one is a genius, it is best to aim at being intelligible.

Anthony Hope (Sir Anthony Hope Hawkins), *The Dolly Dialogues*, 1894

Genius . . . has been defined as a supreme capacity for taking trouble . . . It might be more fitly described as a supreme capacity for getting its possessors into trouble of all kinds.

Samuel Butler, *Notebooks*, 1912

We define genius as the capacity for productive reaction against one's training.

Bernard Berenson

Skill is fine, and genius is splendid, but the right contacts are more valuable than either.

Sir Archibald McIndoe, quoted in *The Wit of Medicine*, ed. L. and M. Cowan, 1972

See also INTELLECTUALS

GENTLEMEN

A thief passes for a gentleman when stealing has made him rich.

Thomas Fuller, M.D., *Gnomologia*, 1732

The only infallible rule we know is, that the man who is always talking about being a gentleman never is one.

Robert Surtees, *Ask Mamma*, 1858

There is no such thing as a democratic gentleman. The adjective and the noun are hyphenated by a drawn sword.

Joseph Furphy, *Such Is Life*, 1903

I am a gentleman: I live by robbing the poor.

George Bernard Shaw, *Man and Superman*, 1903

A true gentleman is one who knows how to play the bagpipes – but doesn't.

Anonymous

A gentleman is one who never strikes a woman without provocation.

H.L. Mencken, *Sententiae*, 1916

The concept of the gentleman was invented by the aristocrats to keep the middle classes in order.
  Bertrand Russell

The criterion of a gentleman is that however poor he may be, he still refuses to do useful work.
  George Mikes, *How To Be An Alien*, 1946

A gentleman is a man who wouldn't hit a lady with his hat on.
  Evan Esar

A gentleman is a patient wolf.
  Henrietta Tiarks, 1957

My experience of gentlemen's agreements is that, when it comes to the pinch, there are rarely enough bloody gentlemen around.
  Ben Chifley, quoted in *Ben Chifley* by L.F. Crisp, 1961

See also ARISTOCRACY, CLASS

GIRLS

The girl who can't dance says the band can't play.
  Yiddish proverb

After a girl gets too big for Santa Claus, she begins to cast around for an easy mark.
  Kin Hubbard, *Abe Martin's Primer*, 1892

The hardest task in a girl's life is to prove to a man that his intentions are serious.
  Helen Rowland, *Reflections of a Bachelor Girl*, 1909

I like the girls who do,
I like the girls who don't;
I hate the girl who says she will
And then she says she won't.
But the girl that I like best of all
And I think you'll say I'm right –
Is the girl who says she never has
But looks as if she . . .
'Ere, listen . . . !
  Max Miller

There was a little girl
Who had a little curl
When she was good, she was very, very good
And when she was bad, she was very, very popular.

Max Miller

Any girl can be glamorous: all you have to do is stand still and look stupid.

Hedy Lamarr

One girl can be pretty – but a dozen are only a chorus.

F. Scott Fitzgerald, _The Last Tycoon_, 1941

From birth to age eighteen a girl needs good parents, from eighteen to thirty-five she needs good looks, from thirty-five she needs a good personality. From fifty-five on, she needs good cash.

Sophie Tucker, 1953

The girl with a future avoids the man with a past.

Evan Esar, _The Humour of Humour_, 1954

The first girl you go to bed with is always pretty.

Walter Matthau, in _Esquire_ magazine, 1968

Girls who put out are tramps. Girls who don't are ladies. This is, however, a rather archaic use of the word. Should one of you boys happen upon a girl who doesn't put out, do not jump to the conclusion that you have found a lady. What you have probably found is a lesbian.

Fran Lebowitz, _Metropolitan Life_, 1978

When you meet a pretty teenage girl, make a beeline for the mother. I've found it to be usually very rewarding.

Jeffrey Barnard, in _The Spectator_ magazine

See also BOYS, CHILDREN

GOD

God is alive, he just doesn't want to get involved.

Graffito

If God lived on earth, people would break his windows.

Yiddish proverb

If God did not exist, it would be necessary to invent him.
Voltaire, *Letters* vol. xcvi, 1769

The only excuse for God is that he doesn't exist.
Stendhal

God will forgive me, it is his trade.
Heinrich Heine, last words, 1856

We are always making God our accomplice so that we may legalise our own iniquities. Every successful massacre is consecrated by a *Te Deum*, and the clergy have never been wanting in benedictions for any victorious enormity.
Henri-Frédéric Amiel, *Journal intime*, 1885

Priests, kings, statesmen, soldiers, bankers and public functionaries of all sorts; policemen, jailers and hangmen; capitalists, usurers, businessmen and property-owners; lawyers, economists and politicians – all of them, down to the meanest grocer, repeat in chorus the words of Voltaire, that if there were no God it would be necessary to invent Him.
Mikhail Bakunin, *Dieu et l'état*, 1871

Which is it: is man one of God's blunders, or is God one of man's blunders?
Friedrich Wilhelm Nietzsche, *Twilight of the Idols*, 1889

It must be remembered that we have heard only one side of the case. God has written all the books.
Samuel Butler, *Notebooks*, 1912

God is a thought that makes crooked all that is straight.
Friedrich Wilhelm Nietzsche

The soul must have its chosen sewers to carry away its ordure. This function is performed by persons, relationships, professions, the fatherland, the world, or finally, for the really arrogant – I mean our modern pessimists – by the Good God himself.
Friedrich Wilhelm Nietzsche

The Creator is a comedian whose audience is afraid to laugh.
H.L. Mencken

God – the John Doe of philosophy and religion.
   Elbert Hubbard, *The Notebook*, 1927

Those who set out to serve both God and Mammon soon discover that there is no God.
   Logan Pearsall Smith

God, that dumping ground of our dreams.
   Jean Rostand

Every man thinks God is on his side. The rich and powerful know that he is.
   Jean Anouilh, *The Lark*, 1953

Kill one man and you are a murderer. Kill millions and you are a conqueror. Kill all and you are a God.
   Jean Rostand, *Thoughts of a Biologist*, 1955

God is the immemorial refuge of the incompetent, the helpless, the miserable. They find not only sanctuary in His arms, but also a kind of superiority, soothing to their macerated egos; He will set them above their betters.
   H.L. Mencken, *Minority Report*, 1956

It takes a long while for a naturally trustful person to reconcile himself to the idea that after all God will not help him.
   H.L. Mencken, *Minority Report*, 1956

What men usually ask of God when they pray is that two and two not make four.
   Anonymous, quoted in *The Faber Book of Aphorisms*,
   ed. W.H. Auden and L. Kronenberger, 1964

Respectable people believed in God in order to avoid having to speak about him.
   Jean-Paul Sartre, *The Words*, 1964

If you talk to God, you are praying; if God talks to you, you have schizophrenia.
   Thomas Szasz, *The Second Sin*, 1973

God is dead, but fifty thousand social workers have risen to take his place.
   Dr J.D. McCoughey, in *The Bulletin* magazine, 1974

God is not dead. He is alive and working on a much less ambitious project.

Graffito 1975

God is love, but get it in writing.

Gypsy Rose Lee, 1975

See also BELIEF, THE CLERGY, FAITH, HYPOCRISY, MORALS, RELIGION

GOVERNMENT

The punishment which the wise suffer, who refuse to take part in the government, is, to live under the government of worse men.

Plato, 370BC

Whoever desires to found a state and give it laws, must start with assuming that all men are bad and ever ready to display their vicious natures, whenever they may find occasion for it.

Niccolò Machiavelli, *Discourse upon the First Ten Books of Livy*, 1518

No government has ever been, or can ever be, wherein time-servers and blockheads will not be uppermost.

John Dryden

Let the people think they govern and they will be governed.

William Penn, *Some Fruits of Solitude*, 1693

Nothing appears more surprising to those who consider human affairs with a philosophical eye, than the ease with which the many are governed by the few and the implicit submission with which men resign their own sentiments and passions to those of their rulers.

David Hume, *The First Principles of Government*, 1742

To govern mankind one must not over-rate them.

Lord Chesterfield, *Letters to his Son*, 1774

In general, the art of government consists in taking as much money as possible from one party of the citizens to give to the other.

Voltaire

The pleasure of governing must certainly be exquisite, if we may judge from the vast numbers who are eager to be concerned with it.
Voltaire, *Philosophical Dictionary*, 1764

I would not give half a guinea to live under one form of government rather than another. It is of no moment to the happiness of an individual.
Samuel Johnson, 1772

Kings govern by means of popular assemblies only when they cannot do without them.
Charles James Fox, 1776

Society is produced by our wants and government by our wickedness.
Thomas Paine, *Common Sense*, 1776

Every country has the government it deserves.
Joseph de Maistre, letter, 1811

That government is best which governs least.
Henry David Thoreau, *Civil Disobedience*, 1849

The best form of government (setting aside questions of morality) is one where the masses have little power, and seem to have a great deal.
Marquess of Salisbury, *Oxford Essays*, 1858

To be governed is to be watched, inspected, spied upon, directed, law-ridden, regulated, penned up, indoctrinated, preached at, checked, appraised, seized, censured, commanded by beings who have neither title, knowledge nor virtue.
Pierre-Joseph Proudhon

Order means obedience. A government is said to preserve order if it succeeds in getting itself obeyed.
John Stuart Mill, *Representative Government*, 1861

Government is the great fiction, through which everybody endeavours to live at the expense of everybody else.
Frédéric Bastiat, *Essays on Political Economy*, 1872

Government is an association of men who do violence to the rest of us.
Leo Tolstoy, *The Kingdom of God Is Within You*, 1893

Our laws make law impossible, our liberties destroy all freedom, our property is organised robbery, our morality is an impudent hypocrisy, our wisdom is administered by inexperienced or mal-experienced dupes, our power wielded by cowards and weaklings and our honour false in all its points. I am an enemy of the existing order for good reasons.

George Bernard Shaw, *Major Barbara,* **1907**

Opposition, n. In politics the party that prevents the government from running amuck by hamstringing it.

Ambrose Bierce, *The Devil's Dictionary,* **1911**

It is perfectly true that that government is best which governs least. It is equally true that that government is best which provides most.

Walter Lippmann, *A Preface to Politics,* **1914**

All government, in its essence, is a conspiracy against the superior man.

H.L. Mencken, in *The Smart Set* **magazine, 1919**

A well governed people are generally a people who do not think much.

André Siegfried

Government: a kind of legalised pillage.

Kin Hubbard, 1923

The selfish wish to govern is often mistaken for a holy zeal in the cause of humanity.

Elbert Hubbard, *The Notebook,* **1927**

To prevent resentment, governments attribute misfortunes to natural causes; to create resentment, oppositions attribute them to human causes.

Bertrand Russell, *Sceptical Essays,* **1928**

It would be desirable if every government, when it comes to power, should have its old speeches burned.

Philip Snowden

The worst government is the most moral. One composed of cynics is often very tolerant and humane. But when the fanatics are on top there is no limit to oppression.

H.L. Mencken

Universal suffrage almost inevitably leads to government by mass bribery, an auction of the wordly goods of the unrepresented minority.

William R. Inge

The working of great institutions is mainly the result of a vast mass of routine, petty malice, self interest, carelessness and sheer mistake. Only a residual fraction is thought.

George Santayana

Public office is the last refuge of a scoundrel.

Boies Penrose, 1931

Governments last as long as the under-taxed can defend themselves against the over-taxed.

Bernard Berenson

The only good government is a bad one in a hell of a fright.

Joyce Cary, *The Horse's Mouth*, 1944

I will undoubtedly have to seek what is happily known as gainful employment, which I am glad to say does not describe holding public office.

Dean Acheson, on leaving his post as Secretary of State, 1952

Too bad all the people who know how to run the country are busy driving cabs and cutting hair.

George Burns

A politician is a man who understands government and it takes a politician to run a government. A statesman is a politician who's been dead ten or fifteen years.

Harry S. Truman, 1958

Every government is a device by which a few control the actions of many . . . on both sides at the moment complex human societies depend for the final decisions of war and peace on a group of elderly men any sensible plant personnel manager, whether under capitalism or Communism, would hesitate to hire.

I.F. Stone, 1959

The taxpayer, that's someone who works for the federal government, but doesn't have to take a civil service examination.

Ronald Reagan

A government is the only known vessel that leaks from the top.
James Reston

Governments, like individuals, should beware when all men speak well of them.
R.H. Tawney, in the *Guardian*, 1963

It is a function of government to invent philosophies to explain the demands of its own convenience.
Murray Kempton, *America Comes of Middle Age*, 1963

A government that is big enough to give you all you want is big enough to take it all away.
Barry Goldwater, speech, 1964

Government is like a baby. An alimentary canal with a big appetite at one end and no sense of responsibility at the other.
Ronald Reagan, in the *Saturday Evening Post*, 1965

One should be suspicious of 'love' as a political slogan. A government which purports to 'love' its citizens invariably desires all the prerogatives of a lover: to share the loved one's thoughts and to keep him in bondage.
Eric Julber, in *Esquire* magazine, 1969

Any official denial is de facto a confirmation.
John Kifner, in the *New York Times*, 1969

Every government is run by liars and nothing they say should be believed.
I.F. Stone

Governments never learn. Only people learn.
Milton Friedman, 1980

Feeling good about government is like looking on the bright side of any catastrophe. When you quit looking on the bright side, the catastrophe is still there.
P.J. O'Rourke, *Parliament of Whores*, 1991

See also CONSERVATIVES, DEMOCRACY, LEADERS, PARTIES, POLITICIANS, POLITICS, POWER, VOTING

HAPPINESS

Happiness is the perpetual possession of being well deceived.
Jonathan Swift

Amusement is the happiness of those who cannot think.
Alexander Pope

Illusion is the first of the pleasures.
Voltaire

Nothing is more conducive to peace of mind than not having any opinion at all.
Georg Christoph Lichtenberg, *Aphorisms*, 1764–99

Happiness, n: An agreeable sensation arising from contemplating the misery of another.
Ambrose Bierce, *The Devil's Dictionary*, 1911

We must select the illusion which appeals to our temperament and embrace it with passion, if we want to be happy.
Cyril Connolly (Palinurus), *The Unquiet Grave*, 1944

When you jump for joy, beware that no one moves the ground from beneath your feet.
Stanislaw J. Lec, *Unkempt Thoughts*, 1962

Happiness is an imaginary condition, formerly attributed by the living to the dead, now usually attributed by adults to children, and by children to adults.
Thomas Szasz, *The Second Sin*, 1973

Never . . . was any generation of men intent upon the pursuit of happiness more advantageously placed to attain it who yet, with seeming deliberation, took the opposite course – towards chaos, not order, towards breakdown, not stability, towards death, destruction and darkness, not life, creativity and light.
Malcolm Muggeridge, in *Esquire* magazine, 1970

See also LAUGHTER, OPTIMISM

HATRED

Now hatred is by far the longest pleasure;
Men love in haste, but they detest at leisure.
George Gordon, Lord Byron, *Don Juan*, 1819–24

Organised hatred, that is unity.
John Jay Chapman, *Lines on the Death of Bismarck*, 1898

Abhorrence, n. One of the degrees of disapproval due to what is imperfectly understood.
Ambrose Bierce, *The Devil's Dictionary*, 1911

Hate must make one productive. Otherwise one might as well love.
Karl Kraus, *Half Truths and One and a Half Truths*, 1986

It does not matter much what a man hates, provided he hates something.
Samuel Butler, *Notebooks*, 1912

To know all is not to forgive all. It is to despise everybody.
Quentin Crisp, *The Naked Civil Servant*, 1968

See also ENEMIES

HISTORY

Very few things happen at the right time, and the rest do not happen at all. The conscientious historian will correct these defects.
Herodotus, 450BC

The more corrupt the state, the more numerous the laws.
Tacitus, *History*, AD 68–96

If a historian were to relate truthfully all the crimes, weaknesses and disorders of mankind, his readers would take his work for satire rather than for history.
Pierre Bayle, *Dictionary*, 1695–7

All our history . . . is no more than accepted fiction.
Voltaire, *Jeannot et Colin*, 1764

History is just the portrayal of crimes and misfortunes.
Voltaire, *L'Ingénu*, 1767

The history of mankind is little else than a narrative of designs which have failed, and hopes that have been disappointed.

Samuel Johnson, *Works* vol. ix, 1787

History is little more than the register of the crimes, follies and misfortunes of mankind.

Edward Gibbon, *The Decline and Fall of the Roman Empire*, 1776–88

If a man could say nothing against a character but what he can prove, history could not be written.

Samuel Johnson, quoted in *The Life of Samuel Johnson* by J. Boswell, 1791

We learn from history that we do not learn from history.

George Wilhelm Friedrich Hegel

History is the version of past events that people have decided to agree on.

Napoleon Bonaparte, *Maxims*, 1804–15

History in general only informs us what bad government is.

Thomas Jefferson, letter to John Narvell, 1807

For what is history but a kind of Newgate Calendar, a register of the crimes and miseries that man has inflicted on his fellow men? It is a huge libel on human nature.

Washington Irving, *A History of New York*, 1809

The more we know of history, the less shall we esteem the subjects of it, and to despise our species, is the price we must too often pay for our knowledge of it.

Charles Caleb Colton, *Lacon*, 1820

Man is fed with fables through life and leaves it in the belief he knows something of what has been passing, when in truth he has known nothing but what has passed under his own eye.

Thomas Jefferson, letter to Thomas Cooper, 1823

History is nothing but a collection of fables and useless trifles, cluttered up with a mass of unnecessary figures and proper names.

Leo Tolstoy, 1846

Historical phenomena always happen twice – the first time as tragedy, the second as farce.
  Karl Marx

History is all party pamphlets.
  Ralph Waldo Emerson *Journals*, **1909–14**

History is the autobiography of a madman.
  Alexander Herzen

Happy are the people whose annals are blank in the history books.
  Thomas Carlyle, *Frederick the Great*, **1858–65**

There are only two great currents in the history of mankind: the baseness which makes conservatives and the envy which makes revolutionaries.
  Edmond and Jules de Goncourt, *Diary*, **1867**

History is simply a piece of paper covered with print.
  Otto von Bismarck

When a history book contains no lies it is always tedious.
  Anatole France, *Le crime de Sylvestre Bonnard*, **1881**

The only duty we owe history is to rewrite it.
  Oscar Wilde, *The Critic as Artist*, **1891**

The past always looks better than it was; it's only pleasant because it isn't here.
  Finley Peter Dunne

Those who do not remember the past are condemned to repeat it.
  George Santayana, *The Life of Reason*, **1905–6**

History, n. An account mostly false, of events mostly unimportant, which are brought about by rulers, mostly knaves, and soldiers mostly fools.
  Ambrose Bierce, *The Devil's Dictionary*, **1911**

Mythology, n. The body of a primitive people's beliefs, concerning its origin, early history, heroes, deities and so forth, as distinguished from the the true accounts which it invents later.
  Ambrose Bierce, *The Devil's Dictionary*, **1911**

God cannot alter the past, that is why he is obliged to connive at the existence of historians.
Samuel Butler

Human history becomes more and more a race between education and catastrophe.
H.G. Wells, *The Outline of History*, 1920

History . . . is a nightmare from which I am trying to awake.
James Joyce, *Ulysses*, 1922

History is largely concerned with arranging good entrances for people and later exits not always quite so good.
Heywood Broun, *Pieces of Hate*, 1922

History – that little sewer where man loves to wallow.
François Ponge

History repeats itself. Historians repeat each other.
Philip Guedalla, *Supers and Supermen*, 1920

History is attractive to the more timid of us . . . we can recover self-confidence by snubbing the dead.
E.M. Forster, *Abinger Harvest*, 1936

History is full of ignominious getaways by the great and famous.
George Orwell, *Who Are the War Criminals*, 1942

It is sometimes very hard to tell the difference between history and the smell of skunk.
Rebecca West, *Black Lamb and Grey Falcon*, 1941

You don't change the course of history by turning the faces of portraits to the wall.
Jawaharlal Nehru

History is mostly guessing, the rest is prejudice.
Will and Ariel Durant

History is the study of man's unhappiness
Raymond Queneau, *A Model History*, 1966

The history of ideas is the history of the grudges of solitary men.
E.M. Cioran, *Syllogismes de l'amertume*, 1952

What is history after all? History is facts which become legend in the end; legends are lies which become history in the end.
Jean Cocteau, 1957

That men do not learn very much from history is the most important of all the lessons that history has to teach.
Aldous Huxley, *Collected Essays*, 1959

History is littered with wars which everybody knew would never happen.
J. Enoch Powell, 1967

The horror of the twentieth century is the size of each event and the paucity of its reverberation.
Norman Mailer, *Of A Fire on the Moon*, 1970

Crimes of which a people is ashamed constitute its real history. The same is true of man.
Jean Genet, notes for *The Screens*, 1973

Those who don't study the past will repeat its errors; those who do study it will find other ways to err.
Charles Wolf Jr, quoted in the *Wall Street Journal*, 1976

History is an endless repetition of the wrong way of living.
Lawrence Durrell, in *The Listener*, 1978

History repeats itself – the first time as tragi-comedy, the second time as bedroom farce.
Private Eye magazine, 1978

Those who lie on the rails of history must expect to have their legs chopped off.
Rudé Právo, Czech party newspaper, quoted in *The Listener* magazine, 1979

On the whole history tends to be rather poor fiction – except at its best.
Gore Vidal, *Writers at Work* 4th series, 1981

A historian is often only a journalist facing backwards.
Karl Kraus, *Half Truths and One and a Half Truths*, 1986

Once you've made your mark on history those who can't will be so grateful they'll turn it into a cage for you.
Lester Bangs, *Psychotic Reactions and Carburetor Dung*, 1988

That perfect confusion known as history (a.k.a. the survivors' revenge).
Gore Vidal, *A View from the Diner's Club*, 1991

Tradition is just nostalgia walking about fully dressed in public.
Andrew Marr, in the *Independent*, 1993

May you live in interesting times.
Chinese curse

HOLLYWOOD

Hollywood: the place where girls go to look for husbands and husbands go to look for girls.
Anonymous

Hollywood is a carnival where there are no concessions . . . a sewer, with service from the Ritz Carlton.
Wilson Mizner

A leader of public thought in Hollywood wouldn't have sufficient mental acumen anywhere else to hold down a place in the bread line.
Anita Loos

Hollywood impresses me as being ten million dollars worth of intricate and highly ingenious machinery functioning elaborately to put the skin on baloney.
George Jean Nathan

I've spent several years in Hollywood, and I still think the movie heroes are in the audience.
Wilson Mizner

The only 'ism' Hollywood believes in is plagiarism.
Dorothy Parker

In Hollywood the eternal triangle consists of the actor, his wife and himself.
Anonymous

Strip the phoney tinsel off Hollywood and you'll find the real tinsel underneath.
Oscar Levant

The title 'Little Napoleon' in Hollywood is equivalent to the title 'Mister' in any other community.
Alva Johnston

Hollywood is a great place if you're an orange. *(Also cited as* California is a fine place to live in – if you're an orange.)
Fred Allen

Every day, to earn my daily bread
I go to the market where lies are bought
Hopefully
I take up my place among the sellers.
Bertolt Brecht, 'Hollywood' in *Collected Poems 1913–1956,* **1976**

In a novel the hero can lay ten girls and marry a virgin for the finish. In a movie that is not allowed. The villain can lay anybody he wants, have as much fun as he wants cheating and stealing, getting rich and whipping the servants. But you have to shoot him in the end. When he falls with a bullet in the forehead it is advisable that he clutch at the Gobelin tapestry on the wall and bring it down over his head like a symbolic shroud. Also, covered by such a tapestry, the actor does not have to hold his breath while being photographed as a dead man.
Herman Mankiewicz, 1940

Hollywood . . . the most beautiful slave quarters in the world.
Moss Hart

Hollywood buys a good story about a bad girl and changes it to a bad story about a good girl.
Anonymous

There's only one thing that can kill the movies – and that is education.
Will Rogers, *The Autobiography of Will Rogers,* **1949**

Hollywood is a place where people from Iowa mistake each other for a star.
Fred Allen

God felt sorry for actors, so he created Hollywood to give them a place in the sun and a swimming pool. The price they had to pay was to surrender their talent.
Sir Cedric Hardwicke

Hollywood must never permit censorship to collapse – it's far too good for the box office.
Claude Binyon

In Hollywood all marriages are happy. It's trying to live together afterwards that causes the problems.
Shelley Winters

A Hollywood aristocrat is anyone who can trace his ancestry back to his father.
Anonymous

American motion pictures are written by the half-educated for the half-witted.
Sir John Irving, in the *New York Mirror*, 1963

In Hollywood, if you don't have happiness, you send out for it.
Rex Reed

It proves what they say, give the public what they want to see and they'll come out for it.
**Red Skelton, surveying the crowded funeral of loathed
Hollywood mogul, Harry Cohn, 1957; also attributed to Samuel
Goldwyn, attending his rival Louis B. Mayer's obsequies, 1958**

That's what show business is – sincere insincerity.
Benny Hill, in the *Observer*, 1977

Popcorn is the last area of the movie business where good taste is still a concern.
Mike Barfield, in *The Oldie* magazine, 1992

Film directors are people too short to become actors.
Josh Greenfield

A Hollywood marriage is one in which the couple vow to be faithful to each other until after the honeymoon.

Anonymous

See also ACTING

HONESTY

Men keep their agreements when it is to the advantage of neither to break them.

Solon

In this Age, when it is said of a Man, he knows *how to live*, it may be implied that he is not very honest.

George Savile, Marquis of Halifax, *Political, Moral and Miscellaneous Thoughts and Reflexions*, c.1694

To be honest is nothing: the reputation of it is all.

William Congreve, *The Old Bachelor*, 1693

He is only honest who is not discovered.

Susannah Centlivre, *The Artifice*, 1710

He that resolves to deal with none but honest men, must leave off dealing.

Thomas Fuller, M.D., *Gnomologia*, 1732

Honesty is not greater where elegance is less.

Samuel Johnson, *Works* vol. ix, 1787

The surest way to remain poor is to be an honest man.

Napoleon Bonaparte, *Maxims*, 1804–15

Put a rogue in the limelight and he will act like an honest man.

Napoleon Bonaparte, *Maxims*, 1804–15

A moderately honest man with a moderately faithful wife, moderate drinkers both in a moderately healthy house: that is the true middle-class unit.

George Bernard Shaw, *Maxims for Revolutionists*, 1903

Confessions may be good for the soul, but they are bad for the reputation.

Lord Thomas Dewar

Honesty consists not in never stealing, but in knowing when to stop in stealing, and how to make good use of what one does steal.
Samuel Butler, *Notebooks*, 1912

We have to distrust each other. It's our only defence against betrayal.
Tennessee Williams, *Camino Real*, 1953

There is one way to find out if a man is honest – ask him. If he says 'Yes', you know he is crooked.
Groucho Marx, 1954

Experience teaches you that the man who looks you straight in the eye, particularly if he adds a firm handshake, is hiding something.
Clifton Fadiman, *Enter, Conversing*, 1962

The only guy who is honest is the guy who sings in the shower. Everyone else is a prostitute.
Kim Fowley

It's better to be quotable than to be honest.
Tom Stoppard, in the *Guardian*, 1973

See also DECENCY, TRUTH

HOPE

We promise according to our hopes, and perform according to our fears.
François, Duc de La Rochefoucauld, *Maxims*, 1665

Gratitude is merely a secret hope of further favours.
François, Duc de La Rochefoucauld, *Maxims*, 1665

Men should do with their Hopes as they do with tame Fowl, cut their Wings that they may not fly over the Wall.
George Savile, Marquis of Halifax, *Political, Moral and Miscellaneous Thoughts and Reflexions*, c.1694

Hope is the worst of evils, for it prolongs the torment of man.
Friedrich Wilhelm Nietzsche, *Human, All Too Human*, 1878

It is well known that we should not expect something for nothing but we do – and call it Hope.
Edgar Watson Howe, *Country Town Sayings*, 1911

Hope is a pathological belief in the occurrence of the impossible.
H.L. Mencken, *Sententiae*, 1916

Hope must feel that the human breast is amazingly tolerant.
Henry Haskins, *Meditations in Wall Street*, 1940

Hope is an illusion for squares.
Colin Johnson, *Wild Cat Falling*

The hope that springs eternal
Springs right up your behind.
Ian Dury, *This Is What We Find*, 1979

See also OPTIMISM

HUMANITY

Two things only the people anxiously desire: bread and the Circus games.
Juvenal, *Satires*

In brief, we are all monsters, that is, a composition of man and beast.
Sir Thomas Browne, *Religio Medici*, 1642

The truest wild beasts live in the most populous places.
Baltasar Gracian, *The Art of Worldly Wisdom*, 1647

The reason why fools and knaves thrive better in the world than wiser and honester men is because they are nearer to the general temper of mankind, which is nothing but a mixture of cheat and folly.
Samuel Butler, *Prose Observations 1660–1680*, ed. Hugh de Quehen, 1980

It is the Fools and Knaves that make the Wheels of the World turn. *They* are *the World;* those few who have Sense or Honesty sneak up and down single, but never go in Herds.
George Savile, Marquis of Halifax, *Political, Moral and Miscellaneous Thoughts and Reflexions*, c.1694

The most necessary in the World, and yet the least usual, is to reflect that those we deal with may know how to be as arrant knaves as ourselves.
George Savile, Marquis of Halifax, *Political, Moral and Miscellaneous Thoughts and Reflexions*, c.1694

The World is nothing but Vanity cut into several Shapes.
George Savile, Marquis of Halifax, *Political, Moral and Miscellaneous Thoughts and Reflexions*, c.1694

The more I see of men the more I admire dogs.
Marie de Rabutin-Chantal, Marquise de Sévigné, 1725

The world is a vast temple dedicated to Discord.
Voltaire, letter, 1752

That observation which is called knowledge of the world will be found more frequently to make men cunning than good.
Samuel Johnson, *The Rambler*, 1749–52

The world, in its best state, is nothing more than a large assembly of beings, combining to counterfeit happiness, which they do not feel, employing every art and contrivance to embellish life, and to hide their real condition from the eyes of one another.
Samuel Johnson, *The Adventurer*, 1753–4

The first man to fence in a piece of land saying 'This is mine' and who found people simple enough to believe him, was the real founder of civil society.
Jean-Jacques Rousseau, *Discourse on the Origin and Bases of Inequality among Men*, 1755

No sooner are we supplied with everything that nature can demand, than we sit down to contrive artificial appetites.
Samuel Johnson, *The Idler*, 1758–60

All men are born with a sufficiently violent liking for domination, wealth and pleasure, and with much taste for idleness; consequently all men want the money and the wives or daughters of others, to be their master, to subject them to all their caprices, and to do nothing, or at least to do only very agreeable things.
Voltaire, *Philosophical Dictionary*, 1764

Once the people begin to reason, all is lost.
Voltaire, letter, 1766

We are to consider mankind not as we wish them, but as we find them, frequently corrupt and always fallible.
Samuel Johnson, *Works* vol. xi, 1787

The only thing that stops God sending a second Flood is that the first one was useless.

Nicolas de Chamfort, *Characters and Anecdotes*, 1771

The people are that part of the state which does not know what it wants.

Georg Wilhelm Friedrich Hegel

Mankind are an incorrigible race. Give them but bugbears and idols – it is all that they ask.

William Hazlitt, *Lectures on the English Comic Writers*, 1819

Never pity people because they are ill-used. They only wait the opportunity to use others just as ill.

William Hazlitt

That great baby, the world, however it may cry up and pretend to admire its idols, is just like the little girl who, after dressing up her doll in all its finery, and caressing it until she is tired, is not easy until she has pulled it to pieces again and reduced it to its original rags and wool.

William Hazlitt, *The Ruling Passion*, 1829

Human beings cling to their delicious tyrannies and to their exquisite nonsense like a drunkard to his bottle and go on until death stares them in the face.

Sydney Smith

It is an error to suppose that no man understands his own character. Most persons know even their failings very well, only they persist in giving them names different from those usually assigned by the rest of the world.

Sir Arthur Helps, *Thoughts in the Cloister and the Crowd*, 1835

Believe everything you hear about the world; nothing is too impossibly bad.

Honoré de Balzac

Society is a hospital of incurables.

Ralph Waldo Emerson, 1843

The general average of mankind are not only moderate in intellect, but also moderate in inclinations: they have no taste or wishes strong enough to incline them to do anything unusual, and they consequently do not understand those who have, and class all such with the wild and intemperate upon whom they are accustomed to look down.

John Stuart Mill, *On Liberty*, 1859

It is hard for a pure and thoughtful man to live in a state of rapture at the spectacle afforded him by his fellow-creatures.

Matthew Arnold

The Lord prefers common-looking people. That is the reason He makes so many of them.

Abraham Lincoln

Tell me what you think you are and I will tell you what you are not.

Henri-Frédéric Amiel, *Journal intime*, 1866

Whatever you may be sure of, be sure of this: that you are dreadfully like other people.

James Russell Lowell, *My Study Windows*, 1871

That all men should be brothers is the dream of people who have no brothers.

Charles Chincholles, *Pensées de tout le monde*, 1880

People who have no faults are terrible – there is no way of taking advantage of them.

Anatole France

I sometimes think that God, in creating man, somewhat overestimated his ability.

Oscar Wilde

Humanity is a pigsty where liars, hypocrites and the obscene in spirit congregate.

George Moore, *Confessions of a Young Man*, 1888

'Every man has his price.' This is not true. But for every man there exists a bait which he cannot resist swallowing.

Friedrich Wilhelm Nietzsche

Man is a dog's ideal of what God should be.

Holbrook Jackson

It is only shallow people who do not judge by appearances.
  Oscar Wilde, *The Picture of Dorian Gray*, 1891

It is absurd to divide people into good and bad. People are either charming or tedious.
  Oscar Wilde, *Lady Windermere's Fan*, 1892

The great merit of society is to make one appreciate solitude.
  Charles Chincholles, quoted in *Reflections on the Art of Life* by J.R. Solly, 1902

Most people are other people. Their thoughts are someone else's opinions, their lives a mimicry, their passions a quotation.
  Oscar Wilde, *De Profundis*, 1905

The self-made man is often proud of a poor job.
  Addison Mizner and Oliver Herford, *The Entirely New Cynic's Calendar*, 1905

In each human heart there are a tiger, a pig, an ass and a nightingale. Diversity of character is due to their unequal activity.
  Ambrose Bierce, *The Devil's Dictionary*, 1911

The devil is an optimist if he thinks he can make people meaner.
  Karl Kraus, in *Karl Kraus* by H. Zohn, 1971

The world is a prison in which solitary confinement is preferable.
  Karl Kraus, *Half Truths and One and a Half Truths*, 1986

Man, biologically considered, . . . is the most formidable of all beasts of prey, and, indeed, is the only one that preys systematically on its own species.
  William James, *Memories and Studies*, 1911

We think as we do, mainly because other people think so.
  Samuel Butler, *Notebooks*, 1912

The fixity of a habit is generally in direct proportion to its absurdity.
  Marcel Proust, *Remembrance of Things Past*, 1913–27

The world, like an accomplished hostess, pays most attention to those whom it will soonest forget.
  John Churton Collins, in *The English Review*, 1914

Men are the only animals that devote themselves, day in and day out, to making one another unhappy. It is an art like any other. Its virtuosi are called altruists.

H.L. Mencken, *Sententiae*, 1916

The Plain People are worth dying for until you bunch them and give them the cold Once-Over, and then they impress the impartial Observer as being slightly Bovine, with a large Percentage of Vegetable Tissue.

George Ade, *Hand-Made Fables*, 1920

Most human beings are quite likeable if you do not see too much of them.

Robert Lynd

Considering how bad men are, it is wonderful how well they behave.

Salvador de Madariaga

Many people believe they attracted by God, or by Nature, when they are only repelled by man.

William R. Inge, *More Lay Thoughts of a Dean*, 1931

The world consists of the dangerously insane and such that are not.

Mark Twain, *Notebooks*, 1935

I'll give you my opinion of the human race in a nutshell . . . their heart's in the right place, but their head is a thoroughly inefficient organ.

W. Somerset Maugham, *The Summing Up*, 1938

Happy that few of us are aware of the world until we are already in league with it.

Elizabeth Bowen, *The Death of the Heart*, 1938

Most people are such fools that it is really no great compliment to say that a man is above the average.

W. Somerset Maugham, *A Writer's Notebook*, 1949

Humanity, let us say, is like people packed in an automobile which is travelling downhill without lights at terrific speed and driven by a small four-year-old child. The signposts along the way are all marked 'Progress'.

Lord Dunsany, 1954

What men value in this world is not rights, but privileges.
H.L. Mencken, *Minority Report*, 1956

Mankind . . . will not willingly admit that its destiny can be revealed by the breeding of flies or the counting of chiasmata.
Cyril Dean Darlington, lecture, 1960

In a crisis that forces a choice to be made among alternative courses of action, most people will choose the worst one possible.
S.A. Rudin, in the *New Republic*, 1961

He who despairs over an event is a coward, but he who holds hopes for the human condition is a fool.
Albert Camus, *Notebooks*, 1962

Mankind has collected together all the wisdom of his ancestors, and can see what a fool man is.
Elias Canetti

Nothing is the history of the world viewed from a suitable distance. Revolution is a trivial shift in the emphasis of suffering; the capacity for self-indulgence changes hands. But the world does not alter its shape or its course . . . Against such immutability the human struggle takes place on the same scale as the insect movements in the grass.
Tom Stoppard, *Lord Malquist and Mr Moon*, 1966

Human beings seem to have an almost unlimited capacity to deceive themselves and to deceive themselves into taking their own lies for truth.
R.D. Laing, *The Politics of Experience*, 1967

We are all murderers and prostitutes. No matter to what culture, society, class, nation one belongs, no matter how normal, moral or mature one takes oneself to be.
R.D. Laing, *The Politics of Experience*, 1967

If one looks with a cold eye at the mess man has made of his history, it is difficult to avoid the conclusion that he has been afflicted by some built-in mental disorder which drives him towards self-destruction. Murder within the species on an individual or collective scale is a phenomenon unknown in the whole animal kingdom, except for man, and a few varieties of ants and rats.
Arthur Koestler, in the *Observer*, 1968

Though the strongest resist all temptation, all human beings who suffer from any deficiency, real or imagined, are under compulsion to draw attention to it.

Quentin Crisp, *The Naked Civil Servant*, 1968

There is no such thing as a situation so intolerable that human beings must necessarily rise up against it. People can bear anything, and the longer it exists the more placidly they will bear it.

Philip Slater, *The Pursuit of Loneliness*, 1970

People will swim through shit if you put a few bob in it.

Peter Sellers

In the fight between you and the world, back the world.

Frank Zappa

People are always talking about tradition, but they forget we have a tradition of a few hundred years of nonsense and stupidity, that there is a tradition of idiocy, incompetence and crudity.

Hugo Demartini, quoted in *Contemporary Artists*, 1977

Everyone becomes the thing they most despise.

Robert Benchley, quoted in *Wits End* by J.R. Gaines, 1977

All God's children are not beautiful. Most of God's children are, in fact, barely presentable.

Fran Lebowitz, *Metropolitan Life*, 1978

The human race never solves any of its problems. It merely outlives them.

David Gerrold, in *Starlog* magazine, 1978

That old question 'Who are we?' receives a disappointing answer in the world in which we must live. Actually, we are merely the subject of this so-called civilised world, in which intelligence, baseness, heroism and stupidity get on very well together and are alternately being pushed to the fore.

René Magritte, quoted in *Magritte: The True Art of Painting*, ed. H. Torczyner, 1979

We . . . make the modern error of dignifying the Individual. We do everything we can to butter him up. We give him a name, assure him that he has certain inalienable rights, educate him, let him pass on his name to his brats and when he dies we give him a special hole in the ground . . . But after all, he's only a seed, a bloom and a withering stalk among pressing billions. Your Individual is a pretty disgusting, vain, lewd little bastard . . . By God, he has only one right guaranteed to him in Nature, and that is the right to die and stink to Heaven.

Ross Lockridge, quoted in *Short Lives* by Katinka Matson, 1980

If ignorance is bliss, why aren't more people happy.

Leonard Rossiter

People (a group that in my opinion has always attracted an undue amount of attention) have often been likened to snowflakes. This analogy is meant to suggest that each is unique – no two alike. This is quite patently not the case. People . . . are quite simply a dime a dozen. And, I hasten to add, their only similarity to snowflakes resides in their invariable and lamentable tendency to turn, after a few warm days, to slush.

Fran Lebowitz, *Social Studies*, 1981

More than any other time in history, mankind faces a crossroads. One path leads to despair and utter hopelessness. The other, to total extinction. Let us pray we have the wisdom to choose correctly.

Woody Allen, *Side Effects*, 1981

It seemed the world was divided into good and bad people. The good ones slept better . . ., while the bad ones seemed to enjoy the waking hours much more.

Woody Allen, *Side Effects*, 1981

See also LIFE, MEN, WOMEN

HUSBANDS

The bachelor is a peacock, the engaged man a lion, and the married man a jackass.

German proverb

The majority of husbands remind me of an orangutang trying to play the violin.

Honoré de Balzac, *The Physiology of Marriage*, 1829

If there were no husbands, who would look after our mistresses.

George Moore, *Confessions of a Young Man*, 1888

A woman who takes her husband about with her everywhere is like a cat that goes on playing with a mouse long after she's killed it.

Saki (H.H. Munro), *The Watched Pot*, 1924

No woman can endure a gambling husband, unless he is a steady winner.

Lord Thomas Dewar

I know many married men, I even know a few happily married men, but I don't know one who wouldn't fall down the first open coal-hole running after the first pretty girl who gave him a wink.

George Jean Nathan

The man she had was kind and clean
And well enough for everyday,
But, oh, dear friends,
You should have seen
The one that got away.

Dorothy Parker, *The Fisherwoman*, 1931

There you are you see, quite simply, if you cannot have your dear husband for a comfort and a delight, for a breadwinner and a crosspatch, for a sofa, a chair or a hotwater bottle, one can use him as a Cross to be borne.

Stevie Smith

The opera is like a husband with a foreign title – expensive to support, hard to understand and therefore a supreme social challenge.

Cleveland Amory, on NBC-TV, 1961

All husbands are alike, but they have different faces so you can tell them apart.

Anonymous, quoted in *Cassell Book of Humorous Quotations*, 1968

A husband is simply a lover with two days' growth of beard, his collar off and a bad cold in the head.

Anonymous, quoted in *Cassell Book of Humorous Quotations*, 1968

Virginity is supposed to be something you give to your husband, like engraved cufflinks, on your wedding day.
Jilly Cooper, _Super Women_, 1974

See also AFFAIRS, DIVORCE, LOVE, LOVERS, MARRIAGE, WIVES

HYPOCRISY

It is of great consequence to disguise your inclination, and to play the hypocrite well; and men are so simple in their temper and so submissive to their present necessities, that he that is neat and cleanly in his collusions shall never want people to practise them upon.
Niccolò Machiavelli, _The Prince_, 1513

Hypocrisy is the homage that vice pays to virtue.
François, Duc de La Rochefoucauld, _Maxims_, 1665

He must be a perfect _complete hypocrite_, if he will be a _complete tradesman_.
Daniel Defoe, _The Complete English Tradesman_, 1726

Remorse is nothing save the anticipation of the pain to which our offence has exposed us.
C.A. Helvétius, _De l'homme_, 1773

General Good is the plea of the scoundrel, hypocrite and flatterer.
William Blake, _Jerusalem_, 1804–20

Man is no angel. He is sometimes more of a hypocrite and sometimes less, and then fools say he has or has not principles.
Honoré de Balzac, _Old Goriot_, 1835

It is a very noble hypocrisy not to talk of oneself.
Friedrich Wilhelm Nietzsche, _Human, All Too Human_, 1878

What people call insincerity is simply a method by which we can multiply our personalities.
Oscar Wilde, _The Critic as Artist_, 1891

A little sincerity is a dangerous thing, and a great deal of it is absolutely fatal.
Oscar Wilde, _The Critic as Artist_, 1891

There is a good deal to be said for blushing, if one can do it at the proper moment.
Oscar Wilde, *A Woman of No Importance*, 1893

A sentimentalist is simply one who desires to have the luxury of an emotion without paying for it.
Oscar Wilde

To be natural is such a very difficult pose to keep up.
Oscar Wilde, *An Ideal Husband*, 1895

Hypocrite, n: One who, professing virtues that he does not respect, secures the advantage of seeming to be what he despises.
Ambrose Bierce, *The Devil's Dictionary*, 1911

Hypocrisy is the most difficult and nerve-racking vice that any man can pursue; it needs an unceasing vigilance and a rare detachment of spirit. It cannot, like adultery or gluttony, be practised at spare moments; it is a wholetime job.
W. Somerset Maugham, *Cakes and Ale*, 1930

Sentimentality is a superstructure covering brutality.
C.G. Jung, *Reflections*, 1953

We live behind our faces, while they front for us.
Michael Korda, *Power in the Office*, 1976

A hypocrite is a person who . . . but who isn't?
Don Marquis, quoted in *The Oxford Book of Aphorisms*, ed. J. Gross, 1983

See also BELIEF, FAITH, IDEALS, MORALS, RELIGION, TRUE BELIEVERS, TRUTH

IDEALS

The idealist is incorrigible: if he be thrown out of Heaven, he makes an ideal of his Hell.
Friedrich Wilhelm Nietzsche, *Human, All Too Human*, 1878

Do not use that foreign word 'ideals'. We have that excellent native word 'lies'.
Henrik Ibsen, *The Wild Duck*, 1884

Man is a dog's ideal of what God should be.
Holbrook Jackson

An idealist is one who helps the other fellow to make a profit.
Henry Ford

An idealist is one who, on noticing that a rose smells better than a cabbage, concludes that it will also make better soup.
H.L. Mencken, *Sententiae,* **1916**

Idealism increases in direct proportion to one's distance from the problem.
John Galsworthy

It seems to be the fate of idealists to obtain what they have struggled for in a form which destroys their ideals.
Bertrand Russell, *Marriage and Morals,* **1929**

When they come downstairs from their ivory towers, idealists are apt to walk straight into the gutter.
Logan Pearsall Smith, *Afterthoughts,* **1931**

We are all inclined to judge ourselves by our ideals; others by their acts.
Harold Nicolson

Positive ideals . . . can seldom be achieved without someone being killed or maimed or interned.
E.M. Forster, *Two Cheers for Democracy,* **1951**

Idealism is the noble toga that political gentlemen drape over their will to power.
Aldous Huxley, 1963

Idealism is fine, but as it approaches reality the cost becomes prohibitive.
William F. Buckley Jr

An idealist – that implies you aren't going to achieve something.
Arthur Scargill, 1974

Rigorous ideological committment is of greatly negative value for governing a country . . . and is a positive threat to economic tranquility and well-being. Economic and social institutions are in a constant process of change; ideological committment, by its nature and strongly avowed virtue, is static. Accordingly, guidance therefrom is likely to be obsolete, obsolescent or irrelevant.

John Kenneth Galbraith, quoted in the *New York Review of Books*, 1986

See also BELIEF, FAITH, IDEAS, MORALS, RELIGION, TRUE BELIEVERS, TRUTH

IDEAS

A nice man is a man of nasty ideas.

Jonathan Swift, *Thoughts on Various Subjects*, 1706

We use ideas merely to justify our evil, and speech merely to conceal our ideas.

Voltaire

All universal moral principles are idle fancies.

Donatien Alphonse François, Marquis de Sade, *The 120 Days of Sodom*, 1785

One of the greatest pains to human nature is the pain of a new idea.

Walter Bagehot, *Physics and Politics*, 1872

As soon as an idea is accepted it is time to reject it.

Holbrook Jackson

To die for an idea is to place a pretty high price upon conjectures.

Anatole France, *The Revolt of the Angels*, 1914

An idea is putting truth in checkmate.

José Ortega y Gasset, *The Revolt of the Masses*, 1932

Nothing is more dangerous than an idea, when a man has only one idea.

Alain, *Propos de la Réligion*, 1938

Man is ready to die for an idea, provided that idea is not quite clear to him.

Paul Eldridge, *Horns of Glass*, 1943

Few things are as immutable as the addiction of political groups to the ideas by which they have once won office.

John Kenneth Galbraith, *The Affluent Society,* **1958**

Let's remind ourselves that last year's fresh idea is today's cliché.

Austen Briggs

As a rule, the most dangerous ideas are not the ones that divide people but those on which they agree.

Stephen Vizinczey, *The Rules of Chaos,* **1970**

Of all political ideas, perhaps the most dangerous is the wish to make people perfect and happy. The attempt to realise heaven on earth has always produced a hell.

Karl Popper, 1971

See also BELIEF, FAITH, IDEALS, MORALS, RELIGION, TRUE BELIEVERS, TRUTH

INTELLECTUALS

Be wiser than other people if you can, but do not tell them so.

Lord Chesterfield, *Letters to his Son,* **1774**

Clever men are the tools with which bad men work.

William Hazlitt, *Collected Works,* **1904**

An intellectual is a parasite that exudes culture.

Tadeusz Kotarbinski

What is a highbrow? It is a man who has found something more interesting than women.

Edgar Wallace, interview, 1931

A class made up solely of intellectuals will always have a guilty conscience.

Adolf Hitler, on schoolmasters

Intellectuals are like women – they go for the military.

André Malraux

To the man-in-the-street, who, I'm sorry to say
Is a keen observer of life,
The word 'intellectual' suggests right away
A man who's untrue to his wife.

W.H. Auden, *New Year Letter*, 1941

Intellectuals can tell themselves anything, sell themselves any bill of goods, which is why they are so often patsies for the ruling classes.

Lillian Hellman, *An Unfinished Woman*, 1969

Intellectuals are people who believe that ideas are more important than values. That is to say, their own ideas and other people's values.

Gerald Brenan, *Thoughts in a Dry Season*, 1978

If you are sure you understand everything that is going on, you are hopelessly confused.

Walter Mondale, 1978

One time you let people know how much sense you got, right away they quit having anything to do with you.

Chester Burnett (Howlin' Wolf)

Wisdom is deepest platitude.

Gore Vidal, on London Weekend Television, 1981

See also GENIUS

JOURNALISM

News is something someone, somewhere doesn't want you to print – the rest is advertising.

Anonymous

A newswriter is a man without virtue, who writes lies at home for his own profit.

Samuel Johnson, *The Idler*, 1758–60

Perhaps an editor might divide his paper into four chapters, heading the first, Truths; the second, Probabilities; the third, Possibilities and the fourth, Lies.

Thomas Jefferson

A newspaper writer is one who has failed in his calling.

Otto von Bismarck, 1862

There is much to be said in favour of modern journalism. By giving us the opinions of the uneducated, it keeps us in touch with the ignorance of the community.

Oscar Wilde, *The Critic as Artist,* **1891**

The public have an insatiable curiosity to know everything. Except what is worth knowing. Journalism, conscious of this, and having tradesman-like habits, supplies their demands.

Oscar Wilde, *The Soul of Man under Socialism,* **1891**

Journalism largely consists in saying 'Lord Jones Dead' to people who never knew Lord Jones was alive.

G.K. Chesterton, *The Wisdom of Father Brown,* **1914**

Newspapers have roughly the same relationship to life as fortune-tellers to metaphysics.

Karl Kraus, *Half Truths and One and a Half Truths,* **1986**

Journalists write because they have nothing to say, and have something to say because they write.

Karl Kraus

Journalism: a profession whose business is to explain to others what it personally doesn't understand.

Lord Northcliffe

Editor . . . a person employed on a newspaper, whose business it is to separate the wheat from the chaff, and to see that the chaff is printed.

Elbert Hubbard, *Roycroft Dictionary,* **1923**

All newspaper editorial writers ever do is come down from the hills after the battle is over and bayonet the wounded.

Anonymous

You cannot hope
To bribe or twist,
Thank God! the
British journalist.
But seeing what
That man will do
Unbribed, there's
No occasion to.

Humbert Wolfe, *The Uncelestial City,* **1930**

There is more joy in Fleet Street over one sinner that cuts his sweet-heart's throat than over the ninety and nine just men who marry and live happily ever after.
  A.P. Herbert, *Mild and Bitter*, **1936**

There is but one way for a newspaper man to look at a politician, and that is down.
  Frank H. Simonds, quoted in *H.L. Mencken's Dictionary of Quotations*, **1941**

To a newspaper man a human being is an item with skin wrapped around it.
  Fred Allen

A [newspaper] editor should have a pimp for a brother so he'd have someone to look up to.
  Gene Fowler

Journalism . . . drawing sketches in the sand that the sea will wash away.
  Walter Lippmann, *The New Republic*, **1915**

Freedom of the press in Britain is freedom to print such of the pro-prietor's prejudices as the advertisers don't object to.
  Hannen Swaffer, 1902

[The] constant yelping about a free press means, with a few honourable exceptions, freedom to peddle scandal, crime, sex, sensationalism, hate, innuendo and the political and financial uses of propaganda. A news-paper is a business out to make money through advertising revenue. That is predicated on its circulation and you know what circulation depends on.
  Raymond Chandler, *The Long Goodbye*, **1953**

The press conference is the politician's way of being informative with-out actually saying anything.
  Emery Kelen

The interview is an intimate conversation between journalist and politi-cian wherein the journalist seeks to take advantage of the garrulity of the politician and the politician of the credulity of the journalist.
  Emery Kelen

People everywhere confuse what they read in the newspapers with news.

A.J. Liebling, in the *New Yorker* magazine, 1956

The media, far from being a conspiracy to dull the political sense of the people, could be viewed as a conspiracy to disguise the extent of political indifference.

David Riesman

Journalism – an ability to meet the challenge of filling the space.

Rebecca West, in the *New York Herald Tribune*, 1956

I read the newspaper avidly. It is my one form of continuous fiction.

Aneurin Bevan, 1960

You know very well that whether you are on page one or page thirty depends on whether [the press] fear you. It is just as simple as that.

Richard M. Nixon

The important thing about the so-called 'communications industry' is that it is basically concerned with merchandising. News is a kind of by-product and if you want to sell things, you don't want to offend anybody.

I.F. Stone, in *The Listener* magazine, 1963

There are honest journalists like there are honest politicians. When bought they stay bought.

Bill Moyers

To the majority of [newspapermen] a woman is either somebody's mother or a whore.

Alexander King, *Rich Man, Poor Man, Freud and Fruit*, 1965

It is part of the social mission of every great newspaper to provide a refuge and a home for the largest possible number of salaried eccentrics.

Baron Thomson of Fleet

Everything you read in the newspapers is absolutely true, except for that rare story of which you happen to have first-hand knowledge.

Erwin Knoll

The only qualities for real success in journalism are ratlike cunning, a plausible manner and a little literary ability. The capacity to steal other people's ideas and phrases . . . is also invaluable.

Nicholas Tomalin, *Stop the Press, I Want to Get On*, **1969**

Most rock journalism is people who can't write interviewing people who can't talk for people who can't read.

Frank Zappa

Journalism is organised gossip.

Edward Egglestone

The First Law of Journalism: to confirm existing prejudice, rather than contradict it.

Alexander Cockburn, *(more)* **magazine, 1974**

We should always tell the Press, freely and frankly, anything they can easily find out.

Antony Jay and Jonathan Lynn, *Yes, Prime Minister*, **1986**

Journalists are notoriously easy to kid. All you have to do is speak to a journalist in a very serious tone of voice and he will be certain that you are either telling the truth or a big, important lie. It has never occurred to any journalist that he is having his leg pulled.

P.J. O'Rourke, *Parliament of Whores*, **1991**

After politics, journalism has always been the preferred career of the ambitious but lazy second-rater.

Gore Vidal, *A View from the Diners Club*, **1991**

Never trust a smiling reporter.

Ed Koch

Journalism could be described as turning one's enemies into money.

Craig Brown, 1993

See also TELEVISION & RADIO

JUSTICE

The love of justice in most men is nothing more than the fear of suffering injustice.

François, Duc de La Rochefoucauld, *Maxims*, **1665**

To talk of not acting from fear is mere parliamentary cant. From what motive but . . . have all the improvements in our constitution proceeded. I question if justice has ever been done to large masses of mankind from any other motive.

Sydney Smith, *The Letters of Peter Plymley*, **1807**

The only way to make the mass of mankind see the beauty of justice is by showing them in pretty plain terms the consequence of injustice.

Sydney Smith, quoted in *Roads to Ruin*, **by E.S. Turner, 1950**

Justice is the sanction of established injustice.

Anatole France, *Crainquebille*, **1901**

Justice, n. A commodity which in a more or less adulterate condition the State sells to the citizen as a reward for his allegiance, taxes and personal service.

Ambrose Bierce, *The Devil's Dictionary*, **1911**

Justice is being allowed to do whatever I like; injustice is whatever prevents me from doing it.

Samuel Butler, *Notebooks*, **1912**

In the Halls of Justice the only justice is in the halls.

Lenny Bruce

Justice is like a train that's nearly always late.

Yevgeny Yevtushenko, *A Precocious Autobiography*, **1963**

See also CRIME, LAW, LAWYERS

LAUGHTER

He who laughs at everything is as big a fool as he who weeps at everything.

Baltasar Gracian, *The Art of Worldly Wisdom*, **1647**

Laughter is nothing else but sudden glory arising from some sudden conception of some eminency in ourselves, by comparison with the infirmity of others, or with our own formerly.

Thomas Hobbes, *On Human Nature*, **1650**

Laughter is the hiccup of a fool.

John Ray, *A Collection of English Proverbs*, **1670**

Laughter is little more than an expression of self-satisfied shrewdness.
Georg Wilhelm Friedrich Hegel, *The Philosophy of Right*, 1820

He who laughs has not yet heard the bad news.
Bertolt Brecht

Nothing shortens a journey so pleasantly as an account of misfortunes at which the hearer is permitted to laugh.
Quentin Crisp, *How To Become a Virgin*, 1981

See also HAPPINESS

LAW

Laws are like spiders' webs which, if anything small falls into them they ensnare it, but large things break through and escape.
Solon, quoted in *Lives and Opinions of Eminent Philosophers* by Diogenes Laertius, c.AD225

Sir, executions are intended to draw spectators. If they do not draw spectators they don't answer their purpose.
Samuel Johnson, quoted in *The Life of Samuel Johnson* by J. Boswell, 1791

Laws are now maintained in credit, not because they are essentially just, but because they are laws. It is the mystical foundation of their authority; they have none other. They are often made by fools; more often by men who in hatred of equality have want of equity; but ever by men who are vain and irresolute. There is nothing so grossly and largely offending, nor so ordinarily wrongful, as the laws.
Michel de Montaigne, *Essays*, 1595

Necessity hath no law.
Oliver Cromwell, 1654

Law is but a heathen word for power.
Daniel Defoe, *The History of the Kentish Rebellion*, 1701

Liberty is the right to do what the laws permit.
Charles de Secondat, Baron de Montesquieu, *De l'ésprit des lois*, 1748

The law doth punish man or woman
That steals the goose from off the common,
But lets the greater felon loose,
That steals the common from the goose.

Anonymous

Laws are always useful to persons of property.

Jean-Jacques Rousseau, *The Social Contract*, 1762

The mass of the people have nothing to do with the laws but to obey them.

Bishop Samuel Horsley, 1795

Every law which originated in ignorance and malice, and gratifies the passions from which it sprang, we call the wisdom of our ancestors.

Sydney Smith, *The Letters of Peter Plymley*, 1807

What are laws but the expression of some class which has power over the rest of the community?

Thomas Babington Macaulay, Baron Macaulay, *Southey's Colloquies*, 1830

People say law but they mean wealth.

Ralph Waldo Emerson, *Journals*, 1909–14

We bury men when they are dead, but we try to embalm the dead body of laws, keeping the corpse in sight long after the vitality has gone. It usually takes a hundred years to make a law; and then, after it has done its work, takes a hundred years to get rid of it.

Henry Ward Beecher, *Life Thoughts*, 1858

If a man stay away from his wife for seven years, the law presumes the separation to have killed him; yet according to our daily experience, it might well prolong his life.

Charles Darling, *Scintillae Juris*, 1877

A jury is composed of twelve men of average ignorance.

Herbert Spencer

A reasonable man can get out of most any trouble, except marriage, without going to law.

Reflections of a Bachelor, 1878

The law has no claim to human respect. It has no more civilizing mission; its only purpose is to protect exploitation.

Peter Kropotkin, *Paroles d'un révolté*, 1884

The law, in all its majestic equality, forbids the rich as well as the poor to sleep under bridges.

Anatole France, *The Red Lily*, 1894

Law is the expression of the will of the strongest for the time being.

Henry Brooks Adams

Of course there's a different law for the rich and the poor; otherwise, who would go into business.

E. Ralph Stewart

A judge is a lawyer who once knew a politician.

Anonymous

Where there's a will, there's a lawsuit.

Addison Mizner and Oliver Herford, *The Cynic's Calendar*, 1901

Lawful, adj. Compatible with the will of a judge having jurisdiction.

Ambrose Bierce, *The Devil's Dictionary*, 1911

Judge: a law student who marks his own papers.

H.L. Mencken, *Sententiae*, 1916

It has long been noticed that juries are pitiless for robbery and full of indulgence for infanticide. A question of interest, my dear Sir! The jury is afraid of being robbed and has passed the age when it could be a victim of infanticide.

Edmond About, quoted in *A Cynic's Breviary* by J.R. Solly 1925

The Reasonable Man . . . is devoid of any human weaknesses, with not a single saving vice . . . This excellent but odious character stands like a monument in the Courts of Justice.

A.P. Herbert, *Misleading Cases in the Common Law*, 1929

The law, as manipulated by clever and highly respectable rascals, still remains the best avenue for a career of honourable and leisurely plunder.

Gabriel Chevallier, *Clochemerle*, 1936

The law isn't justice. It's a very imperfect mechanism. If you press exactly the right buttons and are also lucky, justice may also turn up in the answer.

Raymond Chandler, _The Long Goodbye_, 1953

Cops never say goodbye. They're always hoping to see you again in the line-up.

Raymond Chandler, _The Long Goodbye_, 1953

I have never seen a situation so dismal that a policeman couldn't make it worse.

Brendan Behan

The dispensing of injustice is always in the right hands.

Stanislaw J. Lec, _Unkempt Thoughts_, 1962

A man's respect for law and order exists in precise relationship to the size of his pay cheque.

Adam Clayton Powell, _Keep the Faith Baby_, 1967

The police and so forth only exist insofar as they can demonstrate their authority. They say they're here to preserve order, but in fact they'd go absolutely mad if all the criminals of the world went on strike for a month. They'd be on their knees begging for a crime. That's the only existence they have.

William S. Burroughs, in the _Guardian_, 1969

One of the greatest delusions in the world is the hope that the evils of this world can be cured by legislation.

Thomas B. Reed

To the right wing 'law and order' is often just a code phrase, meaning 'get the niggers'. To the left wing it often means political oppression.

Gore Vidal, 1975

The quality of legislation passed to deal with a problem is inversely proportional to the volume of media clamour that brought it on.

G. Ray Funkhouser, quoted in _The Official Rules_ by P. Dickson, 1978

Guilty is what the man says when your luck runs out.

Joseph Wambaugh, screenplay for _The Onion Field_, 1979

I don't care what the law is – just tell me who the judge is.
> **Roy Cohn, quoted in *Citizen Cohn* by Nicholas Von Hoffman, 1988**

The Metropolitan Police Force is abbreviated to the 'Met' to give more members a chance of spelling it.
> **Mike Barfield, in *The Oldie* magazine, 1992**

See also CRIME, JUSTICE, LAWYERS

LAWYERS

A bad agreement is better than a good lawyer.
> **Italian proverb**

Lawyers' houses are built on the heads of fools.
> **George Herbert, *Jacula Prudentum*, 1651**

A man without money need no more fear a crowd of lawyers than a crowd of pickpockets.
> **William Wycherley, *The Plain Dealer*, 1674**

Sometimes a man who deserves to be looked down upon because he is a fool is despised only because he is a lawyer.
> **Charles de Secondat, Baron de Montesquieu, *Persian Letters*, 1721**

God works wonders now and then
Behold! a lawyer, an honest man.
> **Benjamin Franklin, *Poor Richard's Almanack*, 1733–58**

Lawyers are the only persons in whom ignorance of the law is not punished.
> **Jeremy Bentham**

Lawyers are the only civil delinquents whose judges must of necessity be chosen from themselves.
> **Charles Caleb Colton, *Lacon*, 1820**

A lawyer is a learned gentleman who rescues your estate from your enemies and keeps it for himself.
> **Henry, Baron Brougham**

Whether you're an honest man or whether you're a thief
Depends on whose solicitor has given me my brief.

W.S. Gilbert, *Utopia Ltd,* **1893**

Lawyer – one who protects us against robbers by taking away the temptation.

H.L. Mencken, *Sententiae,* **1916**

A lawyer: the only man in whom ignorance of the law is not punished.

Elbert Hubbard, *Book of Epigrams,* **1923**

Litigation: a form of hell whereby money is transferred from the pockets of the proletariat into those of lawyers.

Kin Hubbard, 1923

Be frank and explicit with your lawyer . . . it is his business to confuse the issue afterwards.

Anonymous, quoted in *A Cynic's Breviary* **by J.R. Solly, 1925**

There is no better way of exercising the imagination as the study of law. No poet ever interpreted nature as freely as a lawyer interprets truth.

Jean Giraudoux, *Tiger at the Gates,* **1955**

A jury consists of twelve persons chosen to decide who has the better lawyer.

Robert Frost

A lawyer is a learned gentleman who rescues your estate from your enemies and keeps it for himself.

David Lodge, *The British Museum is Falling Down,* **1965**

The best client is a scared millionaire.

Anonymous

See also JUSTICE, LAW

LEADERS

Rulers are a scourge through whom God punishes those whom he decides to punish.

Abu Yusuf, *Kitab Al-Khara,* **850**

A prince who desires to maintain his position must learn to be not always good, but to be so or not, as needs require.

Niccolò Machiavelli, *The Prince*, 1513

The people resemble a wild beast, which, naturally fierce and accustomed to live in the woods, has been brought up, as it were, in a prison and in servitude, and having by accident got its liberty, not being accustomed to search for its food, and not knowing where to conceal itself, easily becomes the prey of the first who seeks to incarcerate it again.

Niccolò Machiavelli, *Discourse upon the First Ten Books of Livy*, 1518

Princes are generous enough if they take nothing from me; and do me much good if they do me no hurt.

Michel de Montaigne, *Essays*, 1595

They say princes learn no art truly, but the art of horsemanship. The reason is, the brave beast is no flatterer. He will throw a prince as soon as his groom.

Ben Jonson, *Timber; or Discoveries Made upon Men and Matter*, 1640

The people would be just as noisy if they were going to see me hanged.

Oliver Cromwell, remarking on the crowds cheering his progress

A prince who writes against flattery is as strange as a pope who writes against infallibility.

Voltaire, letter, 1740

Princes, like beauties, from their youth
Are strangers to the voice of truth.

John Gay, *Fables*, 1727

Whoever is foremost leads the herd.

Johann Christoff Friedrich von Schiller

To succeed in chaining the multitude you must seem to wear the same fetters.

Voltaire, *Philosophical Dictionary*, 1764

It is a general error to suppose the loudest complainer for the public to be the most anxious for its welfare.

Edmund Burke, *Observations on a Publication, 'The present state of the nation'*, 1769

All oppressors attribute the frustration of their desires to the want of sufficient rigour. Then they redouble the efforts of their impotent cruelty.

Edmund Burke, *The Impeachment of Warren Hastings*, 1788

Tyrants seldom want pretexts.

Edmund Burke, *Letter to a Member of the National Assembly*, 1791

When we think we lead most, we are most led.

George Gordon, Lord Byron, *The Two Foscari*, 1821

The conduct and opinions of public men at different periods of their careers must not be curiously contrasted in a free and aspiring society.

Benjamin Disraeli, speech, 1834

To be a leader of men one must turn one's back on men.

Havelock Ellis

There are three sorts of despots. There is the despot who tyrannizes over the body. There is the despot who tyrannizes over the soul. There is the despot who tyrannizes over the soul *and* body alike. The first is called the Prince. The second is called the Pope. The third is called the People.

Oscar Wilde, *The Soul of Man under Socialism*, 1891

The demagogue is one who preaches doctrines he knows to be untrue to men he knows to be idiots.

H.L. Mencken

What luck for the rulers that men do not think.

Adolf Hitler

It is the curse of the great that they have to step over corpses to create new life.

Heinrich Himmler

So long as you suffer any man to call himself your shepherd, sooner or later you will find a crook around your ankle.

H.G. Wells, *Experiment in Autobiography*, 1934

As long as men worship the Caesars and Napoleons, the Caesars and Napoleons will duly rise and make them miserable.

Aldous Huxley, *Ends and Means*, 1937

Those who have had no share in the good fortunes of the mighty
Often have a share in their misfortunes.

Bertolt Brecht, *The Caucasian Chalk Circle*, 1945

A leader is a man who has the ability to get other people to do what
they don't want to do and like it.

Harry S. Truman

When smashing monuments, save the pedestals – they always come in
handy.

Stanislaw J. Lec, *Unkempt Thoughts*, 1962

If Presidents don't do it to their wives, they do it to the country.

Mel Brooks, as the 'Two Thousand Year Old Man', 1962

If someone tells you he is going to make a 'realistic decision', you
immediately understand that he has resolved to do something bad.

Mary McCarthy, *On the Contrary*, 1962

The benevolent despot who sees himself as a shepherd of the people still
demands from others the obedience of sheep.

Eric Hoffer, *The Ordeal of Change*, 1964

People, like sheep, tend to follow a leader – occasionally in the right
direction.

Alexander Chase, *Perspectives*, 1966

When you hear the word 'inevitable', watch out! An enemy of humanity has revealed himself.

Stephen Vizinczey, *The Rules of Chaos*, 1970

Here comes the new boss
Same as the old boss.

Pete Townshend, *Won't Get Fooled Again*, 1971

Anybody that wants the presidency so much that he'll spend two
years organising and campaigning for it is not to be trusted with the
office.

David Broder, in the *Washington Post*, 1973

See also DEMOCRACY, GOVERNMENT, POLITICIANS, POLITICS,
POWER, VOTING

LIBERALS

What is called liberality is often merely the vanity of giving.
François, Duc de La Rochefoucauld, *Maxims*, 1665

I hate liberality – nine times out of ten it is cowardice, and the tenth time lack of principle.
Henry Addington, Viscount Sidmouth

A liberal is a man who leaves a room when the fight begins.
Heywood Broun

Liberal – a power worshipper without power.
George Orwell

We who are liberal and progressive know that the poor are our equals in every sense except that of being equal to us.
Lionel Trilling, *The Liberal Imagination*, 1950

A liberal is a man too broadminded to take his own side in a quarrel.
Robert Frost

It's easier to be a liberal a long way from home.
Don K. Price

We know what happens to people who stay in the middle of the road: they get run over.
Aneurin Bevan, speech, 1953

A liberal is a person whose interests aren't at stake at the moment.
Willis Player

The liberals can understand everything but people who don't understand them.
Lenny Bruce

A rich man told me recently that a liberal is a man who tells other people what to do with their money.
Imamu Amiri Baraka (Everett Leroi Jones), *Kulchur*, 1962

What the liberal really wants is to bring about change that will not in any way endanger his position.
Stokeley Carmichael

The liberal [on pornography] . . . is like a man who loathes whore-houses in practice, but doesn't mind them in principle, providing they are designed by Mies van der Rohe and staffed by social workers in Balenciaga dresses.

Kenneth Tynan, in *Esquire* magazine, 1968

Hell hath no fury like a liberal scorned.

Dick Gregory

If God had been a Liberal there wouldn't have been ten command-ments, there would have been ten suggestions.

Malcolm Bradbury and Christopher Bigsby, *After Dinner Game*, 1982

I have often been called a Nazi, and although it is unfair, I don't let it bother me. I don't let it bother me for one simple reason. No-one has *ever* had a fantasy about being tied to a bed and sexually ravished by someone dressed as a liberal.

P.J. O'Rourke, *Give War a Chance*, 1992

See also CONSERVATIVES, GOVERNMENT, PARTIES, POLITICS

LIFE

Life is an hereditary disease.

Graffito

What do baths bring to your mind? Oil, sweat, dirt, greasy water and everything that is disgusting. Such, then, is life in all its parts and such is every material thing in it.

Marcus Aurelius Antoninus, *Meditations*, AD150

During the time men live without a common power to keep them all in awe, . . . the life of man [is] solitary, poor, nasty, brutish and short.

Thomas Hobbes, *Leviathan*, 1651

The majority of men employ the first part of life in making the rest miserable.

Jean de La Bruyère, *The Characters*, 1688

If thou intendest to live happy, thou must make but few Reflections on Life.

Thomas Fuller, M.D., *Introductio ad Prudentiam*, 1727

We are born crying, live complaining and die disappointed.
Thomas Fuller, M.D., *Gnomologia,* **1732**

In the great game of human life one begins by being a dupe and ends by being a rogue.
Voltaire

Human life is everywhere a state in which much is to be endured and little to be enjoyed.
Samuel Johnson, *Rasselas,* **1759**

Such is the state of life, that none are happy but by the anticipation of change: the change itself is nothing; when we have made it the next wish is to change again.
Samuel Johnson, *Rasselas,* **1759**

Life can then little else supply
But a few good fucks and then we die.
Thomas Potter, *The Essay on Woman,* **1763 (usually attrib. to John Wilkes)**

Nothing can exceed the vanity of our existence but the folly of our pursuits.
Oliver Goldsmith, *The Good-Natured Man,* **1768**

Life is barren enough surely with all her trappings; let us therefore be careful how we strip her.
Samuel Johnson, *Johnsonian Miscellanies,* **ed. G.B. Hills, 1897**

Life is a pill which none of us can bear to swallow without gilding.
Samuel Johnson, *Johnsonian Miscellanies,* **ed. G.B. Hills, 1897**

That kind of life is most happy which affords us most opportunities of gaining our own esteem.
Samuel Johnson

The whole of life is but keeping away the thoughts of death.
Samuel Johnson, *The Life of Samuel Johnson* **by J. Boswell, 1791**

Life to the great majority is only a constant struggle for mere existence – with the certainty of losing it.
Arthur Schopenhauer, *The World as Will and Idea,* **1819**

To desire immortality is to desire the perpetuation of a great mistake.
Arthur Schopenhauer, *The World as Will and Idea,* **1819**

To what point of insignificance may human life not dwindle! To what fine, agonizing threads will it not cling!
William Hazlitt, *Literary Remains,* **ed. W. Hazlitt Jr, 1836**

Life is an apprenticeship to constant renunciations, to the steady failure of our claims, our hopes, our powers, our liberty.
Henri-Frédéric Amiel, *Journal,* **1856**

If God were suddenly condemned to live the life which he has inflicted upon men, he would kill himself.
Alexander Dumas fils

Life is a hospital is which every patient is possessed by the desire to change his bed.
Charles Baudelaire

A man's worst difficulties begin when he is able to do as he likes.
T.H. Huxley

Life is a fatal complaint, and an eminently contagious one.
Oliver Wendell Holmes, *The Poet at the Breakfast-Table,* **1872**

The great pleasure in life is doing what people say you cannot do.
Walter Bagehot, *Literary Studies,* **1879–95**

Life is much too important a thing to talk seriously about it.
Oscar Wilde, *Vera, or the Nihilists,* **1880**

All you need in life is ignorance and confidence and then success is sure.
Mark Twain, letter, 1887

Life is one long process of getting tired.
Samuel Butler, *Notebooks,* **1912**

Almost every person, if you will believe himself, holds a quite different theory of life from the one on which he is patently acting.
Robert Louis Stevenson, *Virginibus Puerisque,* **1881**

All ways end at the same point . . . Disillusion.
Oscar Wilde, *The Picture of Dorian Gray,* **1891**

In this world there are only two tragedies. One is not getting what one wants and the other is getting it.

Oscar Wilde, *Lady Windermere's Fan,* **1892**

The first duty in life is to be as artificial as possible. What the second duty is no one has as yet discovered.

Oscar Wilde, *Phrases and Philosophies for the Use of the Young,* **1894**

Life is a predicament that precedes death.

Henry James

There is always a right and a wrong way, and the wrong way always seems the more reasonable.

George Moore

Life is like an onion: you peel off layer after layer and then you find there is nothing in it.

James Gibbons Huneker

Once your reputation's done
You can live a life of fun.

Wilhelm Busch

Life being what it is, one dreams of revenge.

Paul Gauguin

Experience is a good teacher, but she sends in terrific bills.

Minna Antrim, *Naked Truth and Veiled Allusions,* **1902**

Life is a lease imposed upon the occupant without previous communication of the conditions in the contract.

Guy Delaforest, quoted in *Reflections on the Art of Life* **by J.R. Solly, 1902**

To pass through life tranquilly, one must not be too clear-sighted.

Gustave Droz, quoted in *Reflections on the Art of Life* **by J.R. Solly, 1902**

The great secret in life . . . [is] not to open your letters for a fortnight. At the expiration of that period you will find that nearly all of them have answered themselves.

Arthur Binstead, *Pitcher's Proverbs,* **1909**

The meaning of life is that it stops.
  Franz Kafka

Society is a madhouse where the wardens are the officials and police.
  August Strindberg, Zones of the Spirit, 1913

There is no cure for birth and death save to enjoy the interval.
  George Santayana, Soliloquies in England, 1922

To repent, and then to start all over again, such is life.
  Victor Cherbuliez, quoted in A Cynic's Breviary by J.R. Solly, 1925

Life is a glorious cycle of song
A medley of extemporanea
And love is a thing that can never go wrong
And I am Marie of Roumania
  Dorothy Parker, Comment, 1927

Don't take life too seriously – you will never get out of it alive.
  Elbert Hubbard, The Notebook, 1927

The one dependable law of life: everything is always worse than you thought it was going to be.
  Dorothy Parker, The Waltz, 1936

Life is not a spectacle or a feast; it is a predicament.
  George Santayana, Articles and Essays, 1936–7

Why should not things be largely absurd, futile and transitory? They are so, and we are so, and they and we go very well together.
  George Santayana

There are two things to aim at in life: first, to get what you want, and after that to enjoy it. Only the wisest of mankind achieve the second.
  Logan Pearsall Smith, Afterthoughts, 1931

As a remedy to life in society I would suggest the big city. Nowadays it is the only desert within our means.
  Albert Camus, Notebooks, 1935–42

What is life? Life is stepping down a step or sitting in a chair. And it isn't there.

Ogden Nash, *Good Intentions,* **1942**

We give people a box in the suburbs, it's called a house, and every night they sit in it staring at another box; in the morning they run off to another box called an office, and at the weekends they get into another box, on wheels this time, and grope their way through endless traffic jams.

Caroline Kelly

For the ordinary man is passive. Within a narrow circle . . . he feels himself master of his fate, but against major events he is as helpless as against the elements. So far from endeavouring to influence the future, he simply lies down and lets things happen to him.

George Orwell

Human life begins on the other side of despair.

Jean-Paul Sartre, *The Flies,* **1942**

Life is a maze in which we take the wrong turning before we have learnt to walk.

Cyril Connolly (Palinurus), *The Unquiet Grave,* **1944**

We are all serving a life-sentence in the dungeon of life.

Cyril Connolly (Palinurus), *The Unquiet Grave,* **1944**

If you want a picture of the future, imagine a boot stamping on the human face – forever . . . And remember that is for ever.

George Orwell, *Nineteen Eighty-Four,* **1948**

Most people get a fair amount of fun out of their lives, but on balance life is suffering and only the very young or the very foolish imagine otherwise.

George Orwell, *Shooting an Elephant,* **1950**

To have a grievance is to have a purpose in life.

Eric Hoffer, *The Passionate State of Mind,* **1954**

Take the socalled 'standardofliving'. What do most people mean by 'living'? They don't mean living. They mean the latest and closest plural approximation to the singular prenatal passivity which science, in its finite but unbounded wisdom, has succeeded in selling their wives.

    e.e. cummings, *Poems*, 1923–54

Life always comes to a bad end.

    Marcel Aymé, *Les oiseaux de lune*, 1955

A man can look upon his life and accept it as good or evil; it is far, far harder for him to confess that it has been unimportant in the sum of things.

    Murray Kempton, *Part of Our Time*, 1955

Since all life is futility, then the decision to exist must be the most irrational of all.

    E.M. Cioran, *The Temptation to Exist*, 1956

We're all of us sentenced to solitary confinement inside our own skins, for life.

    Tennessee Williams, *Orpheus Descending*, 1957

We cry when we are born, and what follows can only be an attenuation of this cry.

    Françoise Sagan, in the *Sunday Express*, 1957

Life is an unbroken succession of false situations.

    Thornton Wilder, in the *Observer*, 1957

It takes a kind of shabby arrogance to survive in our time, and a fairly romantic nature to want to.

    Edgar Z. Friedenberg, *The Vanishing Adolescent*, 1959

For most men life is a search for the proper manila envelope in which to get themselves filed.

    Clifton Fadiman, 1960

Life is like a sewer. What you get out of it depends on what you put into it.

    Tom Lehrer, *An Evening Wasted with Tom Lehrer*, 1953

The messiness of experience, that may be what we mean by life.

    Daniel J. Boorstin, *The Image*, 1961

Human life is mainly a process of filling in time until the arrival of death, or Santa Claus, with very little choice, if any, of what kind of business one is going to transact during the long wait.

Eric Berne, *Games People Play*, **1964**

Life is a game at which everybody loses.

Leo Sarkadi-Schuller

Human life . . . is only theatre, and mostly cheap melodrama at that.

Malcolm Muggeridge, *Tread Softly For You Tread on My Jokes*, **1966**

I have always felt that concentration camps . . . are the logical conclusion of contemporary life.

Arthur Miller, in *Writers at Work* **3rd series, 1967**

Life is a gamble at terrible odds – if it was a bet you wouldn't take it.

Tom Stoppard, *Rosencrantz and Guildenstern Are Dead*, **1967**

What is there to say, finally, except that pain is bad and pleasure good, life all, death nothing.

Gore Vidal, in *Esquire* **magazine, 1970**

Most people's lives aren't complex – they're just complicated.

L. Rust Hills, in *Esquire* **magazine, 1970**

Our daily life is a bad serial by which we let ourselves be bewitched.

Michel Butor, *Répertoire II*, **1969**

No one recovers from the disease of being born, a deadly wound if ever there was one.

E.M. Cioran, *The Fall into Time*, **1971**

All that shimmers on the surface of the world, all that we call interesting, is the fruit of ignorance and inebriation.

E.M. Cioran, *The Fall into Time*, **1971**

Life is first boredom, then fear.
Whether or not we use it, it goes,
And leaves what something hidden from us chose,
And age, and then the only end of age.

Philip Larkin, *Dockery and Son*, **1974**

If you just try long enough and hard enough, you can always manage to boot yourself in the posterior.
A.J. Liebling, *The Press*, 1975

Sometimes it seems like that is the choice – either kick ass or kiss ass.
James Caan, in *Playboy* magazine, 1976

Being frustrated is disagreeable, but the real disasters in life begin when you get what you want.
Irving Kristol, 1977

Life is a concentration camp. You're stuck here and there's no way out and you can only rage impotently against your persecutors.
Woody Allen, in *Esquire* magazine, 1977

Life is divided into the horrible and the miserable.
Woody Allen, *Annie Hall*, 1977

Life is what happens to you while you're busy making other plans.
John Lennon, *Beautiful Boy*, 1979

'After she was dead, I loved her.' That is the story of every life – and death.
Gore Vidal, in the *New York Review of Books*, 1980

The very purpose of existence is to reconcile the glowing opinion we hold of ourselves with the appalling things that other people think about us.
Quentin Crisp, *How To Become a Virgin*, 1981

Life is a meaningless comma in the sentence of time.
Chris Garratt and Mick Kidd, *The Essential Biff*, 1982

In my youth I hoped to do great things; now I shall be satisfied to get through without scandal.
Walter Bagehot, quoted in *Selected Letters of Raymond Chandler*, ed. F. MacShane, 1981

Life is an effort that deserves a better cause.
Karl Kraus, *Half Truths and One and a Half Truths*, 1986

The problems of the world, AIDS, cancer, nuclear war, pollution are, finally, no more solvable than the problems of a tree which has borne fruit: the apples are overripe and they are falling – what can be done? . . . What can be done about the problems that beset our life? *Nothing* can be done, and nothing needs to be done.

David Mamet, *Writing in Restaurants*, 1988

Life is generally something that happens elsewhere.

Alan Bennett, *Talking Heads*, 1989

See also EXPERIENCE, HUMANITY, TIME

LOVE

In love there is always one who kisses and one who offers the cheek.

French proverb

Love is the affection of a mind that has nothing better to engage it.

Theophrastus, *c.*300BC

Hunger stops love, or if not hunger, time.

Crates, quoted in *Lives and Opinions of Eminent Philosophers* by Diogenes Laertius, *c.*AD225

Love lasteth as long as the money endureth.

William Caxton, *The Game and Playe of Chesse*, 1474

Oh love will make a dog howl in tune.

Francis Beaumont and John Fletcher, *The Queen of Corinth*, *c.*1612

Out upon it, I have loved
Three whole days together
And am like to love three more
If it prove fair weather.

Sir John Suckling, *Fragmenta Aurea*, 1646

Admiration is a very short-lived passion, that immediately decays upon growing familiar with its object.

Joseph Addison, *The Spectator*, 1711

When poverty comes in at the door, love creeps out at the window.

Thomas Fuller M.D., *Gnomologia*, 1732

The only victory in love is flight.

Napoleon Bonaparte, *Maxims*, 1804–15

Love, in present day society, is just the exchange of two momentary desires and the contact of two skins.

Nicolas de Chamfort, *Maximes et pensées*, 1805

He who cannot love must learn to flatter.

Johann Wolfgang von Goethe

Constancy has nothing virtuous in itself, independently of the pleasure it confers.

Percy Bysshe Shelley, *Queen Mab* (notes), 1813

As that gallant can best affect a pretended passion for one woman, who has no true love for another, so he that has no real esteem for any of the virtues, can best assume the appearance of them all.

Charles Caleb Colton, *Lacon*, 1820

Love is an alchemist that can transmute poison into food – and a spaniel that prefers even punishment from one hand to caresses from another.

Charles Caleb Colton, *Lacon*, 1820

The power of love consists mainly in the privilege that Potentate possesses of coining, circulating, and making current those falsehoods between man and woman, that would not pass for one moment, either between woman and woman, or man and man.

Charles Caleb Colton, *Lacon*, 1820

Love matches are made by people who are content, for a month of honey, to condemn themselves to a life of vinegar.

Marguerite, Countess of Blessington

What is irritating about love is that it is a crime that requires an accomplice.

Charles Baudelaire

The magic of our first love is our ignorance that it can ever end.

Benjamin Disraeli

We study ourselves three weeks, we love each other three months, we squabble three years, we tolerate each other thirty years, and then the children start all over again.

Hippolyte Taine, *Vie et opinions de Thomas Graingorge*, 1868

Love is the desire to prostitute oneself. There is, indeed, no exalted pleasure that cannot be related to prostitution.
Charles Baudelaire, *Intimate Journals,* **1887**

Love matches, so called, have illusion for their father and need for their mother.
Friedrich Wilhelm Nietzsche

Women are well aware that what is commonly called sublime and poetical love depends not upon moral qualities, but on frequent meetings, and on the style in which the hair is done up, and on the colour and the cut of the dress.
Leo Tolstoy, *The Kreutzer Sonata,* **1889**

The only true love is love at first sight; second sight dispels it.
Israel Zangwill

There is only one way to be happy by means of the heart – to have none.
Paul Bourget, *La Physiologie de l'amour moderne,* **1890**

There is always something ridiculous about the passions of people whom one has ceased to love.
Oscar Wilde, *The Picture of Dorian Gray,* **1891**

Always! that is a dreadful word . . . it is a meaningless word too. The only difference between a caprice and a life-long passion is that the caprice lasts a little longer.
Oscar Wilde, *The Picture of Dorian Gray,* **1891**

When one is in love one begins by deceiving oneself. And one ends by deceiving others. This is what the world calls a romance.
Oscar Wilde, *A Woman of No Importance,* **1893**

Romance should never begin with sentiment. It should begin with science and end with a settlement.
Oscar Wilde, *An Ideal Husband,* **1895**

It is well to write love letters. There are certain things it is not easy to ask your mistress for face to face, like money, for instance.
Henri de Régnier

The fickleness of the women whom I love is only equalled by the infernal constancy of the women who love me.
George Bernard Shaw, *The Philanderer,* **1898**

When we want to read of the deeds that are done for love, whither do we turn? To the murder column.

George Bernard Shaw

First love is only a little foolishness and a lot of curiosity, no really self-respecting woman would take advantage of it.

George Bernard Shaw, *John Bull's Other Island*, 1904

Protestations of undying affection are never ridiculous when they are accompanied by emeralds.

W. Somerset Maugham, *Lady Frederick*, 1907

Romance: once upon a time. Seldom twice.

Oliver Herford and John Clay, *Cupid's Cyclopedia*, 1910

Women in love are less ashamed than men; they have less to be ashamed of.

Ambrose Bierce, *The Devil's Dictionary*, 1911

No woman ever falls in love with a man unless she has a better opinion of him than he deserves.

Edgar Watson Howe, *Country Town Sayings*, 1911

Cupid, n. The so-called god of love. This bastard creation of a barbarous fancy . . . of all unbeautiful and inappropriate conceptions, this is the most reasonless and offensive.

Ambrose Bierce, *The Devil's Dictionary*, 1911

Love, n. A temporary insanity curable by marriage or the removal of the patient from the influences under which he incurred the disease . . . it is sometimes fatal, but more frequently to the physician than to the patient.

Ambrose Bierce, *The Devil's Dictionary*, 1911

To live is like to love: all reason is against it and all healthy instinct is for it.

Samuel Butler, *Notebooks*, 1912

A woman we love rarely satisfies all our needs and we deceive her with a woman we do not love.

Marcel Proust, *Remembrance of Things Past*, 1913–27

Love is the delusion that one woman differs from another.
H.L. Mencken, *Sententiae,* **1916**

To be in love is merely to be in a state of perpetual anaesthesia – to mistake an ordinary young man for a Greek god, or an ordinary young woman for a goddess.
H.L. Mencken, *Prejudices* **1st series, 1920**

The only love letters which are of any use are those of goodbye.
Etienne Rey

It's no compliment to be loved by a man who has had no experience.
Ian Hay

Love is what happens to a man and woman who don't know each other.
W. Somerset Maugham

Love is based upon a view of women that is impossible to any man who has had experience of them.
H.L. Mencken, *Prejudices* **4th series, 1924**

You must not love animals, they don't last long enough. You must not love humans, they last too long.
Anonymous, quoted in *A Cynic's Breviary* **by J. R. Solly, 1925**

Lady, lady, should you meet
One whose ways are all discreet,
One who murmers that his wife
Is the lodestar of his life,
One who keeps assuring you
That he never was untrue,
Never loved another one . . .
Lady, lady, better run!
Dorothy Parker, *Social Note,* **1927**

My soul is crushed, my spirit sore;
I do not like me anymore,
I cavil, quarrel, grumble, grouse,
I ponder on the narrow house
I shudder at the thought of men . . .
I'm due to fall in love again.
Dorothy Parker, *Symptom Recital,* **1927**

By the time you swear you're his
Shivering and sighing
And he vows his passion is
Infinite, undying –
Lady, make a note of this:
One of you is lying.

Dorothy Parker, *Unfortunate Coincidence*, 1927

When you're away, I'm restless, lonely,
Wretched, bored, dejected, only
Here's the rub, my darling dear
I feel the same when you are here.

Samuel Hoffenstein, *Poems in Praise of Practically Nothing*, 1929

A husband is what's left of the lover once the nerve has been extracted.

Helen Rowland, *A Guide to Men*, 1929

Love . . . a burnt match skating in a urinal.

Hart Crane, *The Bridge*, 1930

The ideal love affair is conducted by post.

George Bernard Shaw

Every love's the love before
In a duller dress.

Dorothy Parker, *Summary*, 1931

We hate the people we love because they're the only ones that can hurt us.

Lyn Starling, screenplay for *Private Worlds*, 1935

The first man who can think of how he's going to stay in love with his wife and another woman is going to win that prize they're always talking about in Sweden.

Clare Booth Luce, *The Women*, 1936

Love is something that hangs up behind the bathroom door and smells of Lysol.

Ernest Hemingway, *To Have and Have Not*, 1937

The word 'love' bridges for us those chasms of momentary indifference and boredom which gape from time to time between even the most ardent lovers.

Aldous Huxley, *The Olive Tree*, 1937

The voyage of love is all the sweeter for an outside stateroom and a seat at the Captain's table.

Henry Haskins, *Meditations in Wall Street*, 1940

You study one another for three weeks, you love each other for three months, you fight for three years and you tolerate the situation for thirty.

André de Misson

Oh, love is real enough, you will find it some day, but it has one arch-enemy – and that is life.

Jean Anouilh, *Ardèle*, 1948

Love is only a dirty trick played on us to achieve the continuation of the species.

W. Somerset Maugham, *A Writer's Notebook*, 1949

If two people love each other, there can be no happy end to it.

Ernest Hemingway

Love is a hole in the heart.

Ben Hecht, *Winkelberg*, 1950

Love is simple to understand if you haven't got a mind soft and full of holes. It's a crutch, and there isn't one of us who doesn't need a crutch.

Norman Mailer, *Barbary Shore*, 1951

The credulity of love is the most fundamental source of authority.

Sigmund Freud, *Collected Works*, 1955

Many a man has fallen in love with a girl in a light so dim he would not have chosen a suit by it.

Maurice Chevalier, 1955

Every little girl knows about love. It is only her capacity to suffer because of it that increases.

Françoise Sagan, in the *Daily Express*, 1957

Is that what love is? Using people? And maybe that's what hate is. Not being able to use people.

Gore Vidal and Tennessee Williams, screenplay for *Suddenly Last Summer*, 1959

Romance, like alcohol, should be enjoyed, but should not be allowed to become necessary.

Edgar Z. Friedenberg, *The Vanishing Adolescent,* **1959**

Human love is often but the encounter of two weaknesses.

François Mauriac, *Cain, Where Is Your Brother?,* **1962**

A man in love, like Romeo, can no more join his beloved between the sheets than push his dear mother off a roof, at least, not for some time.

Ben Hecht, *Letters from Bohemia,* **1964**

The best love affairs are those we never had.

Norman Lindsay, *Bohemians of the Bulletin,* **1965**

Of course it's possible to love a human being if you don't know them too well.

Charles Bukowski, *Notes of a Dirty Old Man,* **1969**

Love, love, love – all the wretched cant of it, masking egotism, lust, masochism, fantasy under a mythology of sentimental postures, a welter of self-induced miseries and joys, blinding and masking the essential personalities in the frozen gestures of courtship, in the kissing and the dating and the desire, the compliments and the quarrels which vivify its barrenness.

Germaine Greer, *The Female Eunuch,* **1970**

Love is what makes the world go round – that and clichés.

Michael Symons, in the *Sydney Morning Herald,* **1970**

Romance, like the rabbit at the dog track, is the elusive, fake, and never attained reward which, for the benefit and amusement of our masters, keeps us running and thinking in safe circles.

Beverly Jones, *The Florida Paper on Women's Liberation,* **1970**

That desert of loneliness and recrimination that men call love.

Samuel Beckett, quoted in *The New York Review of Books,* **1971**

Love is the victim's response to the rapist.

Ti-Grace Atkinson

What we're all looking for is someone who doesn't live there, just pays for it.

Andy Warhol, *From A to B and Back Again,* **1975**

Perhaps at fourteen every boy should be in love with some ideal woman to put on a pedestal and worship. As he grows up, of course, he will put her on a pedestal the better to view her legs.

Barry Norman, quoted in *The Listener* magazine, 1978

'All I want is us to share the occasional candle-lit dinner and a bit of slap and tickle when your old man's away on business. No involvement. No strings. No complications.' 'Oh Myles, this is too wonderful.' Relief flooded her entire being. Here at last was the casual fling she had always dreamed of.

Posy Simmonds, *True Love*, 1981

Love is like cheap wine . . . it leads you to the stars, but leaves you with the gutrot of tomorrow.

Chris Garratt and Mick Kidd, *The Rainy Day Biff*, 1983

See also AFFAIRS, DIVORCE, HUSBANDS, LOVERS, MARRIAGE, SEX, WIVES

LOVERS

The reason that lovers never weary each other is because they are always talking about themselves.

François, Duc de La Rochefoucauld, *Maxims*, 1665

'Tis an unhappy circumstance that . . . the man so often should outlive the lover.

William Congreve, *The Way of the World*, 1700

All men are thieves in love, and like a woman the better for being another's property.

John Gay, *The Beggar's Opera*, 1728

Wisely a woman prefers to a lover a man who neglects her. This one may love her some day, some day the lover will not.

John Hay

Don't give to lovers you will replace irreplaceable presents.

Logan Pearsall Smith

The sweeter the apple, the blacker the core –
Scratch a lover and find a foe!

Dorothy Parker, *Ballade of a Great Weariness*, 1927

When from time to time I have seen the persons with whom the great lovers satisfied their desires, I have often been more astonished by the robustness of their appetites than envious of their successes. It is obvious that you need not often go hungry if you are willing to dine off mutton hash and turnip tops.

W. Somerset Maugham, *The Summing Up*, **1938**

There is no fury like an ex-wife searching for a new lover.

Cyril Connolly (Palinurus), *The Unquiet Grave*, **1944**

See also AFFAIRS, DIVORCE, HUSBANDS, LOVE, MARRIAGE, SEX, WIVES

LYING

To know how to dissemble is the knowledge of kings.

Cardinal Richelieu, *Mirame*, **c.1625**

When you say you agree to a thing on principle, you mean that you have not the slightest intention of carrying it out in practice.

Otto von Bismarck

The most common sort of lie is that by which a man deceives himself; the deception of others is a relatively rare offence.

Friedrich Wilhelm Nietzsche, *The Antichrist*, **1888**

A lie with a purpose is one of the worst kind, and the most profitable.

Finley Peter Dunne, *Mr Dooley's Opinions*, **1901**

A little inaccuracy sometimes saves tons of explanation.

Saki (H.H. Munro), *The Comments of Moung Ka*, **1924**

Four-fifths of the perjury in the world is expended on tombstones, women and competitors.

Lord Thomas Dewar

The greater the lie, the greater the chance that it will be believed.

Adolf Hitler, *Mein Kampf*, **1924**

Lying is an indispensable part of making life tolerable.

Bergan Evans

When a man you like switches from what he said a year ago, or four years ago, he is a broad-minded person who has courage enough to change his mind with changing conditions. When a man you don't like does it, he is a liar who has broken his promises.

Franklin P. Adams (F.P.A.), *Nods and Becks*, **1944**

The system of organised lying on which society is founded.

George Orwell, outline for *Nineteen Eighty-Four*, **1946**

A lie is an abomination unto the Lord and a very present help in trouble.

Adlai Stevenson, 1951

Society can only exist on the basis that there is some amount of polished lying and that no one says exactly what he thinks.

Lin Yutang

Fraud is the homage that force pays to reason.

Charles P. Curtis, *A Commonplace Book*, **1957**

Conversation is more often likely to be an attempt at deliberate evasion, deliberate confusion, rather than communication. We are all cheats and liars, really.

James Jones, in *Writers at Work* **3rd series, 1957**

The art of living is the art of knowing how to believe lies.

Cesare Pavese, *The Burning Brand*, **1961**

Don't lie if you don't have to.

Leo Szilard, quoted in *Science*, **1972**

You don't tell deliberate lies, but sometimes you have to be evasive.

Margaret Thatcher, 1976

The camera cannot lie. But it can be an accessory to untruth.

Harold Evans, *Pictures on a Page*, **1978**

See also HONESTY, TRUTH

MADNESS

The first step towards madness is to think oneself wise.

Fernando de Rojas, *Celestina, or the Tragi-Comedy of Calisto and Melibea*, **1499–1502**

Men will always be mad, and those who think they can cure them are the maddest of all.
Voltaire, letter, 1762

Mad, adj. Affected with a high degreee of intellectual independence; not conforming to standards of thought, speech and action derived by the conformants from the study of themselves; at odds with the majority; in short, unusual.
Ambrose Bierce, *The Devil's Dictionary*, 1911

A man who is 'of sound mind' is one who keeps the inner madman under lock and key.
Paul Valéry, *Mauvaises pensées et autres*, 1942

To think contrary to one's era is heroism. But to speak against it is madness.
Eugène Ionesco

Whom the mad would destroy, first they make Gods.
Bernard Levin, 1967

Insanity – a perfectly rational adjustment to the insane world.
R.D. Laing, quoted in the *Guardian*, 1972

A madman is also a man whom society did not want to hear and whom it wanted to prevent from uttering certain intolerable truths.
Antonin Artaud, *Selected Writings*, 1976

MANNERS

Politeness is fictitious benevolence.
Samuel Johnson, *The Journal of a Tour to the Hebrides* by J. Boswell, 1785

Manners are the hypocrisy of a nation.
Honoré de Balzac

Politeness is a tacit agreement that peoples' miserable defects, whether moral or intellectual, shall on either side be ignored and not be made the subject of reproach.
Arthur Schopenhauer, *Our Relation to Others*, 1851

A lady: that monster of European civilization and Teutonico-Christian stupidity.
Arthur Schopenhauer, *Parerga und Paralipomena*, 1851

That roguish and cheerful vice, politeness.
Friedrich Wilhelm Nietzsche, *Beyond Good and Evil*, 1886

Politeness, n. The most acceptable hypocrisy.
Ambrose Bierce, *The Devil's Dictionary*, 1911

Politeness is organised indifference.
Paul Valéry, *Tel quel*, 1943

Rudeness is the weak man's imitation of strength.
Eric Hoffer, *The Passionate State of Mind*, 1954

Tact is the art of convincing people that they know more than you do.
Raymond Mortimer

Manners are especially the need of the plain. The pretty can get away with anything.
Evelyn Waugh, in the *Observer*, 1962

Tact consists in knowing how far to go in going too far.
Jean Cocteau, quoted in *The Faber Book of Aphorisms*, ed. W.H. Auden and L. Kronenberger, 1964

Manners are the lowest common denominator of ethical experience.
Victor S. Navasky, *Naming Names*, 1980

MARRIAGE

A wife is one who stands by a man in all the trouble he wouldn't have had if he hadn't married her.
Anonymous

Marriage is the only evil that men pray for.
Greek proverb

Marriage is a romance in which the hero dies in the first chapter.
Anonymous

Asked when a man should marry: For a young man, not yet; for an old man, never at all.

Diogenes, c.350BC

The man who marries for money earns it.

Jewish proverb

Women, deceived by men, want to marry them; it is a kind of revenge as good as any other.

Philip de Remi Beaumanoir

A good marriage would be between a blind wife and a deaf husband.

Michel de Montaigne, Essays, 1595

Marriage is good for nothing but to make friends fall out.

Thomas Shadwell, The Sullen Lovers, 1668

Marriage is a desperate thing. The frogs in Aesop were extreme wise; they had a great mind to some water, but they would not leap into the well, because they could not get out again.

John Selden, Table Talk, 1689

Courtship to marriage, as a very witty prologue to a very dull play.

William Congreve, The Old Bachelor, 1693

Every man plays the fool once in his life, but to marry is to play the fool all one's life long.

William Congreve, The Old Bachelor, 1693

Tho' marriage makes man and wife one flesh, it leaves 'em still two fools.

William Congreve, The Double Dealer, 1694

What cloying meat is love, when matrimony's the sauce to it.

John Vanbrugh, The Provok'd Wife, 1697

Never marry a widow unless her first husband was hanged.

James Kelly, Scottish proverbs, 1721

Keep thy Eyes wide open before Marriage, and half shut afterwards.

Thomas Fuller, M.D., Introductio ad Prudentiam, 1727

Marriage is the only adventure open to the cowardly.
  Voltaire, *Thoughts of a Philosopher*, 1734

His designs were strictly honourable, as the phrase is: that is, to rob a lady of her fortune by way of marriage.
  Henry Fielding, *The History of Tom Jones*, 1749

There is, indeed, nothing that so much seduces reason from vigilance, as the thought of passing life with an amiable woman.
  Samuel Johnson, *The Idler*, 1758–60

Love is blind, but marriage restores its sight.
  Georg Christoph Lichtenberg, *Aphorisms*, 1764–99

It is possible, though not very probable, that there may be joy in marriage.
  Lord Chesterfield, *Letters to his Son*, 1774

'Tis safest in matrimony to begin with a little aversion.
  Richard Brinsley Sheridan, *The Rivals*, 1775

A gentleman who had been very unhappy in marriage married immediately after his wife died: Johnson said it was the triumph of hope over experience.
  Samuel Johnson, *The Life of Samuel Johnson* by J. Boswell, 1791

Love is an ideal thing, marriage a real thing; a confusion of the real with the ideal never goes unpunished.
  Johann Wolfgang von Goethe

Marriage is a good thing, and so is a bone for a dog; but if you tied it to his tail it will drive him mad.
  Colonel George Hanger, *The Life and Adventures and Opinions of Col. George Hanger*, 1801

For the butterfly, mating and propagation involve the sacrifice of life, for the human being, the sacrifice of beauty.
  Johann Wolfgang von Goethe

Next to being married a girl likes to be crossed in love now and then.
  Jane Austen, *Pride and Prejudice*, 1813

A system could not well have been devised more studiously hostile to human happiness than marriage.

Percy Bysshe Shelley, *Queen Mab* **(notes), 1813**

Marriage is a feast where the grace is sometimes better than the dinner.

Charles Caleb Colton, *Lacon,* **1820**

Marriage must incessantly contend with a monster that devours everything: familiarity.

Honoré de Balzac, *The Physiology of Marriage,* **1829**

The married woman is a slave whom one must be able to set upon a throne.

Honoré de Balzac, *The Physiology of Marriage,* **1829**

The music at a wedding procession always reminds me of the music of soldiers going into battle.

Heinrich Heine

The most happy marriage I can picture or imagine to myself would be the union of a deaf man to a blind woman.

Samuel Taylor Coleridge, quoted in *Recollections,*
ed. T. Allsop, 1836

Advice to persons about to marry – don't.

Mr Punch's Almanac, 1845

It doesn't much signify whom one marries, for one is sure to find out the next morning that it was someone else.

Samuel Rogers, *Table Talk,* **ed. A. Dyce, 1856**

Marriage is at best a dangerous experiment.

Thomas Love Peacock, *Gryll Grange,* **1860–1**

No man is regular in his attendance at the House of Commons until he is married.

Benjamin Disraeli

Marriage: a ceremony in which rings are put on the finger of the lady and through the nose of the gentleman.

Herbert Spencer

Every woman should marry – and no man.
  Benjamin Disraeli, *Lothair,* **1870**

If we take matrimony at its lowest . . . if we regard it as no more than a sort of friendship recognised by the police.
  Robert Louis Stevenson, *Virginibus Puerisque,* **1881**

You may carve it on his tombstone, you may cut it on his card
That a young man married is a young man marred.
  Rudyard Kipling, *The Story of the Gadsbys,* **1889**

A man can be happy with any woman as long as he does not love her.
  Oscar Wilde, *The Picture of Dorian Gray,* **1891**

One should always be in love. That is the reason why one should never marry.
  Oscar Wilde

Men marry because they are tired, women because they are curious. Both are disappointed.
  Oscar Wilde, *A Woman of No Importance,* **1893**

The honeymoon is the period when the bride still trusts the groom's word of honour.
  Anonymous

I am not in favour of long engagements. They give people the oporetunity of finding out each other's character before marriage, which I think is never advisable.
  Oscar Wilde, *The Importance of Being Earnest,* **1895**

If we men married the women we deserve, we should have a very bad time of it.
  Oscar Wilde, *An Ideal Husband,* **1895**

Just because a girl's married ain't no sign she hasn't loved and lost.
  Kin Hubbard, *Abe Martin on Things in General,* **1926–30**

If you are afraid of loneliness, don't marry.
  Anton Chekhov

I think it can be stated without denial that no man ever saw a man he would be willing to marry if he were a woman.
George Gibbs, *How to Stay Married*, 1925

It is most unwise for people in love to marry.
George Bernard Shaw

If it were not for the presents, an elopement would be preferable.
George Ade, *Forty Modern Fables*, 1901

When you see what some girls marry, you realise how much they must hate to work for a living.
Helen Rowland, *Reflections of a Bachelor Girl*, 1909

Even if a man was delightful, no woman would marry him if she knew what he was like.
E.F. Benson, *Paul*, 1906

Marriage: the conventional ending of a love affair. A lonesome state.
Oliver Herford and John Clay, *Cupid's Cyclopedia*, 1910

In olden times sacrifices were made at the altar – a practice which is still continued.
Helen Rowland

It isn't tying himself to one woman that a man dreads when he thinks of marrying; it's separating himself from all the others.
Helen Rowland

Marriage – a souvenir of love.
Helen Rowland

Bride, n. A woman with a fine prospect of happiness behind her.
Ambrose Bierce, *The Devil's Dictionary*, 1911

Marriage, n. The state or condition of a community consisting of a master, a mistress and two slaves, making in all, two.
Ambrose Bierce, *The Devil's Dictionary*, 1911

Wedding, n. A ceremony at which two persons undertake to become one, one undertakes to become nothing, and nothing undertakes to become supportable.
Ambrose Bierce, *The Devil's Dictionary*, 1911

Marriage is a good deal like a circus: there is not as much in it as is represented in the advertising.

Edgar Watson Howe, *Country Town Sayings*, 1911

Marriage is distinctly and repeatedly excluded from heaven. Is this because it is thought likely to mar the general felicity?

Samuel Butler, *Notebooks*, 1912

In matrimony to hesitate is sometimes to be saved.

Samuel Butler, *Notebooks*, 1912

The conjugal bedroom is the coexistence of brutality and martyrdom.

Karl Kraus, *Half Truths and One and a Half Truths*, 1986

He marries best who puts it off until it is too late.

H.L. Mencken, *Sententiae*, 1916

If people waited to know each other before they were married, the world wouldn't be so grossly over-populated.

W. Somerset Maugham

When a man marries it is no more than a sign that the feminine talent for persuasion and intimidation . . . has forced him into a more or less abhorrent compromise with his own honest inclinations and best interests.

H.L. Mencken

Marriage, in life, is like a duel in the midst of a battle.

Edmond About, quoted in *A Cynic's Breviary* by J.R. Solly, 1925

Women are always anxious to urge bachelors to matrimony; is it from charity or revenge?

Gustave Vapereau, quoted in *A Cynic's Breviary* by J.R. Solly, 1925

The woman who does not marry makes a blunder than can only be compared to that of the man who does.

Gyp, quoted in *A Cynic's Breviary* by J.R. Solly, 1925

To marry a woman who you love and who loves you is to lay a wager with her as to who will stop loving the other first.

Alfred Capus, *Notes et pensées*, 1926

A man who marries a woman to educate her falls victim to the same fallacy as the woman who marries a man to reform him.
Elbert Hubbard, *The Notebook*, 1927

A marriage is likely to be what is called happy if neither party ever expected to get much happiness out of it.
Bertrand Russell, *Marriage and Morals*, 1929

Many a necklace becomes a noose.
Paul Eldridge

There are various forms of a certain disease, the victim of which is unable to say, 'No'. Some of these forms are more serious than others and often lead to electrocution or marriage.
Robert Benchley

Marriage is the waste paper basket of the emotions.
Sidney Webb, Baron Passfield, quoted in *Autobiography* by Lord Russell, 1967

Marriage always demands the greatest understanding of the art of insincerity possible between two human beings.
Vicki Baum, *Results of an Accident*, 1931

And so they were married – to be more together –
And found they were never again so much together –
Divided by the morning tea,
By the evening paper,
By children and tradesmen's bills.
Louis MacNeice, *Les Sylphides*, 1941

Very few modern women either like or desire marriage, especially after the ceremony has been performed. Primarily women wish attention and affection. Matrimony is something they accept when there is no alternative. Really, it is a waste of time, and hazardous, to marry them. It leaves one open to a rival. Husbands, good or bad, always have rivals. Lovers, never.
Helen Lawrenson, in *Esquire* magazine, 1939

Marriage is like paying an endless visit in your worst clothes.
J.B. Priestley, quoted in *Frank Muir Goes Into* by F. Muir, 1978

The dread of loneliness is greater than the fear of bondage, so we get married.

Cyril Connolly (Palinurus), *The Unquiet Grave,* **1944**

The complaints which anyone voices against his mate indicate exactly the qualities which stimulated attraction before marriage.

Dr Rudolf Dreikurs, *The Challenge of Marriage,* **1946**

All married women should make a habit of saying, 'In spite of everything dear, I'm still devoted to you.'

Eric Linklater, *Private Angelo,* **1946**

Bachelors know more about women than married men. If they didn't, they would be married too.

H.L. Mencken, *A Mencken Chrestomathy,* **1949**

An egotist is a man who expects a woman to marry him for himself alone.

Raymond Mortimer

Marriage is a lottery in which men stake their liberty and women their happiness.

Virginie des Rieux

There is probably nothing like living together for blinding people to each other.

Ivy Compton-Burnett, *Mother and Son,* **1955**

Love, for too many people in our time, consists of sleeping with a seductive woman, one who is properly endowed with the right distribution of curves and conveniences, and one upon whom a permanent lien has been acquired through the institution of marriage.

Ashley Montagu, *The Natural Superiority of Women,* **1953**

Marriage is a vulgar effort on the part of dull people to bring boredom to a fine art.

J.B. Morton ('Beachcomber')

Marriage is based on the theory that when a man discovers a brand of beer exactly to his taste he should at once throw up his job and go to work in the brewery.

George Jean Nathan, 1958

Marriage is give and take. You'd better give it to her, or she'll take it anyway.

Joey Adams, *Cindy and I*, 1959

A man in love is incomplete until he is married. Then he is finished.

Zsa Zsa Gabor, in *Newsweek* magazine, 1960

If you're going to break up with your old lady and you live in a small town, make sure you don't break up at three in the morning. Because you're screwed – there's nothing to do . . . So make it about nine in the morning, . . . bullshit around, worry her a little, then come back at seven in the night.

Lenny Bruce

It is easier to live through someone else than to become complete yourself.

Betty Friedan, *The Feminine Mystique*, 1963

Marriage is a triumph of habit over hate.

Oscar Levant, *Memoirs of an Amnesiac*, 1965

When you're married to someone, they take you for granted . . . when you're living with someone it's fantastic . . . they're so frightened of losing you they've got to keep you satisfied all the time.

Nell Dunn, *Poor Cow*, 1967

The only real argument for marriage is that it remains the best method for getting acquainted.

Heywood Broun, quoted in *Wits End*, ed. R. Drennan, 1968

When you're bored with yourself, marry, and be bored with someone else.

David Pryce-Jones, *Owls and Satyrs*, 1960

Marriage . . . the most advanced form of warfare in the modern world.

Malcolm Bradbury, *The History Man*, 1975

Bigamy is having one husband too many. Monogamy is the same.

**Anonymous woman, quoted as epigraph to *Fear of Flying*
by Erica Jong, 1975**

Marriage is an arrangement by which two people start by getting the best out of each other and often end by getting the worst.

Gerald Brenan, *Thoughts in a Dry Season*, 1978

The glances over cocktails
That seemed to be so sweet
Don't seem quite so amorous
Over Shredded Wheat.

Anonymous rhyme, quoted in *Frank Muir Goes Into* by Frank Muir, 1978

Marriage is an attempt to change a night owl into a homing pigeon.

Anonymous, quoted in *The Penguin Book of Modern Quotations*, ed. Cohen and Cohen, 1981

Marriage is two people agreeing to tell the same lie.

Karen Durbin, 1981

It is explained that all relationships require a little give and take. This is untrue. Any partnership demands that we give and give and give and at the last, as we flop into our graves exhausted, we are told that we didn't give enough.

Quentin Crisp, *How To Become a Virgin*, 1981

After your marriage, my dear, unpleasant things are bound to happen, but take no notice. I never did.

Anonymous aristocrat, advice to her daughter, quoted in *Victorian Women* by Joan Perkin, 1993

See also AFFAIRS, DIVORCE, HUSBANDS, LOVE, LOVERS, WIVES

THE MASSES

A wise fellow who is also worthless always charms the rabble.

Euripides, *Hippolytus*, 428BC

Happy are those who are convinced so as to be of the general Opinions.

George Savile, Marquis of Halifax, *Political, Moral and Miscellaneous Thoughts and Reflexions*, c.1694

If the multitude ever deviate into the right, it is always for the wrong reasons.

Lord Chesterfield, *Letters to his Son*, 1774

About things on which the public thinks long, it commonly attains to think right.

Samuel Johnson, *Works* vol. vii, 1787

Every numerous assembly is *mob*, let the individuals who compose it be what they will . . . Understanding they have collectively none; but they have ears and eyes which must be flattered and seduced.

Lord Chesterfield, *Letters to his Son*, 1774

Ten million ignorances do not constitute one knowledge.

Clemens von Metternich, on democracy

The public is an old woman. Let her maunder and mumble.

Thomas Carlyle, *Journal*, 1835

What the crowd requires is mediocrity of the highest order.

Auguste Préault

Unanimity is almost an indication of servitude.

Charles de Rémusat

Leave this hypocritical prating about the masses. Masses are rude, lame, unmade, pernicious in their demands and influence, and need not to be flattered but to be schooled.

Ralph Waldo Emerson, *The Conduct of Life*, 1860

The majority is always wrong.

Israel Zangwill

When all think alike, then no one is thinking.

Walter Lippmann, quoted in *The Book of Laws* by H. Faber, 1980

Hatred is the most accessible and comprehensive of all unifying agents. Mass movements can rise and spread without belief in a God, but never without belief in a devil.

Eric Hoffer, *The True Believer*, 1951

Mass democracy, mass morality and the mass media thrive independently of the individual, who joins them at a cost of at least a partial perversion of his instinct and insights. He pays for his social ease with what used to be called his soul, his discriminations, his uniqueness, his psychic energy, his self.

Al Alvarez, in *The Listener* magazine, 1971

There's a whiff of the lynch mob or the lemming migration about any over-large concentration of like-thinking individuals, no matter how virtuous their cause.

P.J. O'Rourke, *Parliament of Whores*, 1991

Altruism, a quality as hated by the generality as it is rare.
Gore Vidal, A View from the Diner's Club, 1991

A mob . . . is an ugly thing to see. The audience that's easily moved
to tears is as easily moved to sadistic dementia.
P.J. O'Rourke, Give War a Chance, 1992

See also CLASS

MAXIMS

If you would live innocently seek solitude.
Publilius Syrus, Moral Sayings, c.50BC

All bad precedents began as justifiable measures.
**Gaius Julius Caesar, quoted in The Conspiracy of Catiline
by Sallust, c.50BC**

Severities should be dealt out all at once, so that their suddenness give
less offence; benefits ought to be handed out drop by drop, so that they
may be relished the more.
Niccolò Machiavelli, The Prince, 1513

There are three things that are not to be credited: a woman when she
weeps, a merchant when he swears, nor a drunkard when he prays.
Barnaby Rich, My Lady's Looking Glass, 1616

Do pleasant things yourself, but unpleasant things do through others.
Baltasar Gracian, The Art of Worldly Wisdom, 1647

Fish and visitors smell after three days.
Benjamin Franklin, Poor Richard's Almanack, 1733–58

Promises and pie-crust are made to be broken.
**Jonathan Swift, A Complete Collection of Polite and Ingenious
Conversation, 1738**

One of the pleasures of reading old letters is the knowledge that they
need no answer.
**George Gordon, Lord Byron, quoted in The Oxford Book of
Aphorisms, ed. J. Gross, 1983**

Grant graciously what you cannot refuse safely, and conciliate those you cannot conquer.

Charles Caleb Colton, *Lacon*, 1820

Nothing is so useless as a general maxim.

Thomas Babington Macaulay, Baron Macaulay, in the *Edinburgh Review*, 1827

When you talk to the half-wise, twaddle; when you talk to the ignorant, brag; when you talk to the sagacious, look very humble and ask their opinion.

Edward George Bulwer-Lytton, Baron Lytton, *Paul Clifford*, 1830

We should distrust any enterprise that requires new clothes.

Henry David Thoreau, *Walden*, 1854

The Eleventh Commandment: Thou shalt not be found out.

George Whyte-Melville, *Holmby House*, 1860

There are not many joys in human life equal to the joy of the sudden birth of a generalization.

Peter Kropotkin, 1884

Look for the ridiculous in everything and you will find it.

Jules Renard, *Journal*, 1890

Murder is always a mistake – one should never do anything one cannot talk about after dinner.

Oscar Wilde, *The Picture of Dorian Gray*, 1891

In this world there are only two tragedies. One is not getting what one wants, and the other is getting it. The last is much the worst, the last is a real tragedy.

Oscar Wilde, *Lady Windermere's Fan*, 1892

One should always play fairly when one has the winning cards.

Oscar Wilde, *An Ideal Husband*, 1895

Nothing matters very much, and few things matter at all.

Arthur James, Earl Balfour, attributed

Ade's Law: Anyone can win – unless there happens to be a second entry.

George Ade, *Forty Modern Fables*, 1901

The most delightful day after the one on which you buy a cottage in the country is the one on which you resell it.
J. Brécheux, quoted in *Reflections on the Art of Life* by J.R. Solly, 1902

Take care to get what you like or you will be forced to like what you like.
George Bernard Shaw, *Man and Superman*, 1903

It is dangerous to be sincere unless you are also stupid.
George Bernard Shaw, *Man and Superman*, 1903

It is far better to know too little than to know too much.
Samuel Butler, *Notebooks*, 1912

Always mistrust a subordinate who never finds fault with his superior.
John Churton Collins, in the *English Review*, 1914

Treat a whore like a lady and a lady like whore.
Wilson Mizner, quoted in *The Incredible Mizners* by A. Johnson, 1953

Never gamble – except with a little of the best of it.
Wilson Mizner, quoted in *The Incredible Mizners* by A. Johnson, 1953

'Necessity is the mother of invention' is a silly proverb. 'Necessity is the mother of futile dodges' is much nearer the truth.
Alfred North Whitehead, quoted in *The Faber Book of Aphorisms*, ed. W.H. Auden and L. Kronenberger, 1964

Living well is the best revenge.
Anonymous, 1925

Right or wrong is all the same
When baby needs new shoes.
It isn't how you play the game,
It's whether you win or lose.
John Lardner, replying to Grantland Rice's famous 'It matters not who lost or won . . . but how you played the game'

Don't ever make the same mistake twice – unless it pays.
Mae West

If you aren't rich you should always look useful.
Louis-Ferdinand Céline, *Journey to the End of the Night*, **1932**

The race is not always to the swift, nor the battle to the strong, but that's the way to bet.
Damon Runyon

The finest plans have always been spoiled by the littleness of them that should carry them out.
Bertolt Brecht, *Mother Courage*, **1941**

If it's good, they'll stop making it.
Herbert Block ('Herblock')

You should make a point of trying every experience once – except incest and folk-dancing.
Anonymous Scot, quoted in *Farewell My Youth* **by A. Bax, 1943**

Never eat at a place called Mom's. Never play cards with a man named Doc. And never lie down with a woman who's got more troubles than you.
Nelson Algren

Mistakes are always initial.
Cesare Pavese, quoted in *The Faber Book of Aphorisms*,
ed. W.H. Auden and L. Kronenberger, 1964

Intimacy has its conventions as well as ordinary social intercourse. There are three cardinal rules: don't take somebody's else's boyfriend unless you've been specifically invited to do so, don't take a drink without being asked, and keep a scrupulous accounting in financial matters.
W.H. Auden, *The Table-Talk of W. H. Auden*,
ed. Alan Ansen, 1990

Always fornicate between clean sheets and spit on a well-scrubbed floor.
Christopher Fry, *The Lady's Not for Burning*, **1949**

If you want to get along, go along.
Sam Rayburn, political credo

Be nice to people on the way up, because you'll meet them on your way down.
Wilson Mizner, quoted in *The Incredible Mizners*
by A. Johnson, 1953

To be modern is to potter about in the terminal ward.
E.M. Cioran, *Syllogismes de l'amertume*, **1952**

Logic is the art of going wrong with confidence.
Joseph Wood Krutch

Gumperson's Law: the probability of anything happening is in inverse ratio to its desirability.
John W. Hazard, *Changing Times*, **1957**

A little inaccuracy saves a world of explanation.
C.E. Ayres

More will mean worse.
Kingsley Amis, in *Encounter* **magazine, 1960**

The final delusion is the belief that one has lost all delusions.
Maurice Chapelain

Be careful what you set your heart upon – for it will surely be yours.
James Baldwin, *Nobody Knows My Name*, **1961**

Beware of Greeks bearing gifts, coloured men looking for loans, and whites who understand the negro.
Adam Clayton Powell Jr

The way to a man's heart is through his wife's belly, and don't you forget it.
Edward Albee, *Who's Afraid of Virginia Woolf?*, **1962**

1. Never give anything away for nothing. 2. Never give more than you have to (always catch the buyer hungry and always make him wait). 3. Always take back everything if you possibly can.
William S. Burroughs, on drug pushing in the
Daily Telegraph, **1964**

If you've got them by the balls, their hearts and minds will follow.
The Green Berets, military motto, c.1965

Never sleep three in a bed – or you'll wake up three in a bed.
  Günter Grass, *Dog Years*, 1963

Standards are always out of date – that's what makes them standards.
  Alan Bennett, *Forty Years On*, 1968

A paranoid is a man who knows a little of what's going on.
  William S. Burroughs, in *Friends* magazine, 1970

The chief cause of problems is solutions.
  Eric Sevareid, 1970

Ninety-nine per cent of everything is crap.
  Theodore Sturgeon

If it works, it's obsolete.
  Marshall McLuhan, in *The Listener* magazine, 1971

Do not assume the other fellow has intelligence to match yours. He may have more.
  Terry-Thomas

When in doubt, mumble; when in trouble, delegate; when in charge, ponder.
  James H. Boren, quoted in *The Official Rules* by Paul Dickson, 1972

Blessed is he who expects no gratitude, for he shall not be disappointed.
  W.C. Bennett, quoted in *The Official Rules* by Paul Dickson, 1972

Unhappiness is best defined as the difference between our talents and our expectations.
  Edward de Bono, in the *Observer*, 1977

When anyone says they often think something it means they've just thought of it now.
  Michael Frayn, *Alphabetical Order*, 1975

If anything can go wrong, it will.
  Murphy's Law, quoted in *The Official Rules* by Paul Dickson, 1972

The three questions of greatest concern are – 1. Is it attractive? 2. Is it amusing? 3. Does it know its place?

Fran Lebowitz, *Metropolitan Life*, 1978

You know what they say – the sweetest word in the English language is revenge.

Peter Beard, in *Interview* magazine, 1978

1. You can't win. 2. You can't break even. 3. You can't even quit the game.

Ginsberg's Theorem, quoted in *Murphy's Law* by A. Bloch, 1979

The whole world is a scab. The point is to pick it constructively.

Peter Beard, quoted in *Loose Talk*, ed. L. Botts, 1980

A conclusion is the place where you got tired of thinking.

Matz's Maxim, in *Murphy's Law Book Two* by A. Bloch, 1980

When a man speaks of the need for realism one may be sure that this is always the prelude to some bloody deed.

Sir Isaiah Berlin, quoted in *The Times*, 1981

A good terminology is half the game.

Anonymous, quoted in *Bricks to Babel* by A. Koestler, 1981

Always be nice to those younger than you, because they are the ones who will be writing about you.

Cyril Connolly, *Journal 1928–1937*, ed. D. Pryce-Jones, 1983

Only two things are worth having – money, which you have not had the trouble of earning, and irresponsibility.

Cyril Connolly, *Journal 1928–1937*, ed. D. Pryce-Jones, 1983

So long as there is anything to be gained by saying nothing, it is always better to say nothing than anything.

Antony Jay and Jonathan Lynn, script for *Yes, Prime Minister*, 1986

If you can keep your head when all about you are losing theirs, perhaps you have misunderstood the situation.

Graffito

What you can't have, abuse.
Italian proverb

MEDICINE

He that sinneth before his Maker, Let him fall into the hands of the physician.
The Bible, *Ecclesiasticus (Apocrypha)*, c.AD100

There are more old drunkards than there are old physicians.
François Rabelais, *Gargantua*, 1535

Diseases are the interests of pleasures.
John Ray, *A Collection of English Proverbs*, 1670

Doctors allow one to die; charlatans kill.
Jean de La Bruyère, *The Characters*, 1688

The patient is not likely to recover who makes the doctor his heir.
Thomas Fuller, M.D., *Gnomologia*, 1732

He who was never sick dies the first fit.
Thomas Fuller, M.D., *Gnomologia*, 1732

The art of medicine consists in amusing the patient while nature cures the disease.
Voltaire

Philosophy, like medicine, has plenty of drugs, few good remedies, and hardly any specific cures.
Nicolas de Chamfort, *Maximes et pensées*, 1805

Doctors are the same as lawyers; the only difference is that lawyers merely rob you, wheras doctors rob you and kill you too.
Anton Chekhov

One knows so well the popular idea of health. The English country gentleman galloping after a fox. The unspeakable in full pursuit of the uneatable.
Oscar Wilde, *A Woman of No Importance*, 1893

The animals are not as stupid as one thinks – they have neither doctors nor lawyers.

L. Docquier, quoted in *Reflections on the Art of Life* by J.R. Solly, 1902

You can always read a doctor's bill and you can never read his prescription.

Finley Peter Dunne, *Mr Dooley Says*, 1910

Cured yesterday of my disease
I died last night of my physician.

Matthew Prior

Every man who feels well is a sick man neglecting himself.

Jules Romains, *Knock*, 1923

A really conscientious doctor ought to die with his patient. The captain goes down with his ship, He doesn't survive the wreck!

Eugène Ionesco, *The Bald Prima Donna*, 1948

If Patient turns out to be really ill, after all, it is always possible to look grave at the same time and say 'You realise, I suppose, that twenty-five years ago you'd have been dead.'

Stephen Potter, *One-Upmanship*, 1952

Sociology . . . the study of people who do not need to be studied by people who do.

E.S. Turner

I have a perfect cure for a sore throat – cut it.

Alfred Hitchcock

The beneficient effects of the regular quarter-hour's exercise before breakfast is more than offset by the mental wear-and-tear in getting out of bed fifteen minutes earlier than one otherwise would.

Simeon Strunsky

I don't believe the kindliest of men ever learned about the death of his doctor without a feeling of smugness.

Richard Gordon

Now a Jew, in the dictionary, is one who is descended from the ancient tribes of Judea . . . but you and I know what a Jew is – one who killed

Our Lord . . . A lot of people say to me 'Why did you kill Christ?'
'I dunno, it was one of those parties, got out of hand, you know . . .'
We killed him because he didn't want to become a doctor, that's
why we killed him.

**Lenny Bruce, quoted in *The Essential Lenny Bruce*,
ed. J. Cohen, 1967**

There's no fun in medicine, but there's a lot of medicine in fun.

**Anonymous, quoted in *The Wit of Medicine*, ed. L. and
M. Cowan, 1972**

A drug is a substance that when injected into a guinea pig produces a
scientific paper.

**Anonymous, quoted in *The Wit of Medicine*, ed. L. and
M. Cowan, 1972**

If a patient is poor he is committed to a public hospital as a 'psychotic'.
If he can afford a sanatorium, the diagnosis is 'neurasthenia'. If he is
wealthy enough to be in his own home under the constant watch of
nurses and physicians, he is simply 'an indisposed eccentric'.

**Pierre Janet, quoted in *The Wit of Medicine*, ed. L. and
M. Cowan, 1972**

There is no human activity, eating, sleeping, drinking or sex which
some doctor somewhere won't discover leads directly to cardiac arrest.

John Mortimer, in the *Observer*, 1978

I have always said that exercise is a short cut to the cemetery.

John Mortimer, *Rumpole of the Bailey*, 1978

A young physician can expect nothing but trouble from an important
and original discovery made early in his career. Such an individual
would be wise to attribute his discovery to luck rather than ability. An
even more cynical thought is that a pioneer should develop some
physical handicap (a limp, a stutter or a an eye patch).

Adrian Upton, in *The Vital Probe* by I.S. Cooper, 1982

Medicine: 'Your money and your life!'

Karl Kraus, *Half Truths and One and a Half Truths*, 1986

A virus is a Latin word translated by doctors to mean 'Your guess is
as good as mine'.

Anonymous

Some doctors make the same mistakes for twenty years and call it clinical experience.

Noah Fabricant

Why live like an invalid to die as a healthy man?

Italian proverb

MEN

A man must learn to endure patiently that which he cannot avoid conveniently.

Michel de Montaigne, *Essays*, 1595

Never battle with a man who has nothing to lose, for then the conflict is unequal.

Baltasar Gracian, *The Art of Worldly Wisdom*, 1647

To make a Man tell of some private Grievance, pretend the like Uneasiness, and seem sick of the same Disease.

Thomas Fuller, M.D., *Introductio ad Prudentiam*, 1727

Animals have these advantages over man: they have no theologians to instruct them, their funerals cost them nothing, and no one starts law suits over their wills.

Voltaire

Questioner: 'I wonder what pleasure men can take in making beasts of themselves?'
Johnson: 'He who makes a beast of himself gets rid of the pain of being a man.'

Samuel Johnson, *Murray's Johnsoniana*, 1836

Man's chief merit consists in resisting the impulses of his nature.

Samuel Johnson, *Johnsonian Miscellanies*, ed. G. B. Hill, 1897

Man originates in muck, wades a while in muck, makes muck and in the end returns to muck.

Johann Christoff Friedrich von Schiller, *The Robbers*, 1781

Depend upon it that if a man talks of his misfortunes, there is something in them that is not disagreeable to him.

Samuel Johnson, *The Life of Samuel Johnson* by J. Boswell, 1791

A man can be so much of everything that he is nothing of any thing.
Samuel Johnson, *The Life of Samuel Johnson* by J. Boswell, 1791

Let a man admire himself, and he will infallibly find plenty of simpletons to admire him.
William Hazlitt, *Butts of Different Sorts*, 1829

Yield to a man's tastes and he will yield to your interests.
Edward George Bulwer-Lytton, Baron Lytton, *Paul Clifford*, 1830

If every man were straightforward in his opinions, there would be no conversation.
Benjamin Disraeli

If you pick up a starving dog and make him prosperous, he will not bite you. That is the principal difference between a dog and a man.
Mark Twain

One never dives into the water to save a drowning man more eagerly than when there are others present who dare not take the risk.
Friedrich Wilhelm Nietzsche

I sometimes think that God, in creating man, somewhat overestimated his ability.
Oscar Wilde

It is only the superficial qualities that last. Man's deeper nature is soon found out.
Oscar Wilde, *Phrases and Philosophies for the Use of the Young*, 1894

Why did nature create Man? Was it to show that she is big enough to make mistakes, or was it pure ignorance?
Holbrook Jackson

Man is the only animal that strikes his women-folk.
Jeannie Gunn

[A] 'Grand Old Man'. That means on our continent any one with snow white hair who has kept out of jail till eighty.
Stephen Leacock

Male, n. A member of the unconsidered, or negligible sex. The male of the human race is commonly known to the female as Mere Man. The genus has two varieties: good providers and bad providers.
Ambrose Bierce, *The Devil's Dictionary*, 1911

Never trust a man who speaks well of everybody.
John Churton Collins, in *The English Review*, 1914

Too often the strong, silent man is silent only because he does not know what to say, and is reputed strong only because he has remained silent.
Sir Winston Churchill, 1924

Man is a clever animal who behaves like an imbecile.
Albert Schweitzer

How does a man live? By completely forgetting he is a human being.
Bertolt Brecht, *The Threepenny Opera*, 1928

The only really masterful noise a man makes in a house is the noise of his key, when he is still on the landing, fumbling for the lock.
Colette

If man had created man, he would be ashamed of his performance.
Mark Twain, *Notebooks*, 1935

Man is a useless passion.
Jean-Paul Sartre, *Being and Nothingness*, 1943

Most of us grow up to be the kind of men our mothers warned us against.
Brendan Behan

What is man? A miserable little pile of secrets.
André Malraux

If man is only a little lower than the angels, the angels should reform.
Mary Wilson Little

The only real threat to man is man himself.
Dr Brock Chisholm

There are no great men, buster. There are only men.
Charles Schnee, screenplay for *The Bad and the Beautiful*, 1952

You may be sure that when a man begins to call himself a realist he is preparing to do something that he is secretly ashamed of doing.
Sydney J. Harris

Men are those creatures with two legs and eight hands.
Jayne Mansfield

Always suspect the man who seems to fit every need.
Sir James Darling

Women think of being a man as a gift. It is a duty. Even making love can be a duty. A man has always got to get it up, and love isn't always enough.
Norman Mailer, in *Nova* magazine, 1969

It is chiefly through the instinct to kill that man achieves intimacy with the life of nature.
Lord Clark

Probably the only place where a man can feel really secure is in a maximum security prison, except for the imminent threat of release.
Germaine Greer, *The Female Eunuch*, 1970

Don't accept rides from strange men – and remember that all men are as strange as hell.
Robin Morgan, *Sisterhood is Powerful*, 1970

If you catch a man, throw him back.
Women's Liberation slogan, c.1975

See also HUMANITY, WOMEN

THE MILITARY

It is the blood of the soldier that makes the general great.
Anonymous

If my soldiers began to think, not one would remain in the ranks.
Frederick the Great, attributed

The greatest general is he who makes the fewest mistakes.
  Napoleon Bonaparte, *Maxims,* **1804–15**

There is nothing on earth as stupid as a gallant officer.
  Arthur Wellesley, Duke of Wellington

Generals have never risen from the very learned or erudite class of officers but have mostly been men who, from the circumstances of their position, could not have obtained any great amount of knowledge.
  Karl von Clausewitz, *On War,* **1832**

The louder he talked of his honour, the faster we counted our spoons.
  Ralph Waldo Emerson, *The Conduct of Life,* **1860**

No plan survives contact with the enemy.
  Field-Marshal Helmuth von Moltke

When the military man approaches the world locks up its spoons and packs off its womankind.
  George Bernard Shaw, *Major Barbara,* **1907**

'He's a cheerful old card', grunted Harry to Jack
As they slogged up to Arras with rifle and pack.
. . .
But he did for them both with his plan of attack.
  Siegfried Sassoon, *The General,* **1917**

Nothing raises morale better than a dead general.
  John Masters, *The Road Past Mandalay,* **1961**

We are the unwilling, led by the unqualified, doing the unnecessary for the ungrateful.
  Graffito, Vietnam War, 1970

The army works like this: if a man dies when you hang him, keep hanging him until he gets used to it.
  Spike Milligan

There are three kinds of intelligence – the intelligence of man, the intelligence of animals, and the intelligence of the military. In that order.
  Gottfried Reinhardt

See also BRAVERY

MONEY

There is no fortress so strong that money cannot take it.
Marcus Tullius Cicero

A son might bear with composure the death of his father, but the loss of his inheritance might drive him to despair.
Niccolò Machiavelli, *The Prince*, 1513

There are but two families in the world: Have-much and Have-little.
Miguel de Cervantes, *Don Quixote*, 1615

Plenty of people despise money, but few know how to give it away.
François, Duc de La Rochefoucauld, *Maxims*, 1665

Those who lack money when they come to borrow will also lack money when they come to pay.
Oliver Goldsmith, *The Citizen of the World*, 1762

I would rather trust my money to a man who has no hands, and so a physical impossibility to steal, than to a man of the most honest principles.
Samuel Johnson, *The Life of Samuel Johnson* by J. Boswell, 1791

Is not a Patron . . . one who looks with unconcern on a man struggling for life in the water, and, when he has reached ground, encumbers him with help?
Samuel Johnson, *The Life of Samuel Johnson* by J. Boswell, 1791

The jingling of the guinea helps the hurt that honour feels.
Alfred, Lord Tennyson, *Locksley Hall*, 1842

Few rich men own their property: their property owns them.
Robert G. Ingersoll, 1896

Cash: a sort of window-fastener to keep Love from flying out.
Oliver Herford and John Clay, *Cupid's Cyclopedia*, 1910

Love may laugh at locksmiths, but he has a profound respect for money bags.
Sidney Paternoster, *The Folly of the Wise*, 1907

The most important thing in life is not to have money, but that others have it.
  Sacha Guitry

The two most beautiful words in the English language are 'Cheque Enclosed'.
  Dorothy Parker

Kissing your hand may make you feel very good, but a diamond and safire bracelet lasts for ever.
  Anita Loos, *Gentlemen Prefer Blondes*, 1925

What is robbing a bank compared with founding a bank?
  Bertolt Brecht, *The Threepenny Opera*, 1928

The chief value of money is that one lives in a world in which it is over-estimated.
  H.L. Mencken

The most sensitive part of a man is not his skin but his wallet.
  Adolf Hitler

The avoidance of taxes is the only pursuit that still carries any reward.
  John Maynard Keynes

There are few sorrows, however poignant, in which a good income is of no avail.
  Logan Pearsall Smith, *Afterthoughts*, 1931

A 'sound' banker, alas, is not one who sees danger and avoids it, but one who, when he is ruined, is ruined in a conventional and orthodox way along with his fellows, so that no one can really blame him.
  John Maynard Keynes, *Essays in Persuasion*, 1933

An economist's guess is likely to be as good as anyone else's.
  Will Rogers

No woman marries for money: they are all clever enough, before marrying a millionaire, to fall in love with him first.
  Cesare Pavese, *The Business of Living: Diaries*, 1935–50

Where there is money, there is fighting.
  Marian Anderson, quoted in *Marian Anderson: A Portrait* by Kosti Vehanen, 1941

Money cannot buy
The fuel of love
But is excellent kindling.

W.H. Auden

Economists are people who work with numbers but don't have the personality to be accountants.

Anonymous

An economist is a person who talks about something he doesn't understand and makes you feel you are ignorant.

Herbert Prochnow

A bank is a place where they lend you an umbrella in fair weather and ask for it back when it begins to rain.

Robert Frost

If you would know what the Lord God thinks of money, you have only to look at those to whom he gives it.

Maurice Baring, quoted in *Writers at Work* 1st series, 1958

Wealth is not without its advantages, and the case to the contrary, although it has often been made, has never proved widely persuasive.

John Kenneth Galbraith, *The Affluent Society*, 1958

Economy: cutting down on other people's wages.

J.B. Morton ('Beachcomber')

The most popular labour-saving device today is still a husband with money.

Joey Adams, *Cindy and I*, 1959

Gentility is what is left over from rich ancestors after the money is gone.

John Ciardi

There is no stronger craving in the world than that of the rich for titles, except that of the titled for riches.

Hesketh Pearson, *The Marrying Americans*, 1961

Credit . . . is the only enduring testimonial to man's confidence in man.

James Blish

Those who have some means think that the most important thing in the world is love. The poor know that it is money.

Gerald Brenan, *Thoughts in a Dry Season,* **1978**

No one would remember the Good Samaritan if he had only had good intentions. He had money as well.

Margaret Thatcher, quoted in *The Spectator* **magazine, 1980**

A lot of pain and nuisance might be avoided if the rich would only appreciate the point where love becomes money.

Cyril Connolly, *Journal 1928–1937,* **ed. D. Pryce-Jones, 1983**

The rich, particularly rich women, exist to facilitate things.

Cyril Connolly, *Journal 1928–1937,* **ed. D. Pryce-Jones, 1983**

The trouble about a free market economy is that it requires so many policemen to make it work.

Neal Ascherson, in the *Observer,* **1985**

In all recorded history there has not been one economist who had to worry about where the next meal would come from.

Peter Drucker

See also BUSINESS, POVERTY & THE POOR, THE RICH

MORALS

If we resist our passions, it is more from their weakness than from our strength.

François, Duc de La Rochefoucauld, *Maxims,* **1665**

We reprove others not so much to correct them as to persuade them that we ourselves are free from their faults.

François, Duc de La Rochefoucauld, *Maxims,* **1665**

Repentance is not so much remorse for what we have done as the fear of consequences.

François, Duc de La Rochefoucauld, *Maxims,* **1665**

When vices give us up we flatter ourselves that we are giving them up.

François, Duc de La Rochefoucauld, *Maxims,* **1665**

We often do good that we may do evil with impunity.
François, Duc de La Rochefoucauld, _Maxims_, 1665

Humility is a virtue all preach, none practise, and yet everybody is content to hear. The master thinks it is good doctrine for his servant, the laity for the clergy and the clergy for the laity.
John Selden, _Table Talk_, 1689

Leave morals and honesty to the poor, as they do in London.
John Gay, _The Beggar's Opera_, 1728

It is easier to bear what's amiss than go about to reform it.
Thomas Fuller, M.D., _Gnomologia_, 1732

Be not too hasty to trust or admire the teachers of morality; they discourse like angels but they live like men.
Samuel Johnson, _Rasselas_, 1759

All universal moral principles are idle fancies.
Donatien Alphonse François, Marquis de Sade, _The 120 Days of Sodom_, 1785

It is essential to the triumph of reform that it should never succeed.
William Hazlitt

If I knew for a certainty that man was coming to my house with the conscious design of doing me good, I should run for my life.
Henry Thoreau, _Walden_, 1854

In judging others folks will work overtime for no pay.
Charles Carrothers

We blame in others only those faults by which we do not profit.
Alexander Dumas, père

When Dr Johnson defined patriotism as the last refuge of a scoundrel, he ignored the enormous possibilities of the word 'reform'.
Senator Roscoe Conkling, 1876

Fear is the mother of morality.
Friedrich Wilhelm Nietzsche, _The Genealogy of Morals_, 1887

Morality is the best of all devices for leading mankind by the nose.
Friedrich Wilhelm Nietzsche, *The Antichrist*, 1888

Scandal is gossip made tedious by morality.
Oscar Wilde

A man who moralises is usually a hypocrite and a woman who moralises is invariably plain.
Oscar Wilde, *Lady Windermere's Fan*, 1892

Nothing so needs reforming as other people's habits.
Mark Twain, 1894

Wickedness is a myth invented by good people to account for the curious attractiveness of others.
Oscar Wilde, *Phrases and Philosophies for the Use of the Young*, 1894

I never came across anyone in whom the moral sense was dominant who was not heartless, cruel, vindictive, log-stupid and entirely lacking in the smallest sense of humanity. Moral people, as they are termed, are simply beasts. I would sooner have fifty unnatural vices than one unnatural virtue.
Oscar Wilde, letter to Leonard Smithers, 1897

Morality is simply the attitude we adopt to people whom we personally dislike.
Oscar Wilde, *An Ideal Husband*, 1895

Vice is a creature of such hideous mien that the more you see it the better you like it.
Finley Peter Dunne, *Mr Dooley's Opinions*, 1901

Morality consists in suspecting other people of not being legally married.
George Bernard Shaw, *The Doctor's Dilemma*, 1908

Moral, adj. Conforming to a local and mutable standard of right. Having the quality of general expediency.
Ambrose Bierce, *The Devil's Dictionary*, 1911

Fool, n. A person who pervades the domain of intellectual speculation and diffuses himself through the channels of moral activity.
Ambrose Bierce, *The Devil's Dictionary*, 1911

Immoral, adj. Inexpedient.

Ambrose Bierce, *The Devil's Dictionary*, 1911

If you can't answer a man's argument, all is not lost. You can still call him vile names.

Elbert Hubbard

Moral indignation is jealousy with a halo.

H.G. Wells

Immorality is the morality of those who are having a better time.

H.L. Mencken, *Sententiae*, 1916

Remorse – regret that one waited so long to do it.

H.L. Mencken, *Sententiae*, 1916

The difference between a moral man and a man of honour is that the latter regrets a discreditable act, even when it has worked and he has not been caught.

H.L. Mencken, *Sententiae*, 1916

Morality . . . is what the majority then and there happen to like and immorality is what they dislike.

Alfred North Whitehead

A sense of humour always withers in the presence of the messianic delusion, like justice and truth in front of patriotic passion.

H.L. Mencken, *Prejudices* 1919–27

We like to moralise when we are old because it makes a merit of many deprivations which have become a necessity.

Mme de Salm-Dyck, quoted in *A Cynic's Breviary* by J.R. Solly, 1925

Many people think that virtue consists of severity towards others.

Alphonse Karr, quoted in *A Cynic's Breviary* by J.R. Solly, 1925

We have, in fact, two kinds of morality side by side; one which we preach but do not practise, and another which we practise but seldom preach.

Bertrand Russell, *Sceptical Essays*, 1928

Eats first, morals after.

Bertolt Brecht, *The Threepenny Opera*, 1928

A concern with the perfectibility of mankind is always a symptom of thwarted or perverted development.
Hugh Kingsmill

Fearful is the seductive power of goodness.
Bertolt Brecht, *The Caucasian Chalk Circle*, 1947

Half the harm that is done in this world
Is due to people who want to feel important.
T.S. Eliot, *The Cocktail Party*, 1950

Righteous people terrify me . . . virtue is its own punishment.
Aneurin Bevan

A woman can look both moral and exciting – if she also looks as if it were quite a struggle.
Edna Ferber, in the *Reader's Digest*, 1954

The urge to save humanity is almost always a false front for the urge to rule.
H.L. Mencken, *Minority Report*, 1956

It is in the interest of [film] producers to maintain a certain moral standard since, if they don't do this, the immoral films won't sell.
Jean Renoir

Moral indignation is in most cases two per cent moral, forty-eight per cent indignation and fifty per cent envy.
Vittorio De Sica, in the *Observer*, 1961

Morality's not practical. Morality's a gesture. A complicated gesture learnt from books.
Robert Bolt, *A Man for All Seasons*, 1960

Things have got to be wrong in order that they may be deplored.
Whitney Griswold, quoted in the *New York Times*, 1963

Moral responsibility is what is lacking in a man when he demands it of a woman.
Karl Kraus, *Half Truths and One and a Half Truths*, 1986

Chastity always takes its toll: in some it produces pimples, in others sex laws.
Karl Kraus, *Half Truths and One and a Half Truths*, 1986

The Moral Majority is deeply anti-semitic and will always remain so because the Jews killed our Lord (proving that no good deed goes unpunished . . .).

Gore Vidal, *Armageddon*, 1987

Nor is it remarkable to find a papal encyclical upholding the existence of objective moral standards. A belief in the existence of objective moral standards, authoritatively explained, is, after all, the heritage of all Christians; indeed, of all Jews and Muslims. It helps to explain why they have been able to wage war on each other with good consciences.

Andrew Brown, in the *Independent*, 1993

See also BELIEF, THE CLERGY, FAITH, GOD, IDEALS, IDEAS, RELIGION, TRUE BELIEVERS, TRUTH

MUSIC

The main thing the public demands of a composer is that he be dead.

Arthur Honegger

Song is the licensed medium for bawling in public things too silly or sacred to be uttered in ordinary speech.

Oliver Herford

Composers shouldn't think too much – it interferes with their plagiarism.

Howard Dietz

Classical music is the kind we keep thinking will turn into a tune.

Kin Hubbard, *Abe Martin's Sayings*, 1915

Opera is a loosely connected series of songs designed to make a full evening's entertainment out of an overture.

Miles Kington

NATIONALISM

The first man to fence in a piece of land saying 'This is mine' and who found people simple enough to believe him, was the real founder of civil society.

Jean-Jacques Rousseau, *Discourse on the Origin and Bases of Inequality among Men*, 1754

Happy is the nation that has no history.
Cesare Beccaria, *Of Crimes and Punishments*, 1764

To find a new country and invade it has always been the same thing.
Samuel Johnson, *Works* vol. v, 1787

Kings are for nations in their swaddling clothes.
Victor Hugo, speech, 1848

Immigrant: an unenlightened person who thinks one country better than another.
Ambrose Bierce, *The Devil's Dictionary*, 1911

Nationalism is an infantile disease. It is the measles of mankind.
Albert Einstein, letter, 1921

I know of no existing nation that deserves to live. And I know of very few individuals.
H.L. Mencken

The chief business of the nation, as a nation, is the setting up of heroes, mostly bogus.
H.L. Mencken, *Prejudices* 3rd series, 1922

Countries are like fruit – the worms are always inside.
Jean Giraudoux, *Siegfried*, 1922

Freeing oppressed nationalities is perhaps the most dangerous of all philanthropic enterprises.
William Bolitho, *Twelve Against the Gods*, 1929

The world is divided into two groups of nations: those which want to expel the Jews, and those which do not want to receive them.
Chaim Weizmann, 1938

Unhappy the land that needs heroes.
Bertolt Brecht, *Galileo*, 1937–9

Gratitude, like love, is never a dependable international emotion.
Joseph Alsop, in the *Observer*, 1952

The great nations have always acted like gangsters and the small nations like prostitutes.
Stanley Kubrick, 1963

The hour of their crime does not strike simultaneously for all nations. This explains the permanence of history.

E.M. Cioran, quoted in *The Faber Book of Aphorisms,* **ed. W.H. Auden and L. Kronenberger, 1964**

History teaches us that men and nations behave wisely once they have exhausted all other alternatives.

Abba Eban, 1970

In any country there must be people who have to die. They are the sacrifices any nation has to make to achieve law and order.

Idi Amin Dada, 1976

The length of a country's national anthem is inversely proportional to the importance of that country.

Allen L. Otten, quoted in *The Book of Laws* **by H. Faber, 1980**

I am always fascinated when people talk about 'the forging of a nation'. Most nations are forgeries, perpetrated in the last century or so.

Neal Ascherson, in the *Observer,* **1985**

The unattractive thing about chauvinism is not so much aversion to other nations, but the love of one's own.

Karl Kraus, *Half Truths and One and a Half Truths,* **1986**

See also PATRIOTISM

NEIGHBOURS

Love your neighbour, yet don't pull down your hedge.

Benjamin Franklin

Philosophy may teach us to bear with equanimity the misfortunes of our neighbours.

Oscar Wilde, lecture, 1882

Do not love your neighbour as yourself. If you are on good terms with yourself it as impertinence; if on bad, an injury.

George Bernard Shaw, *Man and Superman,* **1903**

Comfort, n. A state of mind produced by contemplation of a neighbour's uneasiness.

Ambrose Bierce, *The Devil's Dictionary,* **1911**

Do unto yourself as your neighbours do unto themselves and look pleasant.

George Ade, *Hand-Made Fables*, 1920

The propriety of some persons seems to consist in having improper thoughts about their neighbours.

F.H. Bradley, *Aphorisms*, 1930

It's a recession when your neighbour loses his job; it's a depression when you lose yours.

Harry S. Truman, 1958

Don't shout for help at night. You might wake your neighbours.

Stanislaw J. Lec, *Unkempt Thoughts*, 1962

Never keep up with the Jones. Drag them down to your level, it's cheaper.

Quentin Crisp, 1978

See also CHARITY

OPINIONS

Public opinion is a compound of folly, weakness, prejudice, wrong feeling, right feeling, obstinacy and newspaper paragraphs.

Robert Peel

We follow the world in approving others, but go before it in approving ourselves.

Charles Caleb Colton, *Lacon*, 1820

What is a theory but an imperfect generalization caught up by a predisposition.

J.A. Froude, *The Lives of the Saints*, 1852

What we call public opinion is generally public sentiment.

Benjamin Disraeli, speech, 1880

The public buys its opinions as it buys its meat, or takes in its milk, on the principle that it is cheaper to do this than to keep a cow. So it is – but the milk is more likely to be watered.

Samuel Butler, *Notebooks*, 1912

Sound opinions are valueless. What matters is who holds them.
  Karl Kraus, *Half Truths and One and a Half Truths*, 1986

Deliberation, n. The act of examining one's bread to see which side it is buttered on.
  Ambrose Bierce, *The Devil's Dictionary*, 1911

One should respect public opinion insofar as is necessary to avoid starvation and keep out of prison, but anything that goes beyond this is voluntary submission to an unnecessary tyranny.
  Bertrand Russell, *The Conquest of Happiness*, 1930

There is no tyranny so despotic as that of public opinion among a free people.
  Donn Platt

See also ADVICE

OPTIMISM

Optimism, n. An intellectual disorder, yielding to no treatment but death. It is hereditary, but fortunately not contagious.
  Ambrose Bierce, *The Devil's Dictionary*, 1911

The optimist proclaims we live in the best of all possible worlds; and the pessimist fears this is true.
  James Branch Cabell, *The Silver Stallion*, 1926

An optimist is a guy that never had much experience.
  Don Marquis, *Archy and Mehitabel*, 1927

Optimism is the content of small men in high places.
  F. Scott Fitzgerald, *The Crack-Up*, 1936

The optimist thinks that this is the best of all possible worlds, and the pessimist knows it.
  J. Robert Oppenheimer, in *The Bulletin of the Atomic Scientists*, 1951

What passes for optimism is most often the effect of an intellectual error.
  Raymond Aron, *The Opium of the Intellectuals*, 1957

An optimist is one who knows exactly how bad a place the world can be; a pessimist is one who finds out anew every morning.

Peter Ustinov, in *The Illustrated London News*, 1968

The man who smiles when things go wrong has thought of someone he can blame it on.

Jones' Law, quoted in *Murphy's Law* by A. Bloch, 1979

See also PESSIMISM

PARENTS

A man doesn't shoot himself when he's going to be made a lawful father for the first time, unless he can see a long way into the future.

Henry Lawson

A father is a banker provided by nature.

Anonymous, quoted in *The Oxford Book of Aphorisms*, ed. J. Gross, 1983

The first half of our lives is ruined by our parents, and the second half by our children.

Clarence Darrow

The fundamental defect of fathers is that they want their children to be a credit to them.

Bertrand Russell

Kath: Can he be present at the birth of his child?
Ed: It's all any reasonable child can expect if the dad is present at the conception.

Joe Orton, *Entertaining Mr Sloane*, 1964

The mother of the year should be a sterilised woman with two adopted children.

Paul Ehrlich

From the moment of birth, when the Stone Age baby confronts the 20th century mother, the baby is subjected to these forces of violence, called love, as its father and mother, and their parents and their parents before them, have been. These forces are mainly concerned with destroying most of its potential.

R.D. Laing, *The Politics of Experience*, 1967

They fuck you up, your Mum and Dad.
They may not mean to, but they do.
And give you all the faults they had
And add some extra, just for you.
  Philip Larkin, *This Be The Verse*, 1974

Parents are the bones on which children sharpen their teeth.
  Peter Ustinov, *Dear Me*, 1977

Your responsibility as a parent is not as great as you might imagine.
You need not supply the world with the next conqueror of disease or
major motion picture star. If your child simply grows up to be someone
who does not use the word 'collectible' as a noun, you can consider
yourself an unqualified success.
  Fran Lebowitz, *Social Studies*, 1981

Spoil the child
Spare the rod
Open up the caviar and say
Thank God!
  Noël Coward, quoted in *Ritz* magazine, 1984

A father's pride, laid on thick, always makes me wish that the fellow
had at least experienced some pain during procreation.
  Karl Kraus, *Half Truths and One and a Half Truths*, 1986

See also ADULTS, CHILDREN, FAMILIES

PARTIES

Party loyalty lowers the greatest of men to the petty level of the masses
  Jean de La Bruyère, *The Characters*, 1688

The best Party is but a kind of conspiracy against the rest of the
nation . . . Ignorance maketh men go into a party, and shame keepeth
them from going out of it.
  **George Savile, Marquis of Halifax, *Political, Moral and
  Miscellaneous Thoughts and Reflexions*, c.1694**

All political parties die at last of swallowing their own lies.
  John Arbuthnot, 1735

There is no act of treachery or mean-ness of which a political party is not capable; for in politics there is no honour.

Benjamin Disraeli, Vivian Grey, 1826–7

A Conservative government is an organised hypocrisy.

Benjamin Disraeli, speech, 1845

A sect or party is an elegant incognito devised to save a man from the vexation of thinking.

Ralph Waldo Emerson, Journals, 1909–14

English experience indicates that when two great political parties agree about something, it is generally wrong.

G.K. Chesterton, 1919

Party is the madness of the many for the gain of the few.

Alexander Pope

Cease being the slave of a party and you become its deserter.

Jules Simon

The two party system . . . is a triumph of the dialectic. It showed that two could be one and one could be two and had probably been fabricated by Hegel for the American market on a subcontract from General Dynamics.

I.F. Stone, 1968

See also CONSERVATIVES, DEMOCRACY, GOVERNMENT, LIBERALS, POLITICS, VOTING

PATRIOTISM

Patriot: a candidate for place. Politics: the art of getting one.

Henry Fielding, The Covent Garden Journal, 1752

A Patriot is a Fool in ev'ry age.

Alexander Pope, Epistles and Satires of Horace Imitated, 1733–8

Patriotism is the last refuge of a scoundrel.

Samuel Johnson, The Life of Samuel Johnson by J. Boswell, 1791

'God save the King' . . . too often means God save my pension and my place, God give my sisters an allowance out of the privy purse, make me clerk of the irons, let me survey the meltings, let me live upon the fruits of other men's industry, and fatten upon the plunder of the public.

Sydney Smith, *The Letters of Peter Plymley*, 1807

Talking of patriotism, what humbug it is; it is a word which always commemorates a robbery. There isn't a foot of land in the world which doesn't represent the ousting and re-ousting of a long line of successive owners.

Mark Twain, *A Connecticut Yankee at King Arthur's Court*, 1889

Patriotism is the virtue of the vicious.

Oscar Wilde

Patriotism is one of the Monopolist Instincts. And the Monopolist Instincts are the greatest enemies of social life in humanity. They are what we have got in the end to outlive. The test of a man's place in the scale of being is how far he has outlived them.

Grant Allen, quoted in *The Westminster Gazette*, 1894

The less a statesman amounts too, the more he loves the flag.

Kin Hubbard

'My country, right or wrong' is a thing that no patriot would think of saying, except in a desperate case. It is like saying 'My mother, drunk or sober.'

G.K. Chesterton

To be patriotic, hate all nations but your own; to be religious, all sects but your own; to be moral, all pretences but your own.

Lionel Strachey

Whenever you hear a man speak of his love for his country, it is a sign that he expects to be paid for it.

H.L. Mencken, *Sententiae*, 1916

Patriotism is often an arbitrary veneration of real estate above principles.

George Jean Nathan

Patriotism is your conviction that this country is superior to all other countries because you were born in it.

George Bernard Shaw

Love makes fools, marriage cuckolds, and patriotism malevolent imbeciles.
Paul Léautaud

This is the devilish thing about foreign affairs: they are foreign and will not always conform to our whim.
James Reston, 1964

PEACE

Peace, n. In international affairs, a period of cheating between two periods of fighting.
Ambrose Bierce, *The Devil's Dictionary*, 1911

Everlasting peace will come to the world when the last man has slain the last but one.
Adolf Hitler

There is no such thing as inner peace. There is only nervousness or death. Any attempt to prove otherwise constitutes unacceptable behaviour.
Fran Lebowitz, *Metropolitan Life*, 1978

'Peace' is when nobody's shooting. A 'just peace' is when our side gets what it wants.
Bill Mauldin, quoted in *Loose Talk*, ed. L. Botts, 1980

Peace on earth would mean the end of civilization as we know it.
Joseph Heller, *Picture This*, 1986

PESSIMISM

Blessed is he who expects nothing, for he shall never be disappointed.
Alexander Pope, letter, 1727

A pessimist is a man who thinks everybody is as nasty as himself and hates them for it.
George Bernard Shaw, *An Unsocial Socialist*, 1883

It is a matter for regret that so many mean, low suspicions turn out to be well-founded.
Edgar Watson Howe, *Country Town Sayings*, 1911

The most prolific period of pessimism comes at twenty-one, or thereabouts, when the first attempt is made to translate dreams into reality.

Heywood Broun, *Pieces of Hate*, **1922**

A pessimist is a man who has been compelled to live with an optimist.

Elbert Hubbard, *The Notebook*, **1927**

To be a prophet it is sufficient to be a pessimist.

Elsa Triolet

Rowe's Rule: the odds are five to six that the light at the end of the tunnel is the headlight of an oncoming train.

Paul Dickson, *The Official Rules*, **1978**

See also OPTIMISM

PHILOSOPHY

The only difference between graffiti and philosophy is the word 'fuck'.

Graffito

There is nothing so absurd or ridiculous that has not at some time been said by some philosopher.

Marcus Tullius Cicero

There was never yet philosopher
That could endure the toothache patiently.

William Shakespeare, *Much Ado About Nothing*, **1598**

When he who hears doesn't understand him who speaks, and when he who speaks doesn't know what he himself means – that is philosophy.

Voltaire, *Candide*, **1759**

Metaphysics is the finding of bad reasons for what we believe upon instinct.

F.H. Bradley, *Appearance and Reality*, **1893**

Only the shallow know themselves.

Oscar Wilde, *Phrases and Philosophies for the Use of the Young*, **1894**

The more conscious a philosopher is of the weak spots of his theory, the more certain he is to speak with an air of final authority.
Don Marquis

Metaphysics is almost always an attempt to prove the incredible by an appeal to the unintelligible.
H.L. Mencken, *Minority Report*, 1956

Any philosophy that can be put 'in a nutshell' belongs there.
Sydney J. Harris, *Leaving the Surface*, 1968

Being wrong is just an occupational hazard of being a philosopher.
Ronald Laura

PLAGIARISM

Men who borrow their opinions can never repay their debts.
George Savile, Marquis of Halifax, *Political, Moral and Miscellaneous Thoughts and Reflexions*, c.1694

Originality is nothing but judicious imitation.
Voltaire

If we steal thoughts from the moderns, it will be cried down as plagiarism; if from the ancients it will be cried up as erudition.
Charles Caleb Colton, *Lacon*, 1820

About the most originality that any writer can hope to achieve honestly is to steal with good judgement.
Josh Billings

If you steal from one author it's plagiarism; if you steal from many it's research.
Wilson Mizner

Originality is undetected plagiarism.
William R. Inge

We prefer to believe that the absence of inverted commas guarantees the originality of a thought, whereas it may be merely that the utterer has forgotten its source.
Clifton Fadiman, *Any Number Can Play*, 1957

Original thought is like original sin: both happened before you were born to people you could not have possibly met.

Fran Lebowitz, *Social Studies***, 1981**

See also AUTHORS, BOOKS, WRITING

POETS & POETRY

Poetry is the stuff in books that doesn't quite reach the margins.

Anonymous

All poets pretend to write for immortality, but the whole tribe have no objection to present pay and present praise.

Charles Caleb Colton, *Lacon***, 1820**

Immature poets imitate, mature poets steal.

T.S. Eliot, *Philip Massinger***, 1920**

The ideal audience the poet imagines consist of the beautiful who go to bed with him, the powerful who invite him to dinner and tell him secrets of state, and his fellow-poets. The actual audience he gets consists of myopic schoolteachers, pimply young men who eat in cafeterias, and his fellow-poets. This means, in fact, he writes for his fellow-poets.

W.H. Auden, *Poets at Work***, 1948**

It is a sad fact about our culture that a poet can earn much more money writing or talking about his art than he can by practising it.

W.H. Auden, *The Dyer's Hand***, 1963**

If you are of the opinion that the contemplation of suicide is sufficient evidence of a poetic nature, do not forget that actions speak louder than words.

Fran Lebowitz, *Metropolitan Life***, 1978**

The romantic is a spoilt priest, just as the novelist is a spoilt poet.

Cyril Connolly, *Journal 1928–1937***, ed. D. Pryce-Jones, 1983**

See also AUTHORS, BOOKS, WRITING

POLITICIANS

A horrible voice, bad breath, and a vulgar manner – the characteristics of a popular politician.

Aristophanes

Persistence in one opinion has never been considered a merit in political leaders.

Marcus Tullius Cicero, *Ad Familiares*, c.50BC

It is easier for a camel to go through the eye of a needle, or for a rich man to enter the kingdom of heaven than for a politician to lay aside disguise.

James Caulfeild, Earl Charlemont, letter, 1767

An honest politician is one who when he is bought will stay bought.

Simon Cameron, 1860

A politician divides mankind into two classes: tools and enemies. That means he knows only one class – enemies.

Friedrich Wilhelm Nietzsche

The first duty, if not the whole duty, of a private member of the House of Commons is to speak as little and to vote as often as he can.

Herbert Asquith, First Earl of Oxford, speech, 1890

Only people who look dull ever get into the House of Commons, and only people who are dull ever succeed there.

Oscar Wilde, *An Ideal Husband*, 1895

Politicians speak for their parties, and parties never are, never have been and never will be wrong.

Walter Dwight

The politician is an acrobat: he keeps his balance by saying the opposite of what he does.

Maurice Barrès

He knows nothing and thinks he knows everything. That points clearly to a political career.

George Bernard Shaw, *Major Barbara*, 1907

The House of Lords: five hundred men, ordinary men, chosen accidentally from among the unemployed.
David Lloyd George, speech, 1909

The fact of a man's having proclaimed (as leader of a political party, or in any other capacity) that it is wicked to lie obliges him as a rule to lie more than other people.
Marcel Proust, *Remembrance of Things Past*, 1913–27

A gentleman will blithely do in politics what he would kick a man downstairs for doing in ordinary life.
Earl of Rosebery, 1914

It is easy to settle the world upon a soap box.
David Lloyd George

Politician – any man with influence enough to get his old mother a job as a charwoman at City Hall.
H.L. Mencken, *Sententiae*, 1916

The nauseous sham goodfellowship our democratic public men get up for shop use.
George Bernard Shaw, *Back to Methuselah*, 1921

The conception of an 'honest' politician is not altogether a simple one. The most tolerant definition is: one whose political actions are not dictated by a desire to increase his own income.
Bertrand Russell, Presidential Address to LSE students, 1923

When I was a boy I was told that anyone could become President. I'm beginning to believe it.
Clarence Darrow

A wise politician will never grudge a genuflexion or a rapture if it is expected of him by the prevalent opinion.
F.S. Oliver, *The Endless Adventure*, 1930

There's just one rule for politicians all over the world. Don't say in power what you say in opposition. If you do, you'll only have to carry out what the other fellows have found impossible.
John Galsworthy, *Maid in Waiting*, 1931

A politician is a person with whose politics you don't agree; if you agree with him he is a statesman.

David Lloyd George, 1935

Dictators always look good until the last minutes.

Thomas Masaryk

The trouble with this country is that there are too many politicians who believe, with a conviction based on experience, that you can fool all of the people all of the time.

Franklin P. Adams (F.P.A.), *Nods and Becks***, 1944**

When the political columnists say 'every thinking man' they mean themselves; and when the candidates appeal to 'every intelligent voter', they mean everybody who is going to vote for them.

Franklin P. Adams (F.P.A.), *Nods and Becks***, 1944**

A politician is an arse upon which everyone has sat except a man.

e.e. cummings, *One Times One***, 1944**

Have you ever read *Mein Kampf*? It's really the most honest book any politician has ever written.

W.H. Auden, *The Table-Talk of W.H. Auden***,**
ed. Alan Ansen, 1990

Politicians, like prostitutes, are held in contempt. But what man does not run to them when he needs their services?

Brendan Francis

Anyone who says he isn't going to resign, four times, definitely will.

John Kenneth Galbraith

Successful democratic politicians are insecure and intimidated men. They advance politically only as they placate, appease, bribe, seduce, bamboozle or otherwise manage to manipulate the demanding and threatening elements in their constituencies.

Walter Lippmann, *The Public Philosophy***, 1955**

A good politician is quite as unthinkable as an honest burglar.

H.L. Mencken, *Minority Report***, 1956**

The statesman shears the sheep, the politician skins them.

Austin O'Malley

The Left is a group of people who will never be happy unless they can convince themselves that they are about to be betrayed by their leaders.
Richard Crossman, diary, 1959

Politicians are the same all over. They promise to build a bridge even where there is no river.
Nikita Khruschev, 1960

Old politicians, like old actors, revive in the limelight.
Malcolm Muggeridge, in *Esquire* magazine, 1961

Exhortation of other people to do something is the last resort of politicians who are at a loss to know what to do themselves.
Sir Paul Chambers, 1961

Since a politician never believes what he says, he is surprised when others believe him.
Charles de Gaulle, 1962

Don't take a nickel, just hand them your business card.
Richard M. Daley, advising on the safe enjoyment of graft

Congress – these, for the most part, illiterate hacks whose fancy vests are spotted with gravy and whose speeches, hypocritical, unctuous and slovenly, are spotted also with the gravy of political patronage.
Mary McCarthy, *On the Contrary*, 1962

Politics and the fate of mankind are shaped by men without ideals and without greatness. Men who have greatness within them don't go in for politics.
Albert Camus, *Notebooks*, 1962

A little nonsense now and then is not a bad thing. Where would we politicians be if we were not allowed to talk it sometimes?
J. Enoch Powell, 1965

The House of Lords, an illusion to which I have never been able to subscribe – responsibility without power, the prerogative of the eunuch throughout the ages.
Tom Stoppard, *Lord Malquist and Mr Moon*, 1965

Render any politician down and there's enough fat to fry an egg.
Spike Milligan, 1968

These presidential ninnies should stick to throwing out baseballs, and leave the important matters to serious people.

Gore Vidal

The most distinctive characteristic of the successful politician is selective cowardice.

Richard Harris, in the *New Yorker* magazine, 1968

It is dangerous for a national candidate to say things that people might remember.

Senator Eugene McCarthy, 1968

In order to become the master, the politician poses as the servant.

Charles de Gaulle, 1969

A politician is an acrobat: he keeps his balance by saying the opposite of what he does.

Maurice Barrès

A dilemma is a politician trying to save both of his faces at once.

John A. Lincoln

Any American who is prepared to run for President should automatically, by definition, be disqualified from ever doing so.

Gore Vidal

Wisdom is essential in a President; the appearance of wisdom will do in a candidate.

Eric Sevareid

The effectiveness of a politician varies in inverse proportion to his commitment to a principle.

Sam Shaffer, in *Newsweek* magazine, 1971

Politicians who wish to succeed must be prepared to dissemble, at times to lie. All deceit is bad. In politics some deceit or moral dishonesty is the oil without which the machinery would not work.

Woodrow Wyatt, in the *Sunday Times*, 1973

A statesman is a politician who places himself at the service of the nation. A politician is a statesman who places the nation at his service.

Georges Pompidou, in the *Observer*, 1973

Take our politicians: they're a bunch of yo-yos. The presidency is now a cross between a popularity contest and a high school debate, with an encyclopedia of clichés as the first prize.

Saul Bellow, 1980

If you hear someone in public life say that he is going to stand firmly on principle, you should take cover and warn others to do the same. There is going to be suffering.

John Kenneth Galbraith, in *The New York Review of Books*, 1986

In an age of television one must steer clear of presidents who may not know how to act president, and go instead for the best actor available for the job, the one who can read with warm plausibility the commercials that have been written for him.

Gore Vidal, *Armageddon*, 1987

Above any other position of eminence, that of Prime Minister is filled by fluke.

J. Enoch Powell, in the *Observer*, 1987

See also GOVERNMENT, LEADERS, PARTIES, POLITICS, POWER, VOTING

POLITICS

Politics, as the word is commonly understood, are nothing but corruptions.

Jonathan Swift, *Thoughts on Various Subjects*, 1706

Boswell: So, Sir, you laugh at schemes of political improvement.
Johnson: Why, Sir, most schemes of political improvement are very laughable things.

Samuel Johnson

Politics are . . . nothing more than a means of rising in the world.

Samuel Johnson, 1775

In politics, as on the sickbed, people toss fom side to side, thinking they will be more comfortable.

Johann Wolfgang von Goethe

The duty of an opposition [is] very simple – to oppose everything and propose nothing.
Lord Derby, 1841

A Parliament is nothing less than a big meeting of more or less idle people.
Walter Bagehot, *The English Constitution*, 1867

Our differences are policies, our agreements principles.
William McKinley

We have a single system and in that system the only question is the price at which the proletariat is to be bought and sold, the bread and circuses.
Henry Brooks Adams, *The Education of Henry Adams*, 1907

Politics, as a practice, whatever its professions, has always been the systematic organisation of hatreds.
Henry Brooks Adams, *The Education of Henry Adams*, 1907

Practical politics consists in ignoring facts.
Henry Brooks Adams, *The Education of Henry Adams*, 1907

Politics, n. The conduct of public affairs for private advantage.
Ambrose Bierce, *The Devil's Dictionary*, 1911

Alliance, n. In international politics, the union of two thieves who have their hands so deeply inserted into each other's pocket that they cannot safely plunder a third.
Ambrose Bierce, *The Devil's Dictionary*, 1911

Politics, n. A strife of interests masquerading as a contest of principles.
Ambrose Bierce, *The Devil's Dictionary*, 1911

Where you stand depends on where you sit.
Rufus Miles, on political opinions

Communism, like any other revealed religion, is largely made up of prophecies.
H.L. Mencken

A man should always be drunk when he talks of politics – it's the only way in which to make them important.
Sean O'Casey, *The Shadow of a Gunman*, 1923

Politics, as hopeful men practise it in the world, consists mainly of the delusion that a change in form is a change in substance.

H.L. Mencken, *Prejudices* **4th series, 1924**

Socialism . . . is little better than a dusty survival of a plan to meet the problems of fifty years ago based on a misunderstanding of what someone said a hundred years ago.

John Maynard Keynes

The whole aim of practical politics is to keep the populace alarmed (and hence clamorous to be led to safety) by menacing it with an endless series of hobgoblins, all of them imaginary.

H.L. Mencken

In a political fight, when you've got nothing in favour of your side, start a row in the opposition camp.

Huey P. Long

Politics is the art of preventing people from taking part in affairs which properly concern them.

Paul Valéry, *Tel quel,* **1943**

In our time, political speech and writing are largely the defence of the indefensible.

George Orwell, *Politics and the English Language,* **1950**

Political language . . . is designed to make lies sound truthful and murder respectable and to give an appearance of solidarity to pure wind.

George Orwell, *Politics and the English Language,* **1950**

Political thinking consists in deciding upon the conclusion first and then finding good arguments for it. An open mind is considered irresponsible – and perhaps it really is.

Richard Crossman, diary, 1959

Politics is the diversion of trivial men who, when they succeed at it, become important in the eyes of more trivial men.

George Jean Nathan, 1954

Nothing is so admirable in politics as a short memory.

John Kenneth Galbraith

In any assembly the simplest way to stop the transacting of business and split the ranks is to appeal to a principle.
Jacques Barzun, The House of Intellect, 1959

Vote for the man who promises least – he'll be the least disappointing.
Bernard Baruch, quoted in Meyer Berger's New York, 1960

Politics are usually the executive expression of human immaturity.
Vera Brittain, The Rebel Passion, 1964

A citizen is influenced by principle in direct proportion to his distance from the political situation.
Milton Rakove, in The Virginia Quarterly Review, 1965

Political skill . . . the ability to foretell what is going to happen tomorrow, next week, next month and next year. And to have the ability afterwards to explain why it didn't happen.
Sir Winston Churchill, quoted in 1965

Someone has described a technicality as a point of principle which we have forgotten.
Sir Elwyn Jones, 1966

Everything starts as a mystique and ends as politics.
Parisian graffito, 1968

Being in politics is like being a football coach. You have to be smart enough to understand the game and dumb enough to think it's important.
Senator Eugene McCarthy, 1968

Experience suggests that the first rule of politics is never to say never. The ingenious human capacity for manoeuvre and compromise may make acceptable tomorrow what seems outrageous or impossible today.
William V. Shannon, 1968

Politics demands a certain rhetoric. It does not demand moral action to fit the rhetoric. Instead politics demands political action.
Julius Lester, Look Out Whitey!, 1968

All politics are based on the indifference of the majority.
James Reston, 1968

Co-opt is baby-talk for corrupt.

John Leonard, in the New York Times Book Review, 1969

Politics is not the art of the possible. It consists in choosing between the disastrous and the unpalatable.

John Kenneth Galbraith, 1969

The classic prescription for dealing with injustice: give everybody an equal start, above all education, and meanwhile keep the niggers off your porch.

Christopher Lasch

The dirty work at political conventions is almost always done in the grim hours between midnight and dawn. Hangmen and politicians work best when the human spirit is at its lowest ebb.

Russell Baker, The Sayings of Poor Russell, 1972

A group of politicians deciding to dump a President because his morals are bad is like the Mafia getting together to bump off the Godfather for not going to church on Sunday.

Russell Baker, in The New York Times, 1974

In politics, a straight line is the shortest distance to disaster.

John P. Roche, in the Albany Times-Union, 1976

Politics without ideology, and with a strong tendency towards auto-biography, equals Liberalism.

Stephen Spender, The Thirties and After, 1978

I used to say that politics was the second oldest profession, and I have come to know that it bears a gross similarity to the first.

Ronald Reagan, 1979

The first rule of politics: Never Believe Anything Until It's Been Officially Denied.

Antony Jay and Jonathan Lynn, Yes, Prime Minister, 1986

'The truth' in politics means any statement that cannot be proved false.

Antony Jay and Jonathan Lynn, Yes, Prime Minister, 1986

Socialism is about giving people what socialists think is good for them.

Brian Walden, in the Sydney Morning Herald, 1986

Politics are a lousy way for a free man to get things done. Politics are, like God's infinite mercy, a last resort.

P.J. O'Rourke, *Parliament of Whores*, 1991

There's a certain joy in giving away other people's money. That is what drives many people to politics.

Auberon Waugh, in the *Independent*, 1993

See also GOVERNMENT, PARTIES, POLITICIANS

POVERTY & THE POOR

I owe much; I have nothing; the rest I leave to the poor.

François Rabelais, last words, 1533

There's no scandal like rags, nor any crime so shameful as poverty.

George Farquhar, *The Beaux Strategem*, 1707

To be idle and to be poor have always been reproaches, and therefore every man endeavours with his utmost care to hide his poverty from others and his idleness from himself.

Samuel Johnson, *The Idler*, 1758–60

Poverty, like many other miseries of life, is often little more than an imaginary calamity. Men often call themselves poor, not because they want necessaries, but because they have not more than they want.

Samuel Johnson, *Works* vol. ix, 1787

Poverty is an anomaly to rich people. It is very difficult to make out why people who want dinner do not ring the bell.

Walter Bagehot, *Literary Studies*, 1879–95

It is easy enough to say poverty is no crime. If it were, men wouldn't be ashamed of it.

Jerome K. Jerome, *Idle Thoughts of an Idle Fellow*, 1886

I don't know how the poor live. My only regret is that they live at all.

George Moore, *Confessions of a Young Man*, 1888

The very poor are unthinkable and only to be approached by the statistician and the poet.

E.M. Forster, *Howards End*, 1910

The rich bachelor who dines out every evening is what is called a society man; the same poor is a sponger.

Charles Nairey, quoted in *A Cynic's Breviary* **by J.R. Solly, 1925**

It is only the poor who pay cash, and that not from virtue, but because they are refused credit.

Anatole France, quoted in *A Cynic's Breviary* **by J.R. Solly, 1925**

The poor and ignorant will continue to lie and steal as long as the rich and educated show them how.

Elbert Hubbard, *Notebook,* **1927**

Poverty must have its satisfactions, else there would not be so many poor people.

Don Herold

The poor don't know that their function in life is to exercise our generosity.

Jean-Paul Sartre, *The Words,* **1964**

The poor insist on being buried. It's usually the only way they ensure getting a garden of their own.

Derek Marlowe, *A Dandy In Aspic,* **1966**

The best way to help the poor is not to become one of them.

Laing Hancock, in *The Bulletin* **magazine, 1977**

See also CHARITY, MONEY, THE RICH

POWER

Men ought either to be indulged or utterly destroyed, for if you merely offend them they take vengeance, but if you injure them greatly they are unable to retaliate, so that the injury done to a man ought to be such that vengeance cannot be feared.

Niccolò Machiavelli, *The Prince,* **1513**

Treason doth never prosper: what's the reason? For if it prosper, none dare call it treason.

Sir John Harington, *Epigrams,* **1618**

Fortune often makes up for the eminence of office by the inferiority of the office-holder.

Baltasar Gracian, *The Art of Worldly Wisdom*, 1647

So that in the first place I put for a general inclination of all mankind a perpetual and restless desire of power after power, that ceases only in death.

Thomas Hobbes, *Leviathan*, 1651

The opinion of the strongest is always the best.

Jean de La Fontaine, *Fables*, 1668–94

Fear is what is needed in a despotism. Virtue is not at all necessary, and honour would be dangerous.

Charles de Secondat, Baron de Montesquieu, *The Spirit of the Laws*, 1748

There are few minds to which tyranny is not delightful.

Samuel Johnson

It is dangerous to be right in matters on which the established authorities are wrong.

Voltaire, quoted in *A Cynic's Breviary* by J.R. Solly, 1925

I am more and more convinced that man is a dangerous creature and that power, whether vested in many or a few, is ever grasping, and like the grave, cries 'Give, give'.

Abigail Adams, 1775

If you would be powerful, pretend to be powerful.

Horne Tooke

My opinion is that power should be distrusted, in whatever hands it is based.

Sir William Jones, 1782

Necessity is the plea for every infringement of human freedom. It is the argument of tyrants; it is the creed of slaves.

William Pitt the Younger, 1783

Monarchy is only the string which ties the robbers' bundle.

Percy Bysshe Shelley, *A Philosophical View of Reform*, 1820

Power, like the diamond, dazzles the beholder, and also the wearer; it dignifies meanness, it magnifies littleness, to what is contemptible it gives authority, to what is low exaltation.

Charles Caleb Colton, _Lacon_, 1820

The imbecility of men is always inviting the impudence of power.

Ralph Waldo Emerson, _Representative Men_, 1850

That which is called firmness in a king is called obstinacy in a donkey.

Thomas Erskine

Power tends to corrupt and absolute power corrupts absolutely. Great men are almost always bad men, even when they exercise influence and not authority. There is no worse heresy than that the office sanctifies the holder of it.

Sir J.E.E. Dalberg, First Baron Acton, letter to Bishop Mandell Creighton, 1887

There are men who desire power simply for the sake of the happiness it will bring; these belong chiefly to political parties.

Friedrich Wilhelm Nietzsche, _The Will To Power_, 1900

What is the ballot? It is neither more nor less than a paper representative of the bayonet, the billy and the bullet. It is a labour-saving device for ascertaining on which side force lies and bowing to the inevitable. The voice of the majority saves bloodshed, but it is no less the arbitrament of force than is the decree of the most absolute of despots backed by the most powerful of armies.

Benjamin R. Tucker, _Instead of a Book_, 1893

Knowledge is power – if you know it about the right person.

Addison Mizner and Oliver Herford, _The Entirely New Cynic's Calendar_, 1905

Compulsion, n. The eloquence of power.

Ambrose Bierce, _The Devil's Dictionary_, 1911

Next to enjoying ourselves, the next greatest pleasure consists in preventing others from enjoying themselves, or, more generally, the acquisition of power.

Bertrand Russell, _Sceptical Essays_, 1928

Brutality is respected. The people need wholesome fear. They want to fear something. They want someone to frighten them and make them shudderingly submissive . . . Why babble about brutality and get indignant about tortures. The masses want them. They need something that will give them a thrill of horror.

Ernst Röhm

If people say that here and there someone has been taken away and maltreated, I can only reply: You can't make an omelette without breaking eggs.

Hermann Göring, 1933

Mr Salter's side of the conversation was limited to expressions of assent. When Lord Copper was right he said 'Definitely, Lord Copper'; when he was wrong, 'Up to a point.' 'Let me see, what's the name of the place I mean? Capital of Japan? Yokohama, isn't it?' 'Up to a point, Lord Copper.' 'And Hong Kong definitely belongs to us, doesn't it?' 'Definitely, Lord Copper.'

Evelyn Waugh, Scoop, 1933

The exercise of power is agreeable, especially when it is an obscure individual who exercises power over a prominent one.

Bertrand Russell, in the American Mercury, 1940

The future is the only kind of property that the masters willingly concede to slaves.

Albert Camus, The Rebel, 1951

Not only do people accept violence if it is perpetuated by legitimate authority, they also regard violence against certain kinds of people as inherently legitimate, no matter who commits it.

Edgar Z. Friedenberg, 1966

Command is getting people to go the way you want them to go – enthusiastically.

General William Westmoreland

Nothing is impossible for the man who doesn't have to do it himself.

A.H. Weiler, in the New York Times, 1968

People who have the power to make things happen don't do the things that people do, so they don't know what needs to happen.

Russell Baker, The Sayings of Poor Russell, 1972

Women are always attracted to power. I do not think there could ever be a conqueror so bloody that most women would not willingly lie with him in the hope of bearing a son who would be every bit as ferocious as the father.

Gore Vidal, _Creation_, 1981

All power is delightful, and absolute power is absolutely delightful.

Kenneth Tynan, quoted in _the New York Review of Books_, 1982

See also EGOTISM, LEADERS, POLITICIANS, POLITICS

PRAISE

He who refuses praise only wants to be praised again.

François, Duc de La Rochefoucauld, _Maxims_, 1665

We do not like to praise and we never praise without a motive. Praise is flattery, artful, hidden, delicate, which gratifies differently him who praises and him who is praised. The one takes it as the reward of merit, the other bestows it to show his impartiality and discernment.

François, Duc de La Rochefoucauld, _Maxims_, 1665

The praise we give newcomers into the world arises from the envy we bear to those who are established.

François, Duc de La Rochefoucauld, _Maxims_, 1665

Praise is like ambergris: a little whiff of it, and by snatches, is very agreeable; but when a man holds a whole lump of it to our nose, it is a stink, and strikes you down.

Alexander Pope

You must never seem to affect the character in which you have a mind to shine. Modesty is the only sure bait when you angle for praise.

Lord Chesterfield, _Letters to his Son_, 1774

We praise or blame according to whether the one or the other offers a greater opportunity for our power of judgement to shine out.

Friedrich Wilhelm Nietzsche, _Human, All Too Human_, 1878

Nothing is harder to resist than a bit of flattery.

Arnold Lobel, _Fables_, 1980

See also TALK

PROGRESS

Progress is written in the lives of infidels.

Robert G. Ingersoll, speech, 1881

What we call 'progress' is the exchange of one nuisance for another nuisance.

Havelock Ellis

It is the same with men as with horses: those which do the most prancing are generally the ones which make the least progress.

Baron de Stassart, quoted in *Reflections on the Art of Life* by J.R. Solly, 1902

All progress is based upon a universal innate desire of every organism to live beyond its income.

Samuel Butler, *Notebooks*, 1912

Anything that is worth doing has been done frequently. Things hitherto undone should be given, I suspect, a wide berth.

Max Beerbohm, *Mainly on the Air*, 1957

Progress was all right; it just went on too long.

James Thurber

Ours is the age of substitutes: instead of language we have jargon; instead of principles, slogans; and, instead of genuine ideas, bright ideas.

Eric Bentley, *The Dramatic Event*, 1954

Is it progress if a cannibal uses a fork?

Stanislaw J. Lec, *Unkempt Thoughts*, 1962

See also SCIENCE

PROPAGANDA

Propaganda is that branch of lying which often deceives your friends without ever deceiving your enemies.

Walter Lippmann, quoted in *The Laugh's On Me* by B. Cerf, 1911

I shall give a propagandist reason for starting the war, no matter whether it is plausible or not. The victor will not be asked afterwards whether he told the truth or not. When starting and waging war it is not right that matters, but victory.

Adolf Hitler

What I'm out for's a good time. All the rest is propaganda.

Alan Sillitoe, screenplay for *Saturday Night and Sunday Morning*, 1960

We must remember that in time of war what is said on the enemy's side of the front is always propaganda and what is said on our side of the front is truth and righteousness, the cause of humanity and a crusade for peace. Is it necessary for us at the height of our power to stoop to such self-deceiving nonsense?

Walter Lippmann, quoted 1966

Propaganda is a monologue which seeks not a response but an echo.

W.H. Auden, address to International PEN, 1967

Propaganda is the art of persuading others of what one does not believe oneself.

Abba Eban

What's public is propaganda, what's secret is serious.

Charles Bohlen, quoted in the *New York Post*, 1969

Propaganda is that branch of the art of lying which consists in nearly deceiving your friends without quite deceiving your enemies.

F.M. Cornford, quoted in the *New Statesman* magazine, 1978

One ought to acknowledge the significance for mankind of the simultaneous invention of gunpowder and printer's ink.

Karl Kraus, *Half Truths and One and a Half Truths*, 1986

See also LYING

PSYCHOANALYSIS

Psychoanalysis is the disease of emancipated Jews; the religious ones are satisfied with diabetes.

Karl Kraus

Psychoanalysis is that mental illness for which it regards itself as therapy.

Karl Kraus, _Half Truths and One and a Half Truths_, 1986

Psychotherapy – the theory that the patient will probably get well anyhow, and is certainly a damned ijjit.

H.L. Mencken, _Sententiae_, 1916

Psychiatry enables us to correct our faults by confessing our parents' shortcomings.

Laurence J. Peter, _Peter's Principles_, 1977

Group therapy – the theory that a cure will come if a group of similarly afflicted people are rude enough to each other.

Walter Merricks, on BBC-2 TV, 1979

QUOTATIONS

Pointed axioms and acute replies fly loose about the world, and are assigned successively to those whom it may be the fashion to celebrate.

Samuel Johnson, _Works_ vol. vii, 1787

It is with epigrams as with other inventions: the best are those which annoy us because we did not think of them ourselves.

Georg Christoph Lichtenberg, _Reflections_, 1799

France was long a despotism tempered by epigrams.

Thomas Carlyle, _The French Revolution_, 1837

Epigram: a platitude with vine-leaves in its hair.

H.L. Mencken, _A Book of Burlesques_, 1916

Bon mots are perhaps best described as the words other people wish they had said.

Daily Herald, 1964

The nicest thing about quotes is that they give us a nodding acquaintance with the originator which is often socially impressive.

Kenneth Williams, _Acid Drops_, 1980

See also MAXIMS

RACE

A racially integrated community is a chronological term, timed from the entrance of the first black family to the exit of the last white family.
  Saul Alinsky

Black people have never rioted. A riot is what white people think blacks are involved in when they burn stores.
  Julius Lester

RELIGION

Since the masses of the people are inconstant, full of unruly desires, passionate and reckless of consequence, they must be filled with fears to keep them in order. The ancients did well, therefore, to invent gods, and the belief in punishment after death.
  Polybius, *Histories*, c. 125BC

It is for the good of states that men should be deluded by religion.
  Marcus Terentius Varro, *Antiquitates rerum humanarum et divinarum*, c. 40BC

It is when we are in misery that we revere the gods; the prosperous seldom approach the altar.
  Silius Italicus, *Punica*, c. AD75

Fear of power invisible, feigned by the mind or imagined from tales publicly allowed, [is] religion; not allowed, superstition.
  Thomas Hobbes, *Leviathan*, 1651

In matters of religion it is very easy to deceive a man, and very hard to undeceive him.
  Pierre Bayle, *Dictionary*, 1697

When men grow virtuous in their old age, they only make a sacrifice to God of the devil's leavings.
  Jonathan Swift

A man is quickly convinced of the truth of religion, who finds it is not against his interest that it should be true.
  Joseph Addison, in the *Spectator*, 1712

Religion supposed Heaven and Hell, the word of God, and sacraments, and twenty other circumstances which, taken seriously, are a wonderful check to wit and humour.

Jonathan Swift, letter of advice to a young poet, 1720

Theologians are all alike, of whatever religion or country they may be; their aim is always to wield despotic authority over men's consciences; they therefore persecute all of us who have the temerity to tell the truth.

Frederick the Great, letter to Voltaire, 1736

Religion is the idol of the mob: it adores everything it does not understand.

Frederick the Great, letter to Voltaire, 1737

Many a long dispute between divines may thus be abridged: It is so. It is not so. It is so. It is not so.

Benjamin Franklin, *Poor Richard's Almanack*, 1733–58

The Christian religion not only was at first attended by miracles, but even at this day cannot be believed by any reasonable person without one.

David Hume, *On Miracles*, 1748

The truths of religion are never so well understood as by those who have lost the power of reasoning.

Voltaire, *Philosophical Dictionary*, 1764

Whenever an important event, a revolution, or a calamity turns to the profit of the church, such is always signalised as the Finger of God.

Voltaire, *Philosophical Dictionary*, 1764

All religions are ancient monuments to superstitions, ignorance, ferocity; and modern religions are only ancient follies rejuvenated.

Baron d'Holbach, 1772

Prisons are built with stones of law, brothels with bricks of religion.

William Blake, *The Marriage of Heaven and Hell*, 1790–3

What is it the New Testament teaches us? To believe that the Almighty committed debauchery with a woman engaged to be married; and the belief of this debauchery is called faith.

Thomas Paine, *The Age of Reason*, 1793–5

The Bible: a history of wickedness that has served to corrupt and brutalise mankind.

Thomas Paine, *The Age of Reason,* **1793–5**

The study of theology, as it stands in Christian churches, is the study of nothing; it is founded on nothing; it rests on nothing; it proceeds by no authorities; it has no data; it can demonstrate nothing and admits of no conclusion.

Thomas Paine, *The Age of Reason,* **1793–5**

All religions are founded on the fear of the many and the cleverness of the few.

Stendhal

Religion is excellent stuff for keeping common people quiet.

Napoleon Bonaparte

A book is put into our hands when children, called the Bible, the purport of whose history is briefly this: That God made the earth in six days and there planted a delightful garden, in which He placed the first pair of human beings. In the midst of the garden He planted a tree, whose fruit, although within their reach, they were forbidden to touch. That the Devil, in the shape of a snake, persuaded them to eat of this fruit; in consequence of which God condemned both of them and their posterity yet unborn to satisfy His justice by their eternal misery. That, 4000 years after these events the human race in the meantime having gone unredeemed to perdition, God engendered with the betrothed wife of a carpenter in Judaea (whose virginity was nevertheless uninjured), and begat a son, whose name was Jesus Christ; and who was crucified and died in order that no more men might be devoted to hell-fire . . . The book states, in addition, that the soul of whoever disbelieves this sacrifice will be burned with everlasting fire.

Percy Bysshe Shelley, *Queen Mab* **(notes), 1813**

If Jesus Christ were to come today, people would not even crucify him. They would ask him to dinner, and hear what he had to say, and make fun of him.

Thomas Carlyle

Sir Richard Steele has observed, that there is this difference between the Church of Rome and the Church of England: the one professes to be infallible, the other to be never in the wrong.

Charles Caleb Colton, *Lacon,* **1820**

Men will wrangle for religion, write for it, fight for it, die for it, anything but – live for it.
Charles Caleb Colton, *Lacon*, 1820

There is one passage in the Scriptures to which all the potentates of Europe seem to have given their unanimous assent and approbation . . . 'There went out a decree in the days of Caesar Augustus, that all the world should be taxed.'
Charles Caleb Colton, *Lacon*, 1820

There are only two things in which the false professors of all religions have agreed: to persecute all other sects and to plunder their own.
Charles Caleb Colton, *Lacon*, 1820

Look through the whole histories of countries professing the Romish religion and you will uniformly find the leaven of this besetting and accursed principle of action – that the end will sanction any means.
Samuel Taylor Coleridge, *Table-Talk*, 1836

Religion is the opium of the people.
Karl Marx, *A Criticism of the Hegelian Philosophy of Law*, 1844

Monotheistic religions alone furnish the spectacle of religious wars, religious persecutions, heretical tribunals, that breaking of idols and destruction of images of the gods, that razing of Indian temples and Egyptian colossi, which had looked on the sun 3,000 years: just because a jealous god had said, 'Thou shalt make no graven image.'
Arthur Schopenhauer, *Religion: a Dialogue*, 1851

Religion is the masterpiece of the art of animal training, for it trains people as to how they shall think.
Arthur Schopenhauer, *Parerga und Paralipomena*, 1851

Every established fact which is too bad to admit of any other defence is always presented to us as an injunction of religion.
John Stuart Mill, *The Subjection of Women*, 1869

The religion of one age is the literary entertainment of the next.
Ralph Waldo Emerson

All religions, with their gods, demigods, prophets, messiahs and saints, are the product of the fancy and credulity of men who have not yet reached the full development and complete possession of their intellectual powers.

Mikhail Bakunin, *Dieu et l'état,* **1871**

Where it is a duty to worship the sun it is pretty sure to be a crime to examine the laws of heat.

John, Viscount Morley, *Voltaire,* **1872**

Strange but true: those who have loved God most have loved men least.

Robert G. Ingersoll, speech, 1881

The inspiration of the Bible depends upon the ignorance of the gentleman who reads it.

Robert G. Ingersoll, speech, 1881

No man with a sense of humour ever founded a religion.

Robert G. Ingersoll

Whatever a theologian regards as true must be false: there you have almost a criterion of truth.

Friedrich Wilhelm Nietzsche, *The Antichrist,* **1888**

I call Christianity the one great curse, the one enormous and innermost perversion, the one great instinct for revenge, for which no means are too venomous, too underhand, too underground and too petty – I call it the one immortal blemish of mankind.

Friedrich Wilhelm Nietzsche, *The Antichrist,* **1888**

The whole religious complexion of the modern world is due to the absence from Jerusalem of a lunatic asylum.

Havelock Ellis

Truth, in matters of religion, is simply the opinion that has survived.

Oscar Wilde, *The Critic as Artist,* **1891**

Religion is the fashionable substitute for belief.

Oscar Wilde, *The Picture of Dorian Gray,* **1891**

The preponderance of pain over pleasure is the cause of our fictitious morality and religion.

Friedrich Wilhelm Nietzsche

Religion is a sum of scruples which impede the free exercise of our faculties.

Salomon Reinach, *Cultes, mythes et religions,* **1904**

Religion is an illusion . . . it derives its strength from the fact that it falls in with our intellectual desires.

Sigmund Freud

The most serious doubt that has been thrown on the authenticity of the biblical miracles is the fact that most of the witnesses in regard to them were fishermen.

Arthur Binstead, *Pitcher's Proverbs,* **1909**

The man who has no mind of his own lends it to the priests.

George Meredith, in the *Fortnightly Review,* **1909**

Sudden conversion . . . is particularly attractive to the half-baked mind.

E.M. Forster, *Howards End,* **1910**

Saint, n. A dead sinner revised and edited.

Ambrose Bierce, *The Devil's Dictionary,* **1911**

Scriptures, n. The sacred books of our holy religion, as distinguished from the false and profane writings on which all other faiths are based.

Ambrose Bierce, *The Devil's Dictionary,* **1911**

Infidel, n. In New York, one who does not believe in the Christian religion; in Constantinople, one who does.

Ambrose Bierce, *The Devil's Dictionary,* **1911**

A Christian is one who follows the teachings of Christ insofar as they are not inconsistent with a life of sin.

Ambrose Bierce, *The Devil's Dictionary,* **1911**

Heathen, n. A benighted creature who has the folly to worship something he can see and feel.

Ambrose Bierce, *The Devil's Dictionary,* **1911**

Prayers are to men as dolls are to children. They are not without use and comfort, but it is not easy to take them seriously.

Samuel Butler, *Notebooks,* **1912**

Theology – an effort to explain the unknowable by putting it into the terms of the not worth knowing.
    H.L. Mencken, *Sententiae*, 1916

Say what you like about the Ten Commandments, you must always come back to the pleasant fact that there are only ten of them.
    H.L. Mencken, *Sententiae*, 1916

Formal religion was organised for slaves; it offered them consolation which earth did not provide.
    Elbert Hubbard, 1923

We ought to have as great a regard for religion as we can, so as to keep it out of as many things as possible.
    Sean O'Casey, *The Plough and the Stars*, 1926

Many people believe they attracted by God, or by Nature, when they are only repelled by man.
    William R. Inge, *More Lay Thoughts of a Dean*, 1931

By the time a boy has been two years in a church school he is immunised against religion.
    Colin Gordon

Christian ethics are seldom found save in the philosophy of some unbeliever.
    Heywood Broun

Organised Christianity has probably done more to retard the ideals that were its founders than any other agency in the world.
    Richard Le Gallienne

As with the Christian religion, the worst advertisement for Socialism is its adherents.
    George Orwell, *The Road to Wigan Pier*, 1937

A great deal of what passes for current Christianity consists in denouncing other people's vices and faults.
    Henry Williams

The act of worship, as carried on by Christians, seems to me debasing, rather than ennobling. It involves grovelling before a Being who, if he really exists, deserves to be denounced instead of respected.
    H.L. Mencken

People who feel themselves to be exiles in this world are mightily inclined to believe themselves citizens of another.
George Santayana

The only reason the Protestants and Catholics have given up the idea of universal domination is because they've realised they can't get away with it.
W.H. Auden, *The Table-Talk of W. H. Auden*, ed. Alan Ansen, 1990

Maybe this world is just another planet's hell.
Aldous Huxley

The Bible should be taught so early and so thoroughly that it sinks straight to the bottom of the mind where everything that comes along can settle on it.
Northrop Frye

So far as I can remember, there is not one word in the Gospels in praise of intelligence.
Bertrand Russell

Saints should always be judged guilty until they are proved innocent.
George Orwell, *Reflections on Gandhi*, 1949

We must respect the other fellow's religion, but only in the sense and to the extent that we respect his theory that his wife is beautiful and his children smart.
H.L. Mencken, *Minority Report*, 1956

The chief contribution of Protestantism to human thought is its massive proof that God is a bore.
H.L. Mencken, *Minority Report*, 1956

The habit of religion is oppressive, an easy way out of thought.
Peter Ustinov, in *Everybody's* magazine, 1957

Religion is the venereal disease of mankind.
Henry de Montherlant

All Gods were immortal.
Stanislaw J. Lec, *Unkempt Thoughts*, 1962

It is usually when men are at their most religious that they behave with the least sense and the greatest cruelty.

Ilka Chase

Religion is . . . parasitic in the interstices of our knowledge which have not yet been filled.

J.B.S. Haldane, *Science and Life*, 1968

That's all religion is – some principle you believe in . . . man has accomplished far more miracles that the God he invented. What a tragedy it is to invent a God and then suffer to keep him King.

Rod Steiger, in *Playboy* magazine, 1969

Mythology is what grown-ups believe, folklore is what they tell children and religion is both.

Cedric Whitman, 1969

A myth is a religion in which no one any longer believes.

James K. Feibleman, *Understanding Philosophy*, 1973

Why do born-again people so often make you wish they'd never been born the first time.

Katherine Whitehorn, in the *Observer*, 1979

A cult is a religion with no political power.

Tom Wolfe, *In Our Time*, 1980

What's a cult? It just means not enough people to make a minority.

Robert Altman, in the *Observer*, 1981

Heresy is only another word for freedom of thought.

Graham Greene, 1981

See also BELIEF, THE CLERGY, FAITH, GOD, HYPOCRISY, IDEALS, IDEAS, MORALS, TRUE BELIEVERS, TRUTH

REVOLUTION

By a revolution in the state, the fawning sycophant of yesterday is converted into the austere critic of the present hour.

Edmund Burke, *Reflections on the Revolution in France*, 1790

Every successful revolt is termed a revolution, and every unsuccessful one a rebellion.

Joseph Priestley, letter, 1791

In revolutions power always remains in the hands of nobodies.
Georges Danton, on receiving the death sentence, 1794

It is better to abolish serfdom from above than to wait for it to abolish itself from below.
Alexander II, 1856

The New Jerusalem, when it comes, will probably be found so far to resemble the old as to stone its prophets freely.
Samuel Butler, *Notebooks*, 1912

Revolutions have never lightened the burden of tyranny, they have only shifted it to another shoulder.
George Bernard Shaw, *Man and Superman*, 1903

Rebel, n. The proponent of a new misrule who has failed to establish it.
Ambrose Bierce, *The Devil's Dictionary*, 1911

Revolution, n. In politics, an abrupt change in the form of misgovernment.
Ambrose Bierce, *The Devil's Dictionary*, 1911

Insurrection, n. An unsuccessful revolution. Disaffection's failure to substitute misrule for bad government.
Ambrose Bierce, *The Devil's Dictionary*, 1911

The revolutionary spirit is mightily convenient in this: that it frees one from all scruples as regards ideas.
Joseph Conrad, *A Personal Record*, 1912

A revolution only lasts fifteen years – a period which coincides with the effectiveness of a generation.
José Ortega y Gasset, 1930

Few revolutionists would be such if they were heirs to a baronetcy.
George Santayana

Every revolution evaporates and leaves behind only the slime of a new bureaucracy.
Franz Kafka, *The Great Wall of China: Aphorisms 1917–19*, 1931

The successful revolutionary is a statesman, the unsuccessful one is a criminal.
Erich Fromm, *Escape from Freedom*, 1941

Radicalism is the opium of the middle class.

Christina Stead, *Letty Fox, Her Luck*, 1946

The slave begins by demanding justice and ends by wanting to wear a crown. He must dominate in his turn.

Albert Camus, *The Rebel*, 1951

Every revolutionary ends up either by becoming an oppressor or a heretic.

Albert Camus, *The Rebel*, 1951

A revolution requires of its leaders a record of unbroken infallibility. If they do not possess it they are expected to invent it.

Murray Kempton, *Part of Our Time*, 1955

The revolution as myth is the definitive revolution.

Albert Camus, *Notebooks*, 1942–51

It is an illusion to think that you can have a revolution without prisons.

Muhammad Ahmed Ben Bella, 1963

A revolution is interesting insofar as it avoids like the plague the plague it promised to heal.

Daniel Berrigan, in the *New York Review of Books*, 1971

Every successful revolution puts on in time the robes of the tyrant it has deposed.

Barbara Tuchman

There is no surer way of preserving the worst aspects of the bourgeois style than liquidating the bourgeoisie. Whatever else Stalin may or may not have done, he assuredly made Russia safe for the Forsyte Saga.

Malcolm Muggeridge, *Chronicles of Wasted Time* vol. i, 1978

The general law of development for political institutions conceived in revolutionary idealism, which is that they begin as an expression of conscience and become in due course agencies for the issuance of licences and the distribution of patronage.

Murray Kempton, in *Newsday* magazine, 1981

See also DEMOCRACY, FREEDOM

THE RICH

The shortest and best way to make your fortune is to let people see clearly that it is in their interests to promote yours.
Jean de La Bruyère, *The Characters*, 1688

We may see the small value God has for riches by the people he gives them to.
Alexander Pope, *Miscellanies in Prose and Verse*, 1727

There are some men who gain from their wealth only the fear of losing it.
Antoine Rivaroli, Comte de Rivarol, *L'esprit de Rivarol*, 1808

The greatest luxury of riches is, that they enable you to escape so much good advice.
Sir Arthur Helps

God shows his contempt for wealth by the kind of person he selects to receive it.
Austin O'Malley

A rich man's joke is always funny.
Thomas Brown

Rich bachelors should be heavily taxed. It is not fair that some men should be happier than others.
Oscar Wilde

The faults of the burglar are the qualities of the financier.
George Bernard Shaw, *Major Barbara*, 1907

That's it, baby! When you got it, flaunt it! Flaunt it!
Mel Brooks, screenplay for *The Producers*, 1968

The rich are different from you and me because they have more credit.
John Leonard

The parvenu is always someone else.
Anka Muhlstein, *The Rise of the French Rothschilds*, 1983

See also BUSINESS, MONEY, POVERTY & THE POOR

SCIENCE

Professors in every branch of the sciences prefer their own theories to truth: the reason is that their theories are private property, but the truth is common stock.

Charles Caleb Colton, *Lacon*, 1820

Science is the record of dead religions.

Oscar Wilde, *Phrases and Philosophies for the Use of the Young*, 1894

Science is the religion of the suburbs.

W.B. Yeats

The tendency of modern science is to reduce proof to absurdity by continually reducing absurdity to proof.

Samuel Butler, *Notebooks*, 1912

Science in the modern world had many uses; its chief use, however, is to provide long words to cover the errors of the rich.

G.K. Chesterton

A science is said to be useful if its development tends to accentuate the existing inequalities in the distribution of wealth, or more directly promotes the destruction of human life.

Godfrey Hardy, *A Mathematician's Apology*, 1941

We must be aware of needless innovations, especially when guided by logic.

Sir Winston Churchill, 1942

One has to look out for engineers – they begin with sewing machines and end up with the atomic bomb.

Marcel Pagnol, *Critique des critiques*, 1949

A new scientific truth does not triumph by convincing its opponents and making them see the light, but rather because its opponents eventually die, and a new generation grows up that is familiar with it.

Max Planck, *Scientific Autobiography and Other Papers*, 1950

Science is a cemetery of dead ideas.

Miguel de Unamuno

No scientific theory achieves public acceptance until it has been thoroughly discredited.

Douglas Yates

Successful research impedes further successful research.

Keith J. Pendred, in *The Bulletin of the Atomic Scientists*, 1963

Creativity in science could be described as the act of putting two and two together to make five.

Arthur Koestler, *Creation*, 1964

A science is any discipline in which the fool of this generation can go beyond the point reached by the genius of the last generation.

Max Gluckmann, *Politics, Law and Ritual*, 1965

The real accomplishment of modern science and technology consists in taking ordinary men, informing them narrowly and deeply and then, through appropriate action, arranging to have their knowledge combined with that of other specialised but equally ordinary men. This dispenses with the need for genius. The resulting performance, though less inspiring, is far more predictable.

John Kenneth Galbraith, *The New Industrial State*, 1967

There are three roads to ruin – women, gambling and technicians. The most pleasant is with women, the quickest is with gambling, but the surest is with technicians.

Georges Pompidou, in the *Sunday Telegraph*, 1968

Inanimate objects are classified scientifically into three major categories – those that don't work, those that break down and those that get lost.

Russell Baker, in the *New York Times*, 1968

When a distinguished but elderly scientist states that something is possible, he is almost certainly right. When he states that something is impossible, he is very probably wrong.

Arthur C. Clarke, *Profile of the Future*, 1973

A first-rate theory predicts, a second-rate theory forbids and a third-rate theory explains after the event.

Alexander Kitaigorodski, 1975

The progress of science is strewn, like an ancient desert trail, with the bleached skeletons of discarded theories which once seemed to possess eternal life.

Arthur Koestler, address to the PEN Club, 1976

When the lay public rallies round to an idea that is denounced by distinguished but elderly scientists and supports that idea with great fervour and emotion, the distinguished but elderly scientists are then, after all, right.

Isaac Asimov, in *Fantasy and Science Fiction* magazine, 1977

Carson's Consolation: no experiment is ever a complete failure. It can always be used as a bad example.

Paul Dickson, *The Official Rules*, 1978

First Law: if an experiment works, something has gone wrong. Fourth Law: once a job is fouled up, anything done to improve it only makes it worse.

Finagle's Laws, quoted in *Murphy's Law* by A. Bloch, 1979

Enough research will tend to support your theory.

Murphy's Law of Research, quoted in *Murphy's Law* by A. Bloch, 1979

If a scientist uncovers a publishable fact, it will become central to his theory.

Mann's Law, quoted in *Murphy's Law Book Two* by A. Bloch, 1980

Modern science is generally practised by those who lack the flair for conversation.

Fran Lebowitz, *Metropolitan Life*, 1981

See also PROGRESS

SENTIMENTALITY

A sentimentalist is simply one who desires to have the luxury of an emotion without paying for it.

Oscar Wilde

Sentimentality is a superstructure covering brutality.

C.G. Jung, *Reflections*, 1953

SEX

Marriage is the price men pay for sex, sex is the price women pay for marriage.

Anonymous

Filth and old age, I'm sure you will agree
Are powerful wardens upon chastity.

Geoffrey Chaucer, *The Canterbury Tales*, 1387

She is chaste who was never asked the question.

William Congreve

The pleasure is momentary, the position ridiculous and the expense damnable.

Lord Chesterfield, *Letters to his Son*, 1774

What they call 'heart' is located far lower than the fourth waistcoat button.

Georg Christoph Lichtenberg, *Aphorisms*, 1764–99

There are few things that we so unwillingly give up, even in an advanced age, as the supposition that we have still the power of ingratiating ourselves with the fair sex.

Samuel Johnson, *Johnsonian Miscellanies*, ed. G.B. Hill, 1897

Were it not for imagination, Sir, a man would be as happy in the arms of a chambermaid as of a Duchess.

**Samuel Johnson, quoted in *The Life of Samuel Johnson*
by J. Boswell, 1791**

Advice to sexually bored husbands . . . Think of your mistress.

Honoré de Balzac, *The Physiology of Marriage*, 1829

The duration of passion is proportionate with the original resistance of the woman.

Honoré de Balzac

The garter has hanged more men than the halter.

Reflections of a Bachelor, 19th century

Of all the sexual aberrations, perhaps the most peculiar is chastity.
  Rémy de Gourmont

The advantage of being celibate is that when one sees a pretty girl one does not need to grieve over having an ugly one back home.
  Paul Léautaud, *Propos d'un jour,* **1900**

I have a technical objection to making sexual infatuation a tragic theme. Experience proves that it is only effective in the comic spirit.
  George Bernard Shaw, *Three Plays for Puritans,* **1901**

Virginity is the ideal of those who want to deflower.
  Karl Kraus, *Half Truths and One and a Half Truths,* **1986**

There comes a moment in the day, when you have written your pages in the morning, attended to your correspondence in the afternoon, and have nothing further to do. Then comes that hour when you are bored; that's the time for sex.
  H.G. Wells

A man marries to have a home, but also because he doesn't want to be bothered with sex and all that sort of thing.
  W. Somerset Maugham, *The Circle,* **1921**

Give a man a free hand and he'll run it all over you.
  Mae West, *Klondike Annie,* **1936**

Sex: the thing that takes up the least amount of time and causes the most amount of trouble.
  John Barrymore

Anon: Goodness, what beautiful diamonds!
Mae West: Goodness had nothing to do with it, dearie.
  Vincent Lawrence and Mae West, screenplay for *Night After Night,* **1932**

The big difference between sex for money and sex for free is that sex for money usually costs a lot less.
  Brendan Francis

There goes the good time that was had by all.
  Bette Davis, remarking on a passing starlet

That gentlemen prefer blondes is due to the fact that, apparently, pale hair, delicate skin and an infantile expression represent the very apex of a frailty which every man longs to violate.

Alexander King, *Rich Man, Poor Man, Freud and Fruit*, **1945**

Older women are best because they always think they may be doing it for the last time.

Ian Fleming

A fox is a wolf who sends flowers.

Ruth Weston, 1955

Find 'em, feel 'em, fuck 'em and forget 'em.

The Four-F Club, motto of 1950s teenage males

Show me a genuine case of platonic friendship and I shall show you two old or homely faces.

Austin O'Malley

Sex is. There is nothing more to be done about it. Sex builds no roads, writes no novels, and sex certainly gives no meaning to anything in life but itself.

Gore Vidal, *Norman Mailer's Self-Advertisements*, **1960**

Relations between the sexes are so complicated that the only way you can tell if two members of the set are 'going together' is if they are married. Then, almost certainly, they are not.

Cleveland Amory, *Who Killed Society?*, **1960**

Money, it turned out, was exactly like sex. You thought of nothing else if you didn't have it, and thought of other things if you did.

James Baldwin, *Nobody Knows My Name*, **1961**

Literature is mostly about sex and not much about having children, and life is the other way round.

David Lodge, *The British Museum is Falling Down*, **1965**

The man and woman make love, attain climax, fall separate. Then she whispers 'I'll tell you who I was thinking of if you tell me who you were thinking of.' Like most sex jokes the origins of the pleasant exchange are obscure. But whatever the source, it seldom fails to evoke a certain awful recognition.

Gore Vidal, in the *New York Review of Books*, **1966**

I'll be comfortable on the couch. Famous last words.

Lenny Bruce, quoted in *The Essential Lenny Bruce*, ed. J. Cohen, 1967

Love is a way with some meaning; sex is meaning enough.

Charles Bukowski, *Notes of a Dirty Old Man*, 1969

Each man that loves a woman must be prepared for this
For a sexual love is human and betrayal by a kiss
Is a commonplace and not just in the holy book
And it all begins when your eyes take that first long look.

Gavin Ewart

Is sex dirty? Only if it's done right.

Woody Allen, *All You Ever Wanted To Know About Sex*, 1972

I can understand companionship. I can understand bought sex in the afternoon. I cannot understand the love affair.

Gore Vidal, in the *Sunday Times*, 1973

Aren't women prudes if they don't and prostitutes if they do.

Kate Millett, speech, 1975

Love is the answer, but while you are waiting for the answer, sex raises some pretty good questions.

Woody Allen, in the *New York Herald Tribune*, 1975

Don't knock masturbation – it's sex with someone I love.

Woody Allen

Someone once remarked that in adolescence pornography is a substitute for sex, whereas in adulthood sex is a substitute for pornography.

Edmund White, in *New Times* magazine, 1979

The big mistake that men make is that when they turn thirteen or fourteen and all of a sudden they've reached puberty, they believe that they like women. Actually, you're just horny. It doesn't mean you like women any more at twenty-one than you did at ten.

Jules Feiffer, quoted in *Loose Talk*, ed. L. Botts, 1980

What is a promiscuous person – it's usually someone who is getting more sex than you are.

Victor Lownes, quoted in *In and Out: Debrett 1980–81* by N. Mackwood, 1980

The difference between rape and seduction is only one of technique.
  Magnus Magnusson, *Popular Archaeology*, 1981

For certain people, after fifty, litigation takes the place of sex.
  Gore Vidal, in the *Evening Standard*, 1981

From thirty-five to forty-five men go from relative youth to middle age. The transit is often rocky. As a man's life settles into a rut, in mindless rut the man is apt to go.
  Gore Vidal, *Pink Triangle and Yellow Star*, 1982

There is no unhappier creature on earth than a fetishist who yearns for a woman's shoe and has to embrace the whole woman.
  Karl Kraus, *Aphorisms and More Aphorism*, 1909

When the prick stands, the brains get buried in the ground.
  Yiddish proverb

See also AFFAIRS, LOVE, LOVERS

SIN

That which we call sin in others, is experiment for us.
  Ralph Waldo Emerson

The advantage of the emotions is that they lead us astray.
  Oscar Wilde, *The Picture of Dorian Gray*, 1891

Envy is the most stupid of vices, for there is no single advantage to be gained from it.
  Honoré de Balzac, quoted in *Reflections on the Art of Life* by J.R. Solly, 1902

Scandal is merely the compassionate allowance which the gay make to the humdrum.
  Saki (H.H. Munro), *Reginald at the Carlton*, 1904

Only the sinner has the right to preach.
  Christopher Morley

The urge to gamble is so universal and its practice so pleasurable that I assume it must be evil.

Heywood Broun

When choosing between two evils, I always like to take the one I've never tried before.

Mae West, *Klondike Annie*, 1936

Keep a diary and one day it'll keep you.

Mae West, *Everyday's A Holiday*, 1937

Men who make no pretensions to being good on one day out of seven are called sinners.

Mary Wilson Little

We don't call it sin today, we call it self-expression.

Baroness Stocks

Many are saved from sin by being so inept at it.

Mignon McLaughlin, *The Neurotic's Notebook*, 1963

The major sin is the sin of being born.

Samuel Beckett, in the *New York Herald Tribune*, 1964

See also HYPOCRISY, MORALS, RELIGION, VIRTUE

SPORT

Angling – I can only compare it to a stick and a string with a worm at one end and a fool at the other.

Samuel Johnson, 1784

Golf is a good walk spoiled.

Mark Twain

When a man wantonly destroys one of the works of man, we call him a vandal; when he wantonly destroys one of the works of God we call him a sportsman.

Joseph Wood Krutch, on hunting

A sportsman is a man who, every now and then, simply has to go out and kill something.

Stephen Leacock, 1920

Serious sport has nothing to do with fair play. It is bound up with hatred, jealousy, boastfulness, disregard of all rules and sadistic pleasure in witnessing violence: in other words it is war minus the shooting.

George Orwell, *The Sporting Spirit,* **1945**

[Boxing] . . . is the only sport in the world where two guys get paid for doing something they'd be arrested for if they got drunk and did it for nothing.

Carl Foreman, screenplay for *Champion,* **1949**

Show me a good loser in professional sports and I'll show you an idiot. Show me a good sportsman and I'll show you a player I'm looking to trade.

Leo Durocher, 1950

Everyone likes hats when someone else is paying for them.

Willie Ginsberg, testifying on corruption in sport, 1956

Rugby is a beastly game played by gentlemen, soccer is a gentleman's game played by beasts and [US] football is a beastly game played by beasts.

Henry Blaha, 1972

Football is a game designed to keep coalminers off the streets.

Jimmy Breslin, 1973

On the cult of victory at all costs: Last guys don't finish nice.

Stanley Kelley, quoted in *The Official Rules* **by P. Dickson, 1978**

Jogging is for people who aren't intelligent enough to watch Breakfast TV.

Victoria Wood

THE STATE

In taking possession of a state the conqueror should well reflect as to the harsh measures that may be necessary and then execute them at a single blow . . . cruelties should be committed all at once.

Niccolò Machiavelli, *The Prince,* **1513**

Nothing doth hurt more in a state than that cunning men pass for wise.

Francis Bacon, *Essays,* **1625**

Secrecy is the first essential in affairs of state.
  Cardinal Richelieu, *Testament politique,* **1641**

What has always made the state a hell on earth has been precisely that man has tried to make it his heaven.
  Johann Friedrich Hölderlin

The smallest and most inoffensive state is still criminal in its dreams.
  Michael Bakunin

Powerful states can maintain themselves only by crime. Little states are virtuous only because they are weak.
  Mikhail Bakunin, *Proposition motivée,* **1868**

The State is an instrument in the hands of the ruling class for suppressing the resistance of its class enemies.
  Joseph Stalin

It is no part of the State's duty to facilitate the spiritual redemption of rich men by impoverishing them in this life.
  John Grigg, 1964

See also DEMOCRACY, POLITICIANS, POWER

STATESMEN

Consistency is the hobgoblin of little minds, adored by little statesmen and philosophers and divines.
  Ralph Waldo Emerson, *Self-Reliance,* **1841**

A statesman is a successful politician who is dead.
  Thomas B. Reed

In statesmanship get the formalities right, never mind about the moralities.
  Mark Twain

It is amazing how wise statesmen can be when it is ten years too late.
  David Lloyd George, 1932

When you're out of office, then you can be a statesman.
  John Connally, 1971

One man's opportunism is another man's statesmanship.
  Milton Friedman, in *Playboy* magazine, 1973

Statesmen: the word politicians use to describe themselves.
  Antony Jay and Jonathan Lynn, *Yes, Prime Minister*, 1986

See also LEADERS, POLITICIANS, POWER

SUCCESS

What matters is not that I should succeed, but that you should fail.
  Anonymous, attrib. to Gore Vidal inter alios

He that has nothing but merit to support him is in a fair way to starve.
  Anonymous, in *Characters and Observations*, c.1725

To succeed in the world we must look foolish but be wise.
  Charles de Secondat, Baron de Montesquieu, *Mes pensées*, 1722–55

Mediocrity is a hand-rail.
  Charles de Secondat, Baron de Montesquieu, *Mes pensées*, 1722–55

When we examine what glory is we discover that it is nearly nothing. To be judged by the ignorant and esteemed by imbeciles, to hear one's name spoken by a rabble who approve, reject, love or hate without reason – that is nothing to be proud of.
  Frederick the Great, letter to Voltaire, 1773

Be commonplace and creeping and you'll be a success.
  Pierre Augustin Caron de Beaumarchais, *The Barber of Seville*, 1775

One never climbs so high as when he knows not where he is going.
  Napoleon Bonaparte, *Maxims*, 1804–15

If you want to get on in this world make many promises, but don't keep them.
  Napoleon Bonaparte, *Maxims*, 1804–15

No one is so completely disenchanted with the world, or knows it so thoroughly, or is so utterly disgusted with it, that when it begins to smile upon him he does not become partially reconciled to it.
  Giacomo Leopardi, *Pensieri*, 1834–7

Granting our wish is one of Fate's saddest jokes.
James Russell Lowell

Success is the necessary misfortune of life, but it is only to the very unfortunate that it comes early.
Anthony Trollope, *Orley Farm,* **1862**

When the gods wish to punish us they answer our prayers.
Oscar Wilde, *An Ideal Husband,* **1895**

How many 'coming men' has one known! Where on earth do they all go to?
Sir Arthur Pinero

The secret of success in life is known only to those who have not succeeded.
John Churton Collins, in *The English Review,* **1914**

We must believe in luck. For how else can we explain the success of those we don't like.
Jean Cocteau

If at first you don't succeed, try again. Then quit: no use being a damn fool about it.
W.C. Fields

There is no such thing as a great man or woman. People believe in them, just as they used to believe in unicorns and dragons. The greatest man or woman is 99 per cent like yourself.
George Bernard Shaw, interview, 1932

To succeed pre-eminently in public life it is necessary to conform either to the popular image of a bookie or a clergyman.
Malcolm Muggeridge, 1934

Those whom the gods wish to destroy, they first call promising.
Cyril Connolly, *Enemies of Promise,* **1938**

Success is relative: It is what we can make of the mess we have made of things.
T.S. Eliot, *The Family Reunion,* **1939**

Once a guy starts wearing silk pyjamas, it's hard to get up early.
  Eddie Arcaro, 1950

Success listens only to applause. To all else it is deaf.
  Elias Canetti

If A is success in life, then A equals X plus Y plus Z. Work is X, Y is play and Z is keeping your mouth shut.
  Albert Einstein, in the *Observer*, 1950

If you want to sell 'em fish, sell 'em big fish. That's the secret of success.
  Jack Solomons, 1950

We all invent ourselves as we go along, and a great man's myths about himself tend to stick better than most.
  Sir Denis Brogan

The penalty of success is to be bored by people who used to snub you.
  Nancy Astor, quoted, 1956

Anatomise the character of a successful hostess and the knife will lay bare the fact that she owes her position to one of three things: she is liked, or she is feared, or she is important.
  Elsa Maxwell, *How To Do It*, 1957

Many a man owes his success to his first wife and his second wife to his success.
  Jim Backus

Some men are born mediocre, some men achieve mediocrity, and some men have mediocrity thrust upon them.
  Joseph Heller, *Catch-22*, 1961

What is success? It is a toy balloon among children armed with pins.
  Gene Fowler, *Skyline*, 1961

How many of our daydreams would darken into nightmares were there any danger of their coming true.
  Logan Pearsall Smith, quoted in *The Faber Book of Aphorisms*, ed. W.H. Auden and L. Kronenberger, 1964

Having no talent is no longer enough.
  Gore Vidal

The banalities of a great man pass for wit.
   Alexander Chase, *Perspectives*, 1966

Success is the result of a collective hallucination stimulated by the artist.
   Charles Aznavour

The trouble with the rat-race is that even if you win, you're still a rat.
   Lily Tomlin

Success and failure are both difficult to endure. Along with success come drugs, divorce, fornication, bullying, travel, meditation, medication, depression, neurosis and suicide. With failure comes failure.
   Joseph Heller, in *Playboy* magazine, 1975

Nothing succeeds like address.
   Fran Lebowitz, *Metropolitan Life*, 1978

Nothing succeeds like the appearance of success.
   Christopher Lasch, *The Culture of Narcissism*, 1979

A successful man is one who makes more money than his wife can spend. A successful woman is one who can find such a man.
   Lana Turner, 1980

The secret of success is sincerity. Once you can fake that you've got it made.
   **Glyme's Formula, quoted in *Murphy's Law Book Two*
   by A. Bloch, 1980**

See also AMBITION, APPLAUSE, EGOTISM, FAME

TALK

The vanity of being known to be trusted with a secret is generally one of the chief motives to disclose it.
   Samuel Johnson, *The Rambler*, 1749–52

The true use of speech is not so much to express our wants as to conceal them.
   Oliver Goldsmith, *The Citizen of the World*, 1762

Speech was given to man to conceal his thoughts.

Charles-Maurice de Talleyrand, quoted in *Reflections on the Art of Life* by J.R. Solly, 1902

Swans sing before they die; 'twere no bad thing should certain persons die before they sing.

Samuel Taylor Coleridge

A sharp tongue is the only edged instrument that grows keener with constant use.

Washington Irving, *The Sketch Book*, 1820

None are so fond of secrets as those who do not mean to keep them; such persons covet secrets as a spendthrift covets money: for the purpose of circulation.

Charles Caleb Colton, *Lacon*, 1820

A majority is always the best repartee.

Benjamin Disraeli, *Tancred*, 1847

Language, human language, after all is but little better than the croak and cackle of fowls, and other utterances of brute nature – sometimes not as adequate.

Nathaniel Hawthorne, *American Notebook*, 1850

The conversation of men is a mixture of regrets and apprehensions.

Ralph Waldo Emerson

I never deny, I never contradict. I sometimes forget.

Benjamin Disraeli, on dealing with Queen Victoria

Blessed are they that have nothing to say, and who cannot be persuaded to say it.

James Russell Lowell

There is only one thing in the world worse than being talked about and that is not being talked about.

Oscar Wilde, *The Picture of Dorian Gray*, 1891

Arguments are to be avoided; they are always vulgar and often convincing.

Oscar Wilde, *The Picture of Dorian Gray*, 1891

People who want to say merely what is sensible should say it to themselves before they come down to breakfast in the morning, never after.
Oscar Wilde

Darling: the popular form of address used in speaking to a member of the opposite sex whose name you cannot at the moment remember.
Oliver Herford

Three things matter in a speech: who says it, how he says it and what he says – and of the three, the last matters least.
John, Viscount Morley

Confidant, confidante, n. One entrusted by A with the secrets of B, confided to himself by C.
Ambrose Bierce, *The Devil's Dictionary*, 1911

Never say anything remarkable. It is sure to be wrong.
Mark Rutherford, *Last Pages from a Journal*, 1915

Repartee is what you wish you'd said.
Heywood Broun

How awful to reflect that what people say of us is true.
Logan Pearsall Smith, *All Trivia*, 1931

Do you want to injure someone's reputation? Don't speak ill of him, speak too well.
André Siegfried, *Quelques maximes*, 1943

If you can't convince them, confuse them.
Harry S. Truman

The human brain starts working the moment you are born and never stops until you stand up to speak in public.
Sir George Jessel, 1949

What are compliments? They are things you say to people when you don't know what else to say.
Constance Jones

Conversation is anecdote tempered by interruption.
Raymond Mortimer

When there are two conflicting versions of the story, the wise course is to believe the one in which people appear at their worst.
H. Allen Smith, *Let the Crabgrass Grow*, 1960

If you can talk brilliantly about a problem, it can create the consoling illusion that it has been mastered.
Stanley Kubrick

The telephone is a good way to talk to people without having to offer them a drink.
Fran Lebowitz, in *Interview* magazine, 1978

The opposite of talking isn't listening. The opposite of talking is waiting.
Fran Lebowitz, *Social Studies*, 1981

I hate to spread rumours – but what else can one do with them.
Amanda Lear

See also BORES

TELEVISION & RADIO

Television has proved that people will look at anything rather than at each other.
Ann Landers

Television – the bland leading the bland.
Anonymous, quoted in *The Filmgoer's Book of Quotes*, ed. L. Halliwell, 1973

No television performance takes as much preparation as an off-the-cuff talk.
Richard M. Nixon

A television critic is a man forced to be literate about the illiterate, witty about the witless and coherent about the incoherent.
John Crosby, 1955

Television is chewing gum for the eyes.
Fred Allen

Television is summer stock in an iron lung.

Anonymous actor, quoted in the *Manchester Guardian*, 1959

If TV were to do the Second Coming of Christ in full colour for an hour, there would a considerable number of stations which would decline to carry it on the grounds that a Western or a quiz show would be more profitable.

Ed Murrow, 1964

TV is the golden goose that lays scrambled eggs; and it is futile, and probably fatal, to beat it for not laying caviar.

Lee Loevinger, 1966

There is an insistent tendency among serious social scientists to think of any institution which features rhymed and singing commercials, intense and lachrymose voices urging highly improbable enjoyment, caricatures of the human oesophagus in normal or impaired operation, and which hints implausibly at opportunities for antiseptic seduction as inherently trivial. This is a great mistake. The industrial system is profoundly dependent on commercial television and could not exist in its present form without it.

John Kenneth Galbraith, *The New Industrial State*, 1967

Television is the first truly democratic culture – the first culture available to everybody and entirely governed by what the people want. The most terrifying thing is what the people do want.

Clive Barnes, in the *New York Times*, 1969

Television has lifted the manufacture of banality out of the sphere of handicraft and placed it in that of a major industry.

Nathalie Sarraute, in the *Times Literary Supplement*, 1960

Imitation is the sincerest form of television.

Fred Allen, quoted in *Esquire* magazine, 1971

Television is an invention that permits you to be be entertained in your living room by people you wouldn't have in your home.

David Frost, on CBS-TV, 1971

Television – a medium. So called because it is neither rare nor well done.

**Ernie Kovacs, quoted in *The Filmgoer's Book of Quotes*,
ed. L. Halliwell, 1973**

Television . . . the longest amateur night in history.

Robert Carson, quoted in *The Filmgoer's Book of Quotes*, ed. L. Halliwell, 1973

I'm delighted with television because it used to be that films were the lowest form of art. Now we've got something to look down on.

Billy Wilder

Television is democracy at its ugliest.

Paddy Chayevsky

In California they don't throw their garbage away – they make it into television shows.

Woody Allen, *Annie Hall*, 1977

Television is a whore. Any man who wants her full favours can have them in five minutes with a pistol.

Anonymous hijacker, quoted in *Esquire* magazine, 1977

If any reader of this book is in the grip of some habit of which he is deeply ashamed, I advise him not to give way to it in secret but to do it on television. No one will pass him with averted gaze on the other side of the street. People will cross the road at the risk of losing their own lives in order to say 'We saw you on the telly.'

Quentin Crisp, *How To Become a Virgin*, 1981

Television is more interesting than people. If it were not, we should have people standing in the corners of our rooms.

Alan Coren, quoted in *The Penguin Dictionary of Modern Quotations*, ed. J. and M. Cohen, 1981

Radio news is bearable: this is due to the fact that while the news is being broadcast the DJ is not allowed to talk.

Fran Lebowitz

See also JOURNALISM

TIME

Time is a great teacher, but unfortunately it kills all its pupils.

Hector Berlioz

Time is that in which all things pass away; it is the form under which the will to live has revealed to it that its efforts are in vain; it is the agent by which at every moment all things in our hands become as nothing and lose all value.

Arthur Schopenhauer, *The Vanity of Existence*, 1851

Between time and ourselves, it is a struggle as to which shall kill the other.

Guy Delaforest, quoted in *Reflections on the Art of Life* by J.R. Solly, 1902

There is no time like the pleasant.

Addison Mizner and Oliver Herford, *The Entirely New Cynic's Calendar*, 1905

Time is so much kinder to a man than to a woman that a careful bachelor often lives to flirt with the daughter of the woman he once came within an ace of marrying.

Arthur Binstead, *Pitcher's Proverbs*, 1909

Future, n. That period of time in which our affairs prosper, our friends are true and our happiness is assured.

Ambrose Bierce, *The Devil's Dictionary*, 1911

So little time, so little to do.

Oscar Levant

Time: that which man is always trying to kill, but which ends in killing him.

Herbert Spencer

Satire is tragedy plus time.

Lenny Bruce, quoted in *The Essential Lenny Bruce*, ed. J. Cohen, 1967

Hindsight is always 20:20.

Billy Wilder

See also AGE, EXPERIENCE

TRAVEL

Visits always give pleasure: if not in the arrival, then on the departure.
Edouard Le Berquier

Pedestrian: anyone who is knocked down by a motor-car.
J.B. Morton ('Beachcomber')

If you look like your passport photo, in all probability you need the journey.
Earl Wilson, in the Ladies Home Journal, 1961

Holidays are an expensive trial of strength. The only satisfaction comes from survival.
Jonathan Miller, in the Daily Herald, 1962

It is imperative when flying coach that you restrain any tendency toward the vividly imaginative. For although it may momentarily appear to be the case, it is not at all likely that the cabin is entirely inhabited by crying babies smoking inexpensive domestic cigars.
Fran Lebowitz, Social Studies, 1981

TRUE BELIEVERS

Pure in show, an upright holy man,
Corrupt within – and called a Puritan.
Anonymous, A Song of the Puritan, c.1605

A pious man is one who would be an atheist if the king were.
Jean de La Bruyère, The Characters, 1688

No rogue like to the godly rogue.
Thomas Fuller, M.D., The Holy and Profane State, 1732

Suspect, in general, those who remarkably affect any one virtue . . . for they are commonly imposters.
Lord Chesterfield, Letters to his Son, 1774

Bear-baiting was esteemed heathenish and un-christian; the sport of it, not the inhumanity, gave offence.
David Hume, The History of Great Britain, 1754–62

Men whose trade is rat-catching love to catch rats; the bug destroyer seizes on his bug with delight; and the suppressor is gratified by finding his vice.

Sydney Smith, on self-appointed moralists, 1801

We have no doubt but that the immediate effect of a voluntary combination for the suppression of vice is an involuntary combination in favour of the vices to be suppressed.

Sydney Smith, on the newly formed Society for the Suppression of Vice, 1801

As no roads are as rough as those that have just been mended, so no sinners are as intolerant as those that have just turned saints.

Charles Caleb Colton, *Lacon*, 1820

The Puritan hated bear-baiting, not because it gave pain to the bear, but because it gave pleasure to the spectators.

Thomas Babington Macaulay, Baron Macaulay

The Puritans nobly fled from a land of despotism to a land of freedom, where they could not only enjoy their own religion, but prevent everybody else from enjoying *his*.

Artemus Ward (C.F. Browne), *The London Punch Letters*, 1866

The reformer . . . unable to beget or bear, possessing neither fecundity nor virility, endowed with the contempt of men and the disdain of women, and doomed to sterility, isolation and extinction.

J.J. Ingalls, speech, 1885

Any preoccupation with ideas of what is right and wrong in conduct shows an arrested intellectual development.

Oscar Wilde, *Phrases and Philosophies for the Use of the Young*, 1894

The more things a man is ashamed of, the more respectable he is.

George Bernard Shaw, *Man and Superman*, 1903

No people do so much harm as those who go about doing good.

Bishop Mandell Creighton, quoted in *Life and Letters*, 1904

All reformers, however strict their social conscience, live in houses just as big as they can pay for.

Logan Pearsall Smith

Unless the reformer can invent something which substitutes attractive virtues for attractive vices, he will fail.
Walter Lippmann, *A Preface to Politics*, **1914**

Puritanism – the haunting fear that someone, somewhere, may be happy.
H.L. Mencken, *A Book of Burlesques*, **1920**

The infliction of cruelty with a good conscience is a delight to moralists – that is why they invented hell.
Bertrand Russell, *Sceptical Essays*, **1928**

A reformer is a man who rides through a sewer in a glass-bottomed boat.
James J. Walker

The most distressing thing that can happen to a prophet is to be proved wrong. The next most distressing thing is to be proved right.
Aldous Huxley, *Brave New World Revisited*, **1958**

Puritanism . . . helps us enjoy our misery while we are inflicting it on others.
Marcel Ophuls, in *The Listener* **magazine, 1978**

The name 'moralist' sounds like a perversion – one wouldn't be surprised at finding it suddenly in Krafft-Ebing.
Elias Canetti, *The Human Province*, **1978**

Fear prophets . . . and those prepared to die for the truth, for as a rule they make many others die with them.
Umberto Eco, *The Name of the Rose*, **1981**

See also BELIEF, FAITH, HYPOCRISY, IDEALS, IDEAS, MORALS, RELIGION, TRUTH

TRUTH

If you want to annoy your neighbours, tell the truth about them.
Pietro Aretino

Truth always lags behind, limping along on the arm of time.
Baltasar Gracian, *The Art of Worldly Wisdom*, **1647**

Truth . . . never comes into the World, but like a Bastard, to the ignominy of him that brought her forth.

John Milton

Truth does not do so much good in the world as its appearances do evil.

François, Duc de La Rochefoucauld, Maxims, 1665

The exact contrary of what is generally believed is often the truth.

Jean de La Bruyère, The Characters, 1688

A Man that should call everything by its right Name would hardly pass the Streets without being knocked down as a common Enemy.

George Savile, Marquis of Halifax, Political, Moral and Miscellaneous Thoughts and Reflexions, c.1694

Nothing has an uglier look to us than reason, when it is not on our side

George Savile, Marquis of Halifax, Political, Moral and Miscellaneous Thoughts and Reflexions, c.1694

Honour's a fine imaginary notion
That draws in raw and unexperienced men
To real mischiefs.

Joseph Addison, Cato, 1713

Beware of telling an improbable truth.

Thomas Fuller, M.D., Introductio ad Prudentiam, 1727

Seldom any splendid story is wholly true.

Samuel Johnson, Works vol. vii, 1787

To announce truths, to propose something useful to mankind, is an infallible receipt for being persecuted.

Voltaire, quoted in A Cynic's Breviary by J.R. Solly, 1925

Truth lights – but money warms.

Anonymous

A man had rather have a hundred lies told of him, than one truth which he does not wish should be told.

Samuel Johnson, The Life of Samuel Johnson by J. Boswell, 1791

In argument, truth always prevails finally, in politics falsehood always.

Walter Savage Landor

No man speaks the truth or lives a true life two minutes together.
   Ralph Waldo Emerson, *Journals*, 1909–14

Something unpleasant is coming when men are anxious to tell the truth.
   Benjamin Disraeli

It is the customary fate of new truths to begin as heresies and to end as superstitions.
   T.H. Huxley, in *Science and Culture*, 1893–4

When you want to fool the world, tell the truth.
   Otto von Bismarck

All true knowledge contradicts common sense.
   Bishop Mandell Creighton, in *Life and Letters*, 1904

It is always the best policy to tell the truth, unless, of course, you are an exceptionally good liar.
   Jerome K. Jerome

A thing is not necessarily true because a man dies for it.
   Oscar Wilde, *The Portrait of Mr W.H.*, 1889

If one tells the truth, one is sure, sooner or later, to be found out.
   Oscar Wilde, *Phrases and Philosophies for the Use of the Young*, 1894

Vulgarity is simply the conduct of other people, just as falsehoods are the truths of other people.
   Oscar Wilde, *An Ideal Husband*, 1895

The truth is rarely pure and never simple. Modern life would be very tedious if it were either, and modern literature a complete impossibility.
   Oscar Wilde, *The Importance of Being Earnest*, 1895

Liar: one who tells an unpleasant truth.
   Oliver Herford

Tell the truth and shame the – family.
   Addison Mizner and Oliver Herford, *The Entirely New Cynic's Calendar*, 1905

The course of true anything never does run smooth.
Samuel Butler, *Notebooks*, 1912

Some men love truth so much that they seem to be in continual fear lest she should catch a cold on overexposure.
Samuel Butler, *Notebooks*, 1912

Any fool can tell the truth, but it requires a man of some sense to know how to lie well.
Samuel Butler, *Notebooks*, 1912

Truth – something somehow discreditable to someone.
H.L. Mencken, *Sententiae*, 1916

It is unfortunate, considering enthusiasm moves the world, that so few enthusiasts can be trusted to speak the truth.
Arthur James, Earl Balfour, letter, 1918

To die for an idea – it is unquestionably noble. But how much nobler it would be if men died for ideas that were true.
H.L. Mencken

A platitude is simply a truth repeated till people get tired of hearing it.
Stanley Baldwin, First Earl of Bewdley, 1924

By telling the truth one saves oneself from a multitude of fatiguing cares.
E.V. Lucas

What is truth? We must adopt a pragmatic definition: it is what is believed to be the truth. A lie that is put across therefore becomes the truth and may, therefore, be justified. The difficulty is to keep up lying . . . it is simpler to tell the truth and if a sufficient emergency arises, to tell one big thumping lie that will then be believed.
Ministry of Information, memo on the maintenance of British civilian morale, 1939

The nearest approach to immortality for any truth is by its becoming a platitude.
Paul Eldridge, *Horns of Glass*, 1943

True, you can't take it with you, but then, that's not the place where it comes in handy.
Brendan Francis

Believe those who are seeking the truth; doubt those who find it.
André Gide, *So Be It*, 1959

Nagging is the repetition of unpalatable truths.
Dr Edith Summerskill, in the *Observer*, 1960

There aren't any embarrassing questions – only embarrassing answers.
Carl Rowan, in the *New Yorker* magazine, 1963

Truth and Myth are the same thing, . . . you have to simulate passion to feel it, . . . man is a creature of ceremony.
Jean-Paul Sartre, *The Words*, 1964

Truth means not having to guess what a candidate means.
Gerald Ford, 1976

The truth is always libellous.
George Finey, in the *Sydney Morning Herald*, 1981

Truth is what one is obliged to tell policemen.
Bertrand Russell, quoted, 1984

See also BELIEF, FAITH, HONESTY, IDEALS, IDEAS, MORALS, RELIGION, TRUE BELIEVERS

THE UNITED STATES

You can always get the truth from an American statesman after he has turned seventy or given up all hope of the Presidency.
Wendell Philips, 1860

In America the President rules for four years and journalism governs for ever and ever.
Oscar Wilde

When good Americans die, they go to Paris; when bad Americans die, they go to America.
Oscar Wilde, *A Woman of No Importance*, 1893 (based on Thomas G. Appleton's [1812–84] 'When good Americans die, they go to Paris' c.1860)

The American nation in the sixth ward is a fine people; they love the eagle – on the back of a dollar.

Finley Peter Dunne

America is the only nation in history which, miraculously, has gone directly from barbarism to degeneration without the usual interval of civilisation.

Georges Clemenceau

Q: If you find so much that is unworthy of reverence in the United States, why do you live here? Mencken: Why do men go to zoos?

H.L. Mencken, *Prejudices* **5th series, 1926**

America . . . where laws and customs alike are based on the dreams of spinsters.

Bertrand Russell, *Marriage and Morals***, 1929**

All American writing gives me the impression that Americans don't care for girls at all. What the American male really wants is two things: he wants to be blown by a stranger while reading a newspaper and he wants to be fucked by his buddy when he's drunk. Everything else is society.

W.H. Auden, *The Table-Talk of W.H. Auden,*
ed. Alan Ansen, 1990

In America everybody is of the opinion that he has no social superiors, since all men are equal, but he does not admit that he has no social inferiors.

Bertrand Russell, *Unpopular Essays***, 1950**

In America any boy may become President, and I suppose that's just the risk he takes.

Adlai Stevenson, 1952

The organisation of American society is an interlocking system of semi-monopolies notoriously venal, an electorate notoriously unenlightened, misled by a mass media notoriously phoney.

Paul Goodman, *The Community of Scholars***, 1962**

America . . . just a nation of two hundred million used car salesmen with all the money we need to buy guns and no qualms about killing anybody else in the world who tries to make us uncomfortable.

Hunter S. Thompson, *Fear and Loathing on the Campaign Trail***, 1972**

The hatred Americans have for their own government is pathological ... at one level it is simply thwarted greed: since our religion is making a buck, giving a part of that buck to any government is an act against nature.

Gore Vidal

No American who works for the CIA is a spy. A spy is a foreign agent who commits treason.

Jim Keehner, in *New Times* magazine, 1976

If you're going to America, bring your own food.

Fran Lebowitz, *Social Studies*, 1981

Whatever it is that the government does, sensible Americans would prefer that the government do it to somebody else. This is the idea behind foreign policy.

P.J. O'Rourke, *Parliament of Whores*, 1991

The American political system is like fast food – mushy, insipid, made out of disgusting parts of things and everybody wants some.

P.J. O'Rourke, *Parliament of Whores*, 1991

VIRTUE

If you can't be good, be careful.

Anonymous

Everything is good or everything is bad, according to the votes they gain.

Baltasar Gracian, *The Art of Worldly Wisdom*, 1647

Virtue, among other definitions, may thus be defined: an action against the will.

Anonymous, *Characters and Observations*, c.1725

Those whom their virtue restrains from deceiving others are often disposed by their vanity to deceive themselves.

Samuel Johnson, *Works* vol. viii, 1787

To many people virtue consists mainly in repenting faults, not in avoiding them.

Georg Christoph Lichtenberg, *Reflections*, 1799

Fresh air and innocence are good if you don't take too much of them.
Oliver Wendell Holmes

The good (I am convinced, for one)
Is but the bad one leaves undone.
Wilhelm Busch

It is good to be without vice, but it is not good to be without temptations.
Walter Bagehot

No one does good to men with impunity.
Auguste Rodin

Good breeding consists in concealing how much we think of ourselves and how little we think of the other person.
Mark Twain

Few things are harder to put up with than the annoyance of a good example.
Mark Twain

Every virtue has its privileges – for example, that of contributing its own little faggot to the pyre of the condemned.
Friedrich Wilhelm Nietzsche, *Human, All Too Human*, 1878

To be good, according to the vulgar standard of goodness is obviously quite easy. It merely requires a certain amount of sordid terror, a certain lack of imaginative thought, and a certain low passion for middle-class respectability.
Oscar Wilde, *The Critic as Artist*, 1890

Good resolutions are useless attempts to interfere with scientific laws. Their origin is pure vanity. Their result is absolutely nil. They give us, now and then, some of those luxurious sterile emotions that have a certain charm for the weak . . . They are simply cheques that men draw on a bank where they have no account.
Oscar Wilde, *The Picture of Dorian Gray*, 1891

Men become old, but they never become good.
Oscar Wilde, *Lady Windermere's Fan*, 1892

Do not ask me to be kind; just ask me to act as though I were.

Jules Renard, *Journal,* **1898**

Self-denial is not a virtue: it is only the effect of prudence on rascality.

George Bernard Shaw, *Man and Superman,* **1903**

What is virtue but the trades unionism of the married?

George Bernard Shaw, *Man and Superman,* **1903**

Remorse is, after all, a thoroughly wholesome and healthy secretion. With what bitter anguish do we now recall those awful early virtues which we now know to have been only wasted opportunities.

Arthur Binstead, *Pitcher's Proverbs,* **1909**

On virtue: Our vocabulary is defective: we give the same name to woman's lack of temptation and man's lack of opportunity.

Ambrose Bierce, *Collected Works,* **1909–12**

I forget who it was that recommended men for their soul's good to do each day two things they disliked . . . it is a precept that I have followed scrupulously; for every day I have got up and I have gone to bed.

W. Somerset Maugham, *The Moon and Sixpence,* **1919**

A thing called Ethics, whose nature was confusing but if you had it you were a High-Class Realtor and if you hadn't you were a shyster, a piker and a fly-by-night. These virtues awakened Confidence and enabled you to handle Bigger Propositions. But they didn't imply that you were to be impractical and refuse to take twice the value of a house if a buyer was such an idiot that he didn't force you down on the asking price.

Sinclair Lewis, *Babbitt,* **1922**

Nobody's interested in sweetness and light.

Hedda Hopper

Virtue is its own reward – but it has no sale at the box office.

Mae West

Too much of a good thing is simply wonderful.

Mae West

There are no good girls gone wrong – only bad girls found out.

Mae West, screenplay for *Belle of the Nineties*, 1934

So far as we are human, what we do must be either evil or good: so far as we do evil or good, we are human; and it is better, in a paradoxical way, to do evil than to do nothing: at least we exist.

T.S. Eliot, essay on Baudelaire

It's the good girls who keep the diaries; the bad girls never have the time.

Tallulah Bankhead

No good deed goes unpunished.

Clare Booth Luce, quoted in *The Book of Laws* by H. Faber, 1980

Good behaviour is the last refuge of mediocrity.

Henry Haskins, *Meditations in Wall Street*, 1940

There's Mellot. Take a good look at him. A nicer sort of guy never put shoes on. Fine fellow, but he didn't come to win, that's the answer. Nice guys finish last.

Leo Durocher, 1946

Many an attack of depression is nothing but the expression of regret at having to be virtuous.

Dr Wilhelm Stekhel

If you can't say anything good about someone, sit right here by me.

Alice Roosevelt Longworth, general greeting

Saintliness is also a temptation.

Jean Anouilh, *Becket*, 1959

'For your own good' is a persuasive argument that will eventually make a man agree to his own destruction.

Janet Frame, *Faces in the Water*, 1961

Virtue is not photogenic.

Kirk Douglas

Most plain girls are virtuous because of the scarcity of opportunity to be otherwise.

Maya Angelou, *I Know Why the Caged Bird Sings*, 1969

See also SIN

VOTING

I never vote for anyone. I always vote against.
W.C. Fields

Voting is merely a handy device; it is not to be identified with democracy.
G.D.H. Cole, *Essays in Social Theory*, 1950

Voting is simply a way of determining which side is the stronger without putting it to the test of fighting.
H.L. Mencken, *Minority Report*, 1956

Ask a man which way he is going to vote, and he will probably tell you. Ask him, however, why, and vagueness is all.
Bernard Levin, in the *Daily Mail*, 1964

If the people of a democracy are allowed to do so, they will vote away the freedoms which are essential to that democracy.
Snell Putney, *The Conquest of Society*, 1972

The difference between a Democracy and a Dictatorship is that in a Democracy you vote first and take orders later; in a Dictatorship you don't have to waste your time voting.
Charles Bukowski, *Erections, Ejaculations, Exhibitions and Tales of Ordinary Madness*, 1972

If voting changed anything, they'd make it illegal.
Graffito, London, 1979

See also DEMOCRACY, GOVERNMENT, LEADERS, PARTIES, POLITICIANS, POLITICS

WAR

The war is just which is necessary.
Niccolò Machiavelli, *The Prince*, 1513

War is delightful to those who have had no experience of it.
Desiderius Erasmus

Force and fraud are in war the two cardinal virtues.
Thomas Hobbes, *Leviathan*, 1651

Even war is pusillanimously carried on in this degenerate age: quarter is given; towns are taken and the people spared; even in a storm a woman can hardly hope for the benefit of a rape.

Lord Chesterfield, *Letters to his Son*, 1774

War is the faro table of government, and nations the dupes of the games.

Thomas Paine, *The Rights of Man*, 1791-2

A war, or any wild goose chase, is, as the vulgar use the phrase, a lucky turn up of patronage for the minister, whose chief merit is the art of keeping himself in place.

Mary Wollstonecraft, *A Vindication of the Rights of Woman*, 1792

There is more misery inflicted upon mankind by one year of war than by all the civil peculations and oppressions of a century. Yet it is a state into which the mass of mankind rush with the greatest avidity, hailing official murderers, in scarlet, gold and cock's feathers, as the greatest and most glorious of human creatures.

Sydney Smith

A man will fight harder for his interests than for his rights.

Napoleon Bonaparte, *Maxims*, 1804-15

There are no manifestoes like cannon and musketry.

Arthur Wellesley, Duke of Wellington

A great part of the information obtained in war is contradictory, a still greater part is false, and by far the greatest part is of doubtful character.

Karl von Clausewitz, *On War*, 1832

The lower people everywhere desire war. Not so unwisely; there is then a demand for lower people – to be shot!

Thomas Carlyle, *Sartor Resartus*, 1833-4

Such I hold to be the genuine use of gunpowder: that it makes all men alike tall.

Thomas Carlyle

Nothing should be left to an invaded people but their eyes for weeping.

Otto von Bismarck, 1862

As long as war is regarded as wicked it will always have its fascination. When it is looked upon as vulgar, it will cease to be popular.

Oscar Wilde, *Intentions*, 1891

The love of fair play is a spectator's virtue, not a principal's.

George Bernard Shaw, *Maxims for Revolutionists*, 1903

Nothing is ever done in this world until men are prepared to kill one another if it is not done.

George Bernard Shaw, *Major Barbara*, 1907

Battle, n. A method of untying with the teeth a political knot that will not yield to the tongue.

Ambrose Bierce, *The Devil's Dictionary*, 1911

My dear . . . the noise! And the people!

Ernest Thesiger (alleged), commenting on his involvement in the battle of the Somme, 1916

War is a series of catastrophes which result in a victory.

Georges Clemenceau

War hath no fury like a non-combatant.

C.E. Montague, *Disenchantment*, 1922

War is hell . . . when you're getting licked.

Brigadier-General Henry J. O'Reilly, amending General Sherman's famous dictum, 1931

When the leaders speak of peace
The common folk know
That war is coming
When the leaders curse war
The mobilization order is already written out.

Bertolt Brecht, *From a German War Primer*, 1938

War is like love, it always finds a way.

Bertolt Brecht, *Mother Courage*, 1941

On the wall in chalk is written
'They want war'
He who wrote it has already fallen.

Bertolt Brecht, in *Collected Poems 1913–1956*, 1976

It is easier to fight for one's principles than to live up to them.
Alfred Adler, quoted in *Alfred Adler* by P. Bottome, 1939

Naturally the common people don't want war . . . but after all it is the leaders of a country who determine policy, and it is always a simple matter to drag the people along, whether it is a democracy, or a fascist dictatorship, or a parliament, or a communist dictatorship. All you have to do is tell them they are being attacked, and denounce the pacifists for lack of patriotism and exposing the country to danger. It works the same in every country.
Hermann Göring, quoted in *The People's Almanac*, 1976

You can't say civilisation don't advance . . . for in every war they kill you a new way.
Will Rogers, *The Autobiography of Will Rogers*, 1949

People who are vigorous and brutal often find war enjoyable, provided that it is a victorious war and that there is not too much interference with rape and plunder. This is a great help in persuading people that wars are righteous.
Bertrand Russell, *Unpopular Essays*, 1950

A prisoner of war is a man who tries to kill you and fails, and then asks you not to kill him.
Sir Winston Churchill, 1952

War is the unfolding of miscalculations.
Barbara Tuchman, *The Guns of August*, 1962

All wars are popular for the first thirty days.
Arthur Schlesinger Jr

I have never understood this liking for war. It panders to instincts already catered for within the scope of any respectable domestic establishment.
Alan Bennett, *Forty Years On*, 1968

No wars are unintentional or 'accidental'. What is often unintended is the length and bloodiness of the war. Defeat too is unintended.
Geoffrey Blainey, *The Causes of War*, 1973

Violence is the repartee of the illiterate.
Alan Brien, in *Punch* magazine, 1973

People who fight fire with fire usually end up with ashes.
  Abigail van Buren, 1974

War is capitalism with the gloves off.
  Tom Stoppard, *Travesties*, 1974

Only the winners decide what were war crimes.
  Gary Wills, in the *New York Times*, 1975

Usually, when a lot of men get together, it's called war.
  Mel Brooks, in *The Listener* magazine, 1978

Violence is the way of ensuring a hearing for moderation.
  William C. O'Brien, quoted in the *Observer*, 1981

There is no force more terroristic than a national state at war.
  Richard E. Rubenstein, *Alchemists of Revolution: Terrorism in the Modern World*, 1987

WEAKNESS

It's going to be fun to watch and see how long the meek can keep the earth when they inherit it.
  Kin Hubbard, *Abe Martin's Sayings*, 1915

Let the meek inherit the earth – they have it coming to them.
  James Thurber, in *Life* magazine, 1960

The weak have one weapon: the errors of those who think they are strong.
  Georges Bidault, quoted in the *Observer*, 1962

That weakness in human nature which goes by the name of strength.
  Peter Ustinov, in the *Listener* magazine, 1974

See also POWER

WIVES

He knows little who will tell his wife all he knows.
  Thomas Fuller, D.D., *The Holy State and the Profane State*, 1642

Next to no wife, a good wife is best.
Thomas Fuller, D.D., *The Holy State and the Profane State*, 1642

Here lies my wife: here let her lie! Now she's at rest, and so am I.
John Dryden, epitaph intended for his wife

It goes far towards reconciling me to being a woman when I reflect I am thus in no danger of marrying one.
Lady Mary Wortley Montagu

The comfortable estate of widowhood is the only hope that keeps up a wife's spirits.
John Gay, *The Beggar's Opera*, 1728

A dead wife under the table is the best goods in a man's house.
Jonathan Swift, *Polite Conversation*, 1738

The only solid and lasting peace between a man and his wife is, doubtless, a separation.
Lord Chesterfield, *Letters to his Son*, 1774

The man who enters his wife's dressing room is either a philosopher or a fool.
Honoré de Balzac, *The Physiology of Marriage*, 1829

After forty, men have married their habits, and wives are only an item in the list, and not the most important.
George Meredith

He gave way to the queer, savage feeling that sometimes takes by the throat a husband twenty years married, when he sees, across the table, the same face of his wedded wife, and knows that, as he has sat facing it, so must he continue to sit until the day of its death or his own.
Rudyard Kipling, *Plain Tales from the Hills*, 1888

A man likes his wife to be just clever enough to comprehend his cleverness, and just stupid enough to admire it.
Israel Zangwill

It is most dangerous for a husband to pay any attention to his wife in public. It always makes people think that he beats her when they are alone.
Oscar Wilde, *Lady Windermere's Fan*, 1892

A good wife is good, but the best wife is not so good as no wife at all.

Thomas Hardy

Constance: I'm tired of being the modern wife.
Martha: What do you mean by the modern wife?
Constance: A prostitute who doesn't deliver the goods.

W. Somerset Maugham, *The Constant Wife*, 1926

Never feel remorse for what you have thought about your wife. She has thought much worse things about you.

Jean Rostand, *Le mariage*, 1927

A man does not buy his wife a fur coat to keep her warm, but to keep her pleasant.

Sir Seymour Hicks, in the *Observer*, 1946

When a man steals your wife, there is no better revenge than to let him keep her.

Sacha Guitry, *Elles et toi*, 1948

There's nothing like a good dose of another woman to make a man appreciate his wife.

Clare Booth Luce

A man should not insult his wife publicly, at parties. He should insult her in the privacy of the home.

James Thurber, *Thurber Country*, 1953

Of course a platonic relationship is possible – but only between husband and wife.

Ladies Home Journal

A psychiatrist is a fellow who asks you a lot of expensive questions your wife asks you for nothing.

Joey Adams, *Cindy and I*, 1959

A man does not have to be a bigamist to have one wife too many.

Farmer's Almanac, 1966

Happy is the man with a wife to tell him what to do and a secretary to do it.

Lord Mancroft, in the *Observer*, 1966

The husband who doesn't tell his wife everything probably reasons that what she doesn't know won't hurt him.

Leo J. Burke, quoted in *Peter's Quotations*, ed. Dr L. Peter, 1977

See also AFFAIRS, DIVORCE, HUSBANDS, LOVE, LOVERS, MARRIAGE

WOMEN

Don't assume that every sad-eyed woman has loved and lost – she may have got him.

Anonymous

Whether a pretty woman grants or witholds her favours, she always likes to be asked for them.

Ovid, *Ars Amatoria*, c.AD8

For women's tears are but the sweat of eyes.

Juvenal, *Satires*, c.AD100

Trust not a woman when she cries
For she'll pump water from her eyes
With a wet finger, and in faster showers
Than April when he rains down flowers.

Thomas Dekker, *The Honest Whore*, 1604

If that the earth could teem with woman's tears,
Each drop she falls would prove a crocodile.

William Shakespeare, *Othello*, 1604

There's nothing sooner dries than woman's tears.

John Webster, *The White Devil*, 1612

Most virtuous women are like hidden treasures: safe only because they are not sought after.

François, Duc de La Rochefoucauld, *Maxims*, 1665

The cruellest revenge of a woman is to remain faithful to a man.

Jacques Bossuet

Once a woman has given you her heart you can never get rid of the rest of her body.

John Vanbrugh, *The Relapse*, 1696

Men who cherish for women the highest respect are seldom popular with them.
  Joseph Addison

Every day men sleep with women they do not love and do not sleep with women whom they do love.
  Denis Diderot, *Jacques le fataliste,* **1773**

What is woman? Only one of Nature's agreeable blunders.
  Hannah Cowley, *Who's The Dupe?,* **1779**

Women all want to be ladies, which is simply to have nothing to do, but listlessly to go they scarcely care where, for they cannot tell what.
  Mary Wollstonecraft, *Vindication of the Rights of Woman,* **1792**

A woman, if she should have the misfortune of knowing anything, should conceal it as well as she can.
  Jane Austen, *Pride and Prejudice,* **1813**

In her first passion woman loves her lover.
In all the others all she loves is love.
  George Gordon, Lord Byron, *Don Juan,* **1819–24**

It is only the man whose intellect is clouded by his sexual impulses that could give the name of 'the fair sex' to that undersized, narrow-shouldered, broad-hipped and short-legged race.
  Arthur Schopenhauer, *On Women*

Women will pardon any offence rather than a neglect of their charms.
  Charles Caleb Colton, *Lacon,* **1820**

The man's desire is for the woman, but the woman's desire is rarely other than for the desire of the man.
  Samuel Taylor Coleridge, *Table Talk,* **1836**

Man has his will, but woman has her way.
  Oliver Wendell Holmes, *The Autocrat of the Breakfast-Table,* **1857–8**

I'm not denyin' the women are foolish: God Almighty made 'em to match the men.
  George Eliot, *Adam Bede,* **1859**

Was there ever any domination which did not appear natural to those who possessed it.

John Stuart Mill, _The Subjection of Women_, 1869

Woman was God's second mistake.

Friedrich Wilhelm Nietzsche

The only way a woman can ever reform a man is by boring him so completely that he loses all possible interest in life.

Oscar Wilde, _The Picture of Dorian Gray_, 1891

Crying is the refuge of plain women, but the ruin of pretty ones.

Oscar Wilde, _Lady Windermere's Fan_, 1892

One can always recognise women who trust their husbands. They look so thoroughly unhappy.

Oscar Wilde, _Lady Windermere's Fan_, 1892

The history of women is the history of the worst tyranny the world has ever known: the tyranny of the weak over the strong. It is the only tyranny that ever lasts.

Oscar Wilde, _A Woman of No Importance_, 1893

And a woman is only a woman, but a good cigar is a Smoke.

Rudyard Kipling, _The Betrothed_, 1899

A woman will always sacrifice herself if you give her the opportunity. It is her favourite form of self-indulgence.

W. Somerset Maugham

A plain woman will have nothing forgiven her. Her fate is such that the parents of uncomely female infants should be compelled to put them to death at birth.

Miles Franklin, _My Brilliant Career_, 1901

Shame is the feeling you have when you agree with the woman who loves you that you are the man she thinks you are.

Carl Sandburg, _Incidentals_, 1905

Physically there is nothing to distinguish human society from the farm-yard except that children are more troublesome and costly than chickens and women are not so completely enslaved as farm stock.

George Bernard Shaw, _Getting Married_, 1908

Women at least have elegant dresses. But what can men use to cover their emptiness?

Karl Kraus, *Half Truths and One and a Half Truths*, 1986

A woman occasionally is quite a serviceable substitute for masturbation. It takes an abundance of imagination, to be sure.

Karl Kraus

Dream: fem. a term used by a woman discussing a hat; masc. term describing the woman used by the man who is destined to buy the hat.

Oliver Herford and John Clay, *Cupid's Cyclopedia*, 1910

Adam's Rib: the original bone of contention.

Oliver Herford and John Clay, *Cupid's Cyclopedia*, 1910

Woman: the peg on which the wit hangs his jest, the preacher his text, the cynic his grouch and the sinner his justification.

Helen Rowland

Artlessness, n. A certain engaging quality to which women attain by long study and severe practice.

Ambrose Bierce, *The Devil's Dictionary*, 1911

Ugliness, n. A gift of the gods to certain women, entailing virtue without humility.

Ambrose Bierce, *The Devil's Dictionary*, 1911

The woman who is really kind to dogs is always one who has failed to inspire sympathy in men.

Max Beerbohm, *Zuleika Dobson*, 1911

If God considered woman a fit helpmeet for man, he must have had a very poor opinion of man.

Samuel Butler

Brigands demand your money or your life; women require both.

Samuel Butler

When women kiss it always reminds one of prize fighters shaking hands.

H.L. Mencken, *Sententiae*, 1916

A woman can forgive a man for the harm he does her, but she can never forgive him for the sacrifices he makes on her account.

W. Somerset Maugham, *The Moon and Sixpence*, 1919

The allurement that women hold out to men is precisely the allurement that Cape Hatteras holds out to sailors: they are enormously dangerous and hence enormously fascinating.

H.L. Mencken, in the *Smart Set* magazine, 1919

What passes for woman's intuition is often nothing more than man's transparency.

George Jean Nathan

Women are always wonderfully the same. Shapes vary a little, that's all.

Aldous Huxley, *Crome Yellow*, 1921

Most women are not as young as they are painted.

Max Beerbohm, *A Defence of Cosmetics*, 1922

A man's women folk, whatever their outward show of respect for his merit and authority, always regard him secretly as an ass, and with something akin to pity . . . In this fact, perhaps, lies one of the best proofs of feminine intelligence or, as the common phrase makes it, feminine intuition.

H.L. Mencken, *In Defence of Women*, 1923

Women with 'pasts' interest men because men hope that history will repeat itself.

Mae West

When one knows women one pities men, but when one studies men, one excuses women.

Achille Tournier, quoted in *A Cynic's Breviary* by J.R. Solly, 1925

Women, as they grow older, rely more and more on cosmetics. Men, as they grow older, rely more and more upon a sense of humour.

George Jean Nathan, in the *American Mercury*, 1925

The only nice women are the ones who have had no opportunities.

Frederick Lonsdale, *The Last of Mrs Cheyney*, 1925

Women are like elephants to me: I like to look at them, but I wouldn't
want to own one.

W.C. Fields

To win a woman in the first place one must please her, then undress
her, and then somehow get her clothes back on her. Finally, so she will
allow you to leave her, you've got to annoy her.

Jean Giraudoux, *Amphitryon 38*, 1929

No man who says 'I am as good as you' believes it. The St. Bernard
never says it to the toy dog, nor the scholar to the dunce, nor the
employable to the bum, nor the pretty woman to the plain. The claim
to equality is made only by those who feel themselves to be in some way
inferior.

C.S. Lewis, *Screwtape Proposes a Toast*, 1961

No woman should know more than a man. If she wants to be loved,
that's to say.

Virginia Graham

A woman's best protection is a little money of her own.

Clare Booth Luce

An intelligent woman is one with whom one can be as stupid as one
wants.

Paul Valéry, *Mauvaises pensées et autres*, 1942

Women never refer to their age until it would be wiser to ignore it.

**Anonymous, quoted in *Thesaurus of Epigrams*, ed. E. Fuller,
1943**

God created man, and finding him not sufficiently alone, gave him a
companion to make him feel his solitude more.

Paul Valéry, *Tel quel*, 1943

There is one woman whom fate has destined for each of us. If we miss
her we are saved.

Anonymous, quoted in the *New York Times*, 1948

Woman's virtue is man's greatest invention.

Cornelia Otis Skinner

What a man enjoys about a woman's clothes are his fantasies of how she would look without them.
Brendan Francis

Women like silent men. They think they're listening.
Marcel Achard, in *Quote* magazine, 1956

Women want mediocre men, and men are working hard to become as mediocre as possible.
Margaret Mead, in *Quote* magazine, 1958

There is no sincerity like a woman telling a lie.
Norman Krasna, screenplay for *Indiscreet*, 1958

The woman whose behaviour indicates that she will make a scene if she is told the truth asks to be deceived.
Elizabeth Jenkins, quoted in *The Faber Book of Aphorisms*, ed. W.H. Auden and L. Kronenberger, 1964

A woman needs a man like a fish needs a bicycle.
Anonymous feminist slogan, 1970

Woman is: finally screwing and your groin and buttocks and thighs ache like hell and you're all wet and maybe bloody and it wasn't like a Hollywood movie at all but Jesus at least you're not a virgin any more but is this what it's all about? And meanwhile, he's asking 'Did you come?'
Robin Morgan, *Sisterhood is Powerful*, 1970

The vast majority of women who pretend vaginal orgasms are faking it to 'get the job'.
Ti-Grace Atkinson

A woman's a woman until the day she dies, but a man's only a man as long as he can.
Moms Mabley, in the *New York Daily News*, 1975

Any woman who has a lot to offer the world is in trouble.
Hazel Scott, in *Ms* magazine, 1976

Whatever women do they must do twice as well as men to be thought half as good. Luckily this is not difficult.
Charlotte Whitton, *Canada Month*, 1963

Being a woman is of special interest only to aspiring male trans-sexuals. To actual women it is merely a good excuse not to play football.

Fran Lebowitz, *Metropolitan Life*, 1978

The decisive economic contribution of women in the developed industrial society is rather simple . . . It is, overwhelmingly, to make possible a continuing and more or less unlimited increase in the sale and use of consumer goods.

John Kenneth Galbraith, *Annals of an Abiding Liberal*, 1980

The greatest problem with women is how to contrive that they should seem our equals.

Cyril Connolly, *Journal 1928–1937*, ed. D. Pryce-Jones, 1983

The major achievement of the Women's Movement in the 1970s was the Dutch treat.

Nora Ephron, *Heartburn*, 1983

Women's all right. The only place you can beat one and not get thrown in jail is at the poker table.

'Amarillo Slim' Preston, quoted in *The Biggest Game in Town* by A. Alvarez, 1983

See also HUMANITY, MEN

WORK

It is easier to appear worthy of a position one does not hold, than of the office which one fills.

François, Duc de La Rochefoucauld, *Maxims*, 1665

Every profession has its secrets . . . if it hadn't it wouldn't be a profession.

Saki (H.H. Munro), *The Story of St Vespalius*, 1911

Labor, n. One of the processes whereby A acquires property for B.

Ambrose Bierce, *The Devil's Dictionary*, 1911

Is it hot in the rolling mill? Are the hours long? Is $15 a day not enough? Then escape is very easy. Simply throw up your job, spit on your hands, and write another 'Rosenkavalier'.

H.L. Mencken, *Sententiae*, 1916

I am a friend of the working man, and I would rather be his friend than be one.

Clarence Darrow

Unionism seldom, if ever, uses such power as it has to ensure better work – almost always it devotes a large part of that power to safeguarding bad work.

H.L. Mencken, *Prejudices* 3rd series, 1922

Most people perform essentially meaningless work. When they retire that truth is borne in upon them.

Brendan Francis

The miracles that have been held up to us in praise of work are a little unfortunate. 'How doth the little busy bee improve each shining hour, and gather honey all the day from every opening flower.' Well, he does not. He spends most of the day in buzzing and aimless aerobatics, and gets about a fifth of the honey he would collect if he organised himself.

Sir Heneage Ogilvie

So much of what we call management consists in making it difficult for people to work.

Peter Drucker

The longer the title, the less important the job.

George McGovern, 1960

The price one pays for pursuing any profession or calling is an intimate knowledge of its ugly side.

James Baldwin, *Nobody Knows My Name*, 1961

The world is full of willing people. Some willing to work, the rest willing to let them.

Robert Frost, in *Quote and Unquote*, 1970

We are an indispensable team; you are overmanned; they are redundant.

Anthony Sampson, in the *Observer*, 1981

WRITING

No man but a blockhead ever wrote except for money.

Samuel Johnson, *The Life of Samuel Johnson* by J. Boswell, 1791

An old tutor of a college said to one of his pupils: Read over your compositions, and whenever you meet with a passage which you think is particularly fine, strike it out.

Samuel Johnson, *The Life of Samuel Johnson* **by J. Boswell, 1791**

Gentlemen, I agree with you that Napoleon is a tyrant, a monster, the sworn foe of our nation. But gentlemen – he once shot a publisher.

Thomas Campbell, toast to Napoleon

People do not deserve to have good writing, they are so pleased with bad.

Ralph Waldo Emerson, *Journals,* **1909–14**

The basis of literary friendship is mixing the poisoned bowl.

Oscar Wilde

Write without pay until somebody offers pay. If nobody offers within three years, the candidate may look upon this circumstance with the most implicit confidence as the sign that sawing wood is what he was intended for.

Mark Twain

A literary movement consists of five or six people who live in the same town and hate each other cordially.

George Moore

A favourite dodge to get your story read by the public is to assert that it's true, and then add that Truth is stranger than Fiction.

O. Henry

Modern literature: prescriptions written by patients.

Karl Kraus, *Half Truths and One and a Half Truths,* **1986**

Posterity is what you write for after being turned down by many publishers.

George Ade, *Hand-Made Fables,* **1920**

If you want to get rich from writing, write the sort of thing that's read by persons who move their lips when they're reading to themselves.

Don Marquis

Everything's great in this good old world;
(This is the stuff they can always use.)
God's in his heaven, the hill's dew-pearled;
(This will provide for baby's shoes.)
Hunger and War do not mean a thing;
Everything's rosy where'er we roam;
Hark, how the little birds gaily sing!
(This is what fetches the bacon home.)

Dorothy Parker, *The Far Sighted Muse*, 1925

In the same way that a woman becomes a prostitute. First I did it to please myself, then I did it to please my friends, and finally I did it for money.

Ferenc Molnár, asked how he became a writer

Coleridge was a drug addict. Poe was an alcoholic. Marlowe was killed by a man whom he was treacherously trying to stab. Pope took money to keep a woman's name out of a satire then wrote a piece so that she could still be recognised anyhow. Chatterton killed himself. Byron was accused of incest. Do you still want to be a writer – and if so, why?

Bennett Cerf, *Shake Well before Using*, 1948

Translations (like wives) are seldom faithful if they are in the least attractive.

Roy Campbell, in the *Poetry Review*, 1949

Those who write clearly have readers; those who write obscurely have commentators.

Albert Camus, *Notebooks*, 1942–51

It is the rule, not the exception, that otherwise unemployable public figures inevitably take to writing for publication.

Richard Condon

Good swiping is an art in itself.

Jules Feiffer

People who write fiction, if they had not taken it up, might have become very successful liars.

Ernest Hemingway, *This Week*, 1959

If there's one major cause for the spread of mass illiteracy, it's the fact that everybody can read and write.

Peter De Vries, *The Tents of Wickedness*, 1959

The profession of book writing makes horse racing seem like a solid, stable business.
  John Steinbeck, in Newsweek magazine, 1962

A writer is congenitally unable to tell the truth and that is why we call what he writes fiction.
  William Faulkner, quoted in his obituary, 1962

Only a minor talent can be a perfect gentleman; a major talent is always more than a bit of a cad. Hence the importance of minor writers – as teachers of good manners
  W.H. Auden, The Dyer's Hand, 1963

There are no dull subjects. There are only dull writers.
  H.L. Mencken, quoted in Esquire magazine, 1965

I can make it longer if you like the style
I can change it round and I want to be a paperback writer.
  John Lennon and Paul McCartney, Paperback Writer, 1966

There is always one thing to remember: writers are always selling somebody out.
  Joan Didion, Slouching Towards Bethlehem, 1968

There are three reasons for becoming a writer: the first is that you need the money; the second that you have something to say that you think the world should know; the third is that you can't think what to do with the long winter evenings.
  Quentin Crisp, The Naked Civil Servant, 1968

Writing is turning one's worst moments into money.
  J.P. Donleavy, 1968

A synonym is a word you use when you can't spell the word you first thought of.
  Burt Bacharach, in Quote and Unquote, 1970

Writing . . . locking yourself in a room and inventing conversations, no way for a grown-up to behave. Then your book is published, the sun comes up, as usual, and the sun goes down, as usual, and the world is in no way altered, and it must be someone's fault.
  John Leonard, in Esquire magazine, 1975

Hell hath no fury like a hustler with a literary agent.
Frank Sinatra, 1977

Contrary to what you might imagine, a career in letters is not without its drawbacks – chief among them is the unpleasant fact that one is frequently called upon to sit down and write.
Fran Lebowitz, *Metropolitan Life*, 1978

Writers don't need love, all they require is money.
John Osborne, in the *Observer*, 1980

A freelance is one who gets paid by the word – per piece or perhaps.
Robert Benchley, quoted in *Selected Letters of James Thurber*, ed. H. Thurber and J. Weeks, 1981

The only way for writers to meet is to share a quick pee over a common lamp-post.
Cyril Connolly, *Journal 1928–1937*, ed. D. Pryce-Jones, 1983

See also AUTHORS, BEST-SELLERS, BOOKS

THE YOUNG

Cultivate vices when you are young, and when you are old they will not forsake you.
Anonymous

Young men think old men are fools; but old men know young men are fools.
George Chapman, *All Fools*, 1605

The heart never grows better by age; I fear rather worse, always harder. A young liar will only be an old one, and a young knave will only be a greater knave as he grows up.
Lord Chesterfield, *Letters to his Son*, 1774

Youth is a blunder, manhood a struggle, old age a regret.
Benjamin Disraeli, *Coningsby*, 1844

The disappointment of manhood succeeds to the delusion of youth.
Benjamin Disraeli

Young men want to be faithful and are not; old men want to be faithless and cannot.

Oscar Wilde, _The Picture of Dorian Gray_, 1891

Young people, nowadays, imagine that money is everything, and when they grow older, they know it.

Oscar Wilde, _The Picture of Dorian Gray_, 1891

To get back one's youth one has merely to repeat one's follies.

Oscar Wilde, _The Picture of Dorian Gray_, 1891

The young have aspirations that never come to pass, the old have reminiscences of what never happened.

Saki (H.H. Munro), _Reginald at the Carlton_, 1904

Only the young die good.

Addison Mizner and Oliver Herford, _The Entirely New Cynic's Calendar_, 1905

There is a tide in the affairs of young men, which, if not skillfully dodged, effectually drowns them.

Arthur Binstead, _Pitcher's Proverbs_, 1909

It is a lamentable but incontrovertible solecism that many young men who are highly moral . . . are inwardly never happier than when suspected of disreputable tendencies.

Arthur Binstead, _Pitcher's Proverbs_, 1909

Blush: a weakness of youth and an accomplishment of experience.

Oliver Herford and John Clay, _Cupid's Cyclopedia_, 1910

All that the young can do for the old [is] to shock them and keep them up to date.

George Bernard Shaw, _Fannie's First Play_, 1911

From the earliest times the old have rubbed it into the young that they are wiser than they, and before the young had discovered what nonsense this was they were old too, and it profited them to carry on the imposture.

W. Somerset Maugham, _Cakes and Ale_, 1930

What is more enchanting than the voices of young people when you can't hear what they say.

Logan Pearsall Smith, _All Trivia_, 1933

The good die young – because they see it's no use living if you've got to be good.

John Barrymore

Adolescence: a stage between infancy and adultery.

Anonymous, quoted in *H.L. Mencken's Dictionary of Quotations*, 1942

But then, that's what young men are there for.

Adolf Hitler, commenting on exceptionally heavy casualty lists

A youth with his first cigar makes himself sick; a youth with his first girl makes others sick.

Mary Wilson Little

Every young man should have a hobby: learning how to handle money is the best one.

Jack Hurley, 1961

The young always have the same problem – how to rebel and conform at the same time. They have now solved this by defying their parents and copying one another.

Quentin Crisp, *The Naked Civil Servant*, 1968

All adolescents should be given a thoroughly beastly time of it, in order to give them something to look forward to when they grow up.

Richard Gordon, *Doctor in the Swim*, 1962

Youth is a disease from which we all recover.

Dorothy Fuldheim, *A Thousand Friends*, 1974

It has been said that there is no fool like an old fool, except a young fool. But the young fool has first to grow up to be an old fool to realise what a damn fool he was when he was a young fool.

Harold Macmillan, Earl of Stockton

Youth is a period of missed opportunities.

Cyril Connolly, *Journal 1928–1937*, ed. D. Pryce-Jones, 1983

See also AGE

INDEX